The Psyche as Interaction

Electromagnetic Patterns of Conscious Energy

Manya J. Long

Copyright © 2014 Manya J. Long

All rights reserved. No part of this book may be reproduced, stored, or transmitted by any means—whether auditory, graphic, mechanical, or electronic—without written permission of both publisher and author, except in the case of brief excerpts used in critical articles and reviews. Unauthorized reproduction of any part of this work is illegal and is punishable by law.

ISBN: 978-1-4834-1156-9 (sc)
ISBN: 978-1-4834-1155-2 (e)

Because of the dynamic nature of the Internet, any web addresses or links contained in this book may have changed since publication and may no longer be valid. The views expressed in this work are solely those of the author and do not necessarily reflect the views of the publisher, and the publisher hereby disclaims any responsibility for them.

Any people depicted in stock imagery provided by Thinkstock are models, and such images are being used for illustrative purposes only.
Certain stock imagery © Thinkstock.

Lulu Publishing Services rev. date: 04/24/2014

"When certain areas of the brain are stimulated by the secret processes of the Mysteries, the consciousness of man is extended and he is permitted to behold the Immortals and enter into the presence of the superior gods. The Book of Thoth describes the method whereby the stimulation was accomplished. In truth, therefore, it was the 'Key to Immortality'."

<u>An Encyclopedic Outline of Masonic Hermetic Qabbalistic and Rosicrucion Philosophy</u> by Manly P. Hall

Dedication

For: Dad, Mama, and her mama, too.

For: Tugg, Beulah, Gertie, Wrinkles, Abe, Teddy, Sunny, Sondra, Buckeye, Zeus, Pansy, Xian, Gwen, Bertha, Dixie, Trixie, Pixie, Gus, Midge, Buddy, Pete, Bammer, Clara, Claire, Rachel, Leona, Blackie, Isaac, Peking, Bubba, Zachariah, Perry, Hippocrates, Mort, Eddie, Larry, Curly, Moe, Biscuit, Auggie Doggie, Dinky, Hilda, Wilson, Ragsie, Beijing, Tess, Chelsea, Miranda, Omaha, Bandit, Irving, Maude, Gus, Cisco, Romero, Caesar, Shiloh, Tasha, Sam, Sasha, Tinkerbell, Snow White, Gomer, Jesse, Nome, Euripides, Archimedes, Sparky, Hypathia, Homer, Blackie, Ike, Spike, Chester, Homer, Scream, Bertha, Pansy, Patty, Sedona, Mirage, Toledo, Oscar, Cyrano, Orville, Simba, San, Fran, Clytemnestra, Wilhemina, Guinevere, Philip and Buddy, Rollie, Mary, Pal, Brutus, Mufkin, Patches, Allie, Chelsea, Morris, Miranda, Wanda, Letty, Harold, Hilda, Tigger, Bill, Billy, James, Zorro, Lucky, Yippy, Skippy, Tippy, Max, Sondra, Lucy, Yettie, Timmy, Elijiah, Edgar, Aristotle, Pinto, Bronson, Baby Louise, Pal, Gordan, Poncho, Cleve, Rocky, Omaha, Lady, Dusty, Cleatus, Odysseus, Soupy Sales, Pepper, Snickers, and all the rest of our children.

And for John.

Contents

PREFACE ix
HYPOTHESIS xi

PART 1: THE COLLECTIVE UNCONSCIOUS
    Chapter 1: Definition of psyche; zodiacal signs; reverse speech 1
    Chapter 2: Archetypes 1 through 4; Myths as science, religion, and fairytales 12
    Chapter 3: The Importance of ritual; fractal geometry; the Chaos Theory; dissipative structures 18
    Chapter 4: The Numerical Field Structure of Thought Cantor's Continuum Hypothesis: $2\aleph_0 = \aleph_1$ 24

PART 2: THE PERSONAL UNCONSCIOUS
    Chapter 1: Bridge between idea and matter 39
    Chapter 2: Image Maker 42
    Chapter 3: The Senses as Channels for an Idea's Projection 50
    Chapter 4: Non-linear Mathematical Organizers of Form 54

PART 3: THE CONSCIOUS MIND
    Chapter 1: Consciousness as a process 59
    Chapter 2: Rule, Boundary and Distinction Maker 60
    Chapter 3: Language as Reality's Morphological Tool 64
    Chapter 4: Reality as a Projected Hologram 67

PART 4: ORGANIZERS OF FORM FOR THE CONSCIOUS MIND
    Chapter 1: Number as frequency 73
    Chapter 2: Color as frequency and number 83
    Chapter 3: Sound/Language 87
    Chapter 4: Emotion 92

CONCLUSION 95

APPENDICES
    Chapter 5:   Scientific Concepts 107
    Chapter 6:   Mathematical Concepts 115
    Chapter 7:   Neurological Concepts......................... 136
    Chapter 8:   Musical Concepts 162

GLOSSARY 171
BIBLIOGRAPHY 179
POSTSCRIPT 189
ENDNOTES 221

Preface

"The sine-wave is the sum total of the waveform (thoughtform)." That sentence, complete with the punctuation, acted as a catalyst in my twenty-year journey in search of a comprehensive structure in which to understand the nature of the paranormal phenomena that I have experienced since I was two years old. Originally, I thought I had seen that sentence in a book that I had been reading before I fell asleep one night. However, the next morning, I searched through the entire book and could not find it. This event happened in November, 1990.

Prior to that time, in 1984, I began seeing tiny, iridescent bits of energy as an overlay of objects, such as people, plants, animals; inanimate objects, too. At first, I only saw these energy shapes once or twice a year. I found the experiences fascinating, but at the same time, I wanted explanations. These events created a vacuum in my imagination and intellect which inevitably needed to be filled: hence, this journey. Beginning in 1996 and continuing until the present, the frequency of the energy experiences increased to between twenty and thirty times a day. Having an inquisitive nature, I wanted to understand the "hows" and "whys" for those phenomena.

My intellectual travels also have been in search of other explanations for the "awake" dreams (lucid dreams) I have experienced, my physically empathetic reactions when I was in proximity to certain people, and three out of body experiences. The first of the out of body experiences occurred when I was only two years old; the second was when I was thirteen years old playing in a volleyball game; and the third was when I was nineteen years of age.

My journey took me to college courses and studies in physics, mathematics, philosophy, psychology and religion. In addition, I delved into books on the occult, parapsychology and "New Age" topics. Some common themes and patterns started to emerge from these seemingly diverse subjects. Connections appeared between mathematics, physics, psychology, music, religion, neurophysiology and parapsychology.

This search has culminated in an accumulation, analysis and integration of strands of conclusions from different disciplines in order to weave a fabric explaining an individual's participation in personal and mass reality. Concepts in quantum mechanics, fractal geometry, the Chaos

Theory, philosophy, religion, music and parapsychology are interwoven with astrology, numerology, holography, topography, matrices, dissipative structures, reverse speech and the Santiago Theory of cognition, with its auto poetic concept and the Fourier Transform (metaphorically).

The road map in researching the destination for this journey was unknown to me until 1992, when I thought that I had read the following sentence in a book, only to go back the next day and find it was not there: "In other words, there is no exteriorization of nature; everything is the mental, spiritual and psychic manifestation of All That Is." This sentence, too, was complete with punctuation.

Hypothesis

The psyche (soul/mind), of which there is an aura camera photo proving the linear succession of images, which the soul creates as part of the psychological realm of All That Is, emotionally propels conscious energy outward as waves from the thought pattern field of the collective unconscious so that "The sinewave is the sum total of the waveform (thought form)," via the frequency image by the subconscious. These thought images correspond to the frequency range of 5-8 cps, which is the range of our theta brainwave patterns. These represent the materialization of objects for each of our conscious intervals. This actualization of objects starts at 5 billionth of a second or when there is 10^7 to 10^8 photons 5 feet away from the source: the source meaning your unactualized body which is pure energy consciousness. (see Part One Chapter Four: Numerical Field Structure of Thought.) These thoughtforms represent all earthly phenomena at their natural resonant frequency. So, in other words, the world of appearances, "the land of 1,000 forms," is a holographic image that is formed individually and *en masse* as a physical expression of a spiritual and psychological realm and can be empirically proven with EEGs, EKGs and the aura camera. Our same senses (for example, sight, hearing, taste, touch and feel) that project the energy outward also act as analyzers of that same frequency, again by isomorphically utilizing the Fourier Transform, and transforming it at higher frequencies (by the conscious mind at 16 to 40 cps, beta waves), in order to create the illusion of density, which is matter (*i.e.*, how a whirling propeller appears solid but is really composed of individual blades).

Therefore, our conscious minds form a cohesive and coherent framework of the thought/frequency realm due to the limiting and screening ability of the reticular activating system (r. a. s.), (see: neurophysiological concepts) in order to promote effective survival behavior, which depends on linear time reactions.

"In other words, there is no exteriorization of nature; everything is the mental, spiritual and psychic manifestation of All That Is."

PART ONE

The Collective Unconscious

Chapter One

Definition of psyche; zodiacal signs; reverse speech

The collective unconscious is composed of awareized (*i.e.*, conscious) energy as thoughtforms.

In <u>The Individual and The Nature of Mass Events</u> by Jane Roberts, as she channels for the "energy personality" called Seth, his description of Jung and Freud's collective unconscious is Framework 2. "Framework 1 is simply a term representing the everyday, linear, conscious 'working reality' we take for granted, the one in which 'time' and events automatically unfold in moment after undeniable moment." [1]

"Framework 2 is the psychological medium in which the consciousness of the world exists," Seth explains. Continuing, he states, "The individuals who have to one extent or another perceived Framework 2 have, then, described it according to their own beliefs, taking it for granted 'that the part was a representative sample of the whole.' Plato conceived [of] it as the world of ideals, seeing within it the perfect model behind each imperfect physical phenomenon."[2]

Referring again to our conscious mind's reality, Seth adds, "Your world is populated by individuals concentrating upon physical activities [*i.e.*, Framework 1], dealing with events that are 'finished products' - at least in usual terms."[3] In other words, the probable versions of a particular activity would be actualized in other branches of reality, according to the Many Worlds Theory of quantum mechanics. In 1957, a Princeton physics student, Hugh Everett, invented a solution to the notorious quantum measurement problem. He called it the many-worlds theory of quantum mechanics, because each time that a decision is made to collapse the sine wave, so that a probability became an actuality (i.e. each conscious interval in which we perceive alleged "solid" objects) then whatever other probabilities aren't actualized in parallel universes with 10^{100} possibilities constantly splitting off into further possibilities. "Your inner egos populate Framework 2, and deal with the actual creation of those events that are then objectified."[4]

Clarifying Framework 2's process, Seth explains, "Your own senses bring you information each moment, and that information is in a way already invisibly processed according to your own beliefs, desires, and intents."[5]

Adding an extra dimension of explanation regarding the interwovenness of the collective unconscious and the conscious mind as Framework 1 and 2, Seth explains, "So far, I have been speaking of Frameworks 1 and 2 separately, and I will continue to do so for your convenience and understanding. Actually the two merge, of course, for your Framework 1 existence is immersed in Framework 2. Again, your body itself is constantly replenished in Framework 1 because of its simultaneous reality in Framework 2. Framework 2 is ever exteriorizing itself, appearing in your experience as Framework 1."[6]

In addition to Plato, Seth comments on Jung's glimpse into Framework 2, "Jung's collective unconscious was an attempt to give your world its psychological roots, but Jung could not perceive the clarity, organization, and deeper context in which that collective unconscious has its own existence."[7]

"This deeper layer I call the collective unconscious. I have chosen the term 'collective' because this part of the unconscious is not individual but universal in contrast to the personal psyche, it has contents and modes of behavior that are more or less the same everywhere and in all individuals,"[8] writes Jung in The Archetypes and the Collective Unconscious. He explains that his mentor, Freud was aware of the collective unconscious, but viewed it as merely representing "forgotten and repressed contents," even though "he was aware of its archaic and mythological thoughtforms."[9]

Jung defines the concept of an archetype as "essentially an unconscious content that is altered by becoming conscious and by being perceived, and it takes its colour from the individual consciousness in which it happens to appear."[10]

Delineating Jung's concept of the collective unconscious, Marie von Franz in Psyche & Matter points out, "For Jung, however, the unconscious is, in addition, a realm in which subliminal perceptions, incipient processes of psychic development that is, anticipations of future conscious processes - and in general all creative contents are constellated." (von Franz, 1988, p. 1) She describes Jung's view of the mingling of the conscious and unconscious realms: "The psychic processes flow or merge into the physical processes; how and where are still unclear in many respects."[11]

Further illustrating his concept of the collective unconscious, Jung, in On The Nature of The Psyche, points out, "The unconscious depicts an extremely fluid state of affairs: everything of which I know, but of which I am not at the moment thinking; everything of which I was once conscious but have now forgotten; everything perceived by my senses, but not noted by my conscious mind; everything which, involuntarily and without paying attention to it, I feel, think, remember, want, and do; all the future things that are taking shape in me and will sometime come to consciousness: all this is the content of the unconscious… But, as I say, we must also include in the unconscious the psychoid functions that are not capable of consciousness and of whose existence we have only indirect knowledge."[12]

Delving into the specifics of what Jung meant by the psychoid function, Marie von Franz explains, "In his view, the psychoid system is the part of the psychic realm where the psychic element appears to mix with inorganic matter."[13]

Jung referred to the associative thought/energy patterns of the collective unconscious as archetypes. "The archetypes are more or less the inborn normal complexes that we all have. Thus Jung understood archetypes to be inborn disposition or unobservable psychic structures that in recurring typical situations produce similarly structured ideas, thoughts, emotions, and fantasy motifs. The Jungian archetypes have often been compared with the Platonic ideas," notes von Franz.[14]

Clarifying the difference between the structure and the image that the archetype takes, she says, "There is no doubt that the archetypal structures are inherited; this is not, however, the case with the images… The disposition is passed down, the structures are passed on, and they then always produce the same or similar images afresh. When an inborn archetypal structure passes into the manifest form of an archetypal fantasy or image, the psyche makes use of impressions from the external surroundings for its means of expression; therefore, the individual images are not entirely identical but only similar in structure."[15]

"Who formed the things of sense after the pattern of the ideas?" was a question posed by Plato in one of his dialogues. Also, in Timaeus, Plato states "that the Creator of the world did this in looking on the eternal archetypes."[16]

Just as Plato proposed in his theory of forms that ideas or thoughtforms were the models or archetypes from which objects were structured, his Doctrine of a World Soul is tantamount to Jung's collective unconscious and Seth's Framework 2.

Plato states in Timaeus that "there was a massive simultaneity of mathematical forms present in the 'body of ideas' following the example of which the visible world was created. Since these could not be translated into actual reality all at once, the demiurge created a revolving model so that the individual forms could manifest in a temporal succession, and in fact in accordance with the sequential arrangement of the natural numbers," wrote Marie von Franz in Psyche and Matter.[17]

The immortality and transmigration of the soul is hinted at in the Meno Dialogue, along with the concept that ideas or thoughtforms were associative -- implying that they are circular and consequently magnetic by nature. The concept of the transmigration of the soul implies that ideas or thoughtforms are circular (i.e. a rotating electron as a circle produces simultaneously both electricity and magnetism) and consequently recurring in a linear sequence (i.e. time).

In The Essential Plato by Alain De Botton, the author in his introduction to Meno, one of Platos dialogues, summarizes that "This Dialogue contains the first intimation of the doctrine of reminiscence and of the immortality of the soul. It may be observed that the fanciful motion of preexistence is combined with a true view of the unity of knowledge, and of the association of ideas."[18] Socrates, in the dialogue is addressing a question posed by Meno:

> "Meno: What did they say?
> Soc: They spoke of a glorious Truth, as I conceive.
> Meno: What was that? And who were they?
> Soc: Some of them were priests and priestesses; who have studied how they might be able to give reason of their profession: there have been poets also, such as the poet Pindar and other inspired men. And what they say is – mark now, and see whether their words are true – they say that the soul of man is immortal, and at one time has an end, which is termed dying, and at another time is born again, but is never destroyed. And the moral is that a man ought to live always in perfect holiness."[19]

These philosophic concepts are dusted off and put back in the spotlight 2,500 years later by Jung, a psychologist, and Seth, a channeled energy source.

Possibly alluding to the subconscious and conscious mind, in The Republic, Plato refers to the sphere of the intellect as having two subdivisions, "There are two subdivisions, in the lower of which the soul uses the figures given by the former division as images; the inquiry can only be hypothetical, and instead of going upwards to a principle descends to the other end; in the higher of the two, the soul passes out of hypothesis, and goes up to a principle which is above hypothesis, making no use of images as in the former case, but proceeding only in and through the ideas themselves."[20]

Other ancient civilizations also had similar concepts for "the undifferentiated matrix of the unconscious, an existence bathed in the pre-egoid memories of the watery abyss of our life within the womb,"[21] describes Jill Purce in The Mystic Spiral. "In ancient Egypt the primordial vibrational field (called *nada* in India) is called Nun, the primal ocean. It is the One imaged as undifferentiated cosmic substance,"[22] explains Robert Lawlor in Sacred Geometry.

Modern physicists, such as David Bohm refer to a "sea of electrons", or to an "energy sea"[23], as Heinz Pagels does in The Cosmic Code, or a "simultaneous everywhere present matrix" per Ken Wilber in The Holographic Paradigm; These physicists sense of the wholeness of reality can be echoed in the concept used to describe awareized thought/energy fields of the collective unconscious as framework 1 (i.e. the unconscious interval of .8s-1.25s) from where the individual conscious minds form the objects and events in framework 2 (i.e. the conscious interval of .95s-1s) In order to describe the awareized thought/energy fields of the collective unconscious as Framework 2 from where the individual conscious minds form objects and events.[24],[25]

Seth refers to these "blueprints" or models of objects as "patterns-out-of-focus" in The Seth Material[26] and, echoing this concept in The Dancing Wu Li Masters, Gary Zukav refers to "'matter' [as] actually a series of patterns out of focus." In order to explain that, he says, "According to particle physics, the world is fundamentally dancing energy; energy that is everywhere and incessant assuming first this form and then that."[27]

Demonstrating the interconnectedness of the collective unconscious from a chemist's molecular viewpoint, Hans Jenny in Cymantics says, "In the vibrational field it can be shown that every part is, in the true sense, implicated in the whole. If we single out a detail, if we follow an individual part, it will be found on careful observation that the sum total of connections, albeit specifically transformed, is reflected in it."[28]

Offering a remark of Nietzsche's to explain the thought/energy field that composes us, and that we compose with, Deepak Chopra in Unconditional Life quotes, "All philosophy is based upon the premise that we think, but it is equally possible that we are being thought."[29]

Chopra also comments, "Instead of viewing the brain as a series of chemical relays that can be brightened or dimmed like a TV monitor, we should explore much more deeply its role as a creator."[30]

A physicist who has delved into Jungian synchronicities in order to construct a holographic view of reality, F. David Peat says in his book, Synchronicity: The Bridge Between Matter and Mind, "Synchronicities take the form of patterns that emerge by chance out of a general background of chance and contingency and hold a deep meaning for the person who experiences them."[31]

He also observes, as did Jung, that, "Often these coincidences occur at critical points in a person's life and can be interpreted as containing the seeds of future growth. Synchronicities could, therefore, be said to involve the meaningful unfoldment of potential."[32]

In Psyche & Matter, Marie von Franz refers to the infinite scope of knowledge contained in the collective unconscious as being the source for the phenomenon of synchronicity and ESP per Jung: "Whether we like it or not, we find ourselves in this embarrassing position as soon as we begin seriously to reflect on the teleological processes in biology or to investigate the compensatory function of the unconscious, not to speak of trying to explain the phenomenon of synchronicity. Final causes, twist them as you will, postulate a foreknowledge of some kind."[33]

Von Franz adds, "Only in cases of ESP (extrasensory perception), which cancel out time, space, and causality, can we speak with certainty of a synchronistic relationship."[34] And, "In dreams, says Seth, we write the script for our daily lives and perceive other levels of existence that our physical focus usually obscures",[35] writes Jane Roberts in the preface to her book, Dreams and Projection of Consciousness.

Later, as she channels Seth, she adds, "Sleep is the entity's rest from physical idea construction. Only enough energy is used to keep the personal image construction in existence. The entity withdraws into basic energy realms and is comparatively free from time since idea construction is at a minimum level. The entity is in contact with other entities at a subconscious area."[36]

Referring to the source of inspiration, intuitive thought or ESP, Seth comments, "In most cases the stimuli [toward healing] come from deeper levels of the self, where they may be translated into terms that the personal subconscious can use. In such cases, these perceptions may find their way to the ego, appearing as inspirations or intuitive thought."[37]

Although it took Jung twenty years, as he says in the foreword of The Interpretation of Nature and the Psyche, to address the existence of ESP as the basis for synchronicity, he acknowledges that, "Meaningful coincidences - which are to be distinguished from meaningless chance groupings - therefore seem to rest on an archetypal foundation."[38] In summation, von Franz clarifies, "In other words, the archetype sometimes preconsciously organizes our train of ideas."[39]

Consequently, the thought/energy patterns, organized in circular associative archetypal concept clusters of the global collective unconscious, operates telepathically, in both the waking and the dream state, providing a basis of coherence and similarity for the experiences of reality.

"Thoughts have what we will for now term electromagnetic properties. In those terms your thoughts mix and match with others in Framework 2, creating mass patterns that form the overall psychological basis behind world events,"[40] expresses Seth.

Thoughts are both electrical (in the brain) and magnetic (electromagnetism). Electricity and electromagnetism are opposite sides of the same coin produced by a rotating electron, with the x-axis simultaneously representing time (as a progressive linear sequence of images) and electricity; and the y-axis simultaneously representing the concepts of space and magnetism.

Since thoughts are magnetic, Jung discovered that they are associative and hence his theory of gigantic clusters of similar thoughts representing archetypal concepts originating in the collective unconscious before being individually perceived by the conscious mind.

"C.G. Jung not only used astrology as a psychological tool in his practice, but also spent years doing research into the psychological aspects of alchemical symbolism,"[41] explains Dr. Stephen Arroyo in his book Astrology, Psychology, and the Four Elements.

Illustrating the concept that the twelve astrological signs of the zodiac express the personality traits, behaviors and themes from the archetypal thought patterns and are reflected by the metaphoric content of reverse speech in each person's conscious perception of reality, Arroyo states, "In fact, astrology can be viewed as the most comprehensive mythological framework that has ever arisen in human culture."[42]

Just as the ancient Sumerians, Babylonians and Egyptians viewed astrology as a link with the One, Arroyo states, "It is just this unity of process seen in all particular forms that astrology provides man. In astrology, every individual is considered a whole and unique expression of universal principles, patterns, and energies. The zodiac was considered by ancient astrologers and philosophers as the 'soul of nature,' that which gives form and order to life."[43]

In an interview with a magazine, Jung said "One can expect with considerable assurance that a given well-defined psychological situation will be accompanied by an analogous astrological configuration. Astrology consists of configurations symbolic of the collective unconscious which is the subject matter of psychology: the 'planets' are the gods, symbols of the powers of the unconscious."[44]

Noting that, "In many of his writings, Jung emphasized that astrology includes the sum total of all ancient psychological knowledge, including both the innate predisposition of individuals and an accurate way of timing life crises:

> 'I have observed many cases where a well-defined psychological phase or an analogous event has been accompanied by a transit (particularly the afflictions of Saturn and Uranus). (Jung, 1954)'"[45]

Arroyo demonstrates, "Astrology actually comprises both the mathematical and the symbolic languages of life, synthesizing both into one harmonic system, the uses of which are far broader than any other system, mathematical or symbolic."[46]

In Archetypes of The Zodiac, Kathleen Burt defines the theme song of each of the twelve zodiacal signs, for example:

- "Aries: The Search for a Separate Identity;
- Taurus: The Search for Value and Meaning;
- Gemini: The Search for Variety:
- Cancer: The Search for the Mother Goddess;
- Leo: The Search for Being and Wholeness;
- Virgo: The Search for Meaningful Service;
- Libra: The Search for the Soul Mate;
- Scorpio: The Search for the Transformation;
- Sagittarius: The Search for Wisdom;
- Capricorn: The Search for Dharma;
- Aquarius: The Search for the Holy Grail;
- and Pisces: The Search for the Castle of Peace."[47]

She explains, "In taking one form, the idea (archetype) goes through a story development process. The Leo king has to reclaim his throne; the Aries hero goes off to fight his battles in the outer world. The Scorpio hero descends into himself (the inner world) to fight his demons and rescue his Persephone. Taurus encounters his/her obstacles to create a comfortable, secure world, or has to let go of his world once he creates it solidly. There are many definitions of myth."[48]

These same astrological archetypes contained within the collective unconscious were accidentally discovered by David John Oates to be speech reversals underlying our verbal forward speech patterns.

In the 1960s, Beatle John Lennon accidentally created a new recording technique called backward masking. Then, in 1984, psychologist-hypnotist David John Oates discovered that reversals are naturally a part of a human's forward speech patterns.

He explains in Reverse Speech, "Reverse speech is unconscious in nature. Automatic brain functions are involved in the delivery and reception of speech reversals. It is an intricate part of spoken language and always relates to, or is complementary with, the forward dialogue."[49]

He says in his findings, "Its complementary nature seems to indicate that Reverse Speech draws upon many different areas of the mind to correct and enhance what is spoken forwards, effectively serving as the brain's own editor of forward speech."[50]

Due to his experimental observations he determined that the right-brain hemisphere, which "is emotional, imaginative and creative in nature" and "is thought to be responsible for unconscious mental activity and the emotional emphasis placed in speech",[51] was the source of Reverse speech.

Oates continues, "Everything contained within the unconscious mind - what is now and what has been in the past - has the potential to appear in Reverse Speech. Reverse Speech, using its metaphors and primordial images, exposes the total Self and the three areas of the mind as defined by Carl Jung."[52]

Oates acknowledges the significance of his discovery when he says, "It, [Reverse Speech], reveals not just a single aspect of the psyche, but encompasses the totality of the whole. At its deepest levels, it describes a universal mind, revealing that all of us are linked inexorably, and forever, with one another."[53] In summary, he says, "As human beings, we share a collective unconscious and this collective identity, with its limitless knowledge, is expressed and handed down, in part, using speech reversals."[54]

According to Deepak Chopra, each person has 60,000 thoughts per day, or 41+ per minute. We are only consciously aware of a percentage of those thoughts. Those electromagnetic thoughts surrounding a person constitute archetypal concept patterns from the collective unconscious, as a colored, numbered frequency (aura) containing the probable objects/events of the person's next conscious .95 - 1s interval.

The colored energy field surrounding all objects has been noticed by ancient civilizations for over 5,000 years. In 1908, Dr. Walter Kilner "conceived the idea that the human aura might be made visible if viewed through a suitable substance, and he experimented with dicyanin, a remarkable coal-tar dye. This dye appeared to have a definite effect upon eyesight, making the observer temporarily near-sighted and therefore more readily able to perceive radiation in the ultra-violet band,"[55] for humans, visible light, is 10^{14} of the electromagnetic spectrum, - a very small segment of the energy domain. (see: Part C: Neurophysiological Concepts)

In The Chakras, C.W. Leadbeater refers to the auric field as "clearly visible to the clairvoyant as a mass of faintly-luminous violet-grey mist, interpenetrating the denser part of the body, and extending very slightly beyond it."[56]

Guy Coggins, president of the Progen Company and inventor of the Aura Camera 3000 to 6000, explains the chronological development of how his interest in Kirlian photography led to his own aura camera invention: "I became interested in the 'New Age' movement through Kirlian photography. I discovered that an aura camera was developed in Russia in the 1930's that could photograph the energy - or corona discharge - of your fingertips and toes. I was practicing meditation and yoga at the time, too."[57]

Coggins continues, "My interest in auras was mystical, spiritual, and scientific. It seemed natural to me to blend together what I knew from each discipline. I built my first Kirlian-style aura camera in 1970."[58]

He adds, "To me, it just seemed like the most logical step to develop existing technology into a system that could show the energy field around someone's portrait." Coggins states "that his camera doesn't actually 'see' auras, rather it perceives them electronically," by "transmitting radio waves through the subject's electromagnetic field, then converts the waves into electrical energy which can be processed as light and color." Finally, Coggins reiterates his purpose: "As an inventor, my ideal is to make this technology so popular that everyone will learn to tell the truth."[59]

Consequently, the 60,000 thoughts per person per day times approximately 7 billion people worldwide constitutes the wave pattern interference of the collective unconscious as a person's energy field. Then the subconscious, as an image maker, actualizes or manifests an object/event at the natural base resonant frequency of 5-8 cps, which corresponds with our brain's theta waves, utilizing the archetypal information clusters. Then the conscious mind mathematically constructs an object/event during the conscious interval of .95s - 1s which it then views.

The varying frequencies of the "everywhere present energy domain" is referred to as the electromagnetic spectrum ranging from 10^1 to 10^{24}. Its logarithmic design is harmonic, or represented as octaves. The electromagnetic spectrum represents segments of electricity cycles per second (cps) and simultaneously magnetism as nanometers measured in wavelengths. For example, visible light to humans is within the 10^{14} segment of the electromagnetic spectrum where the color red is approximately 429 trillion (4.29×10^{14}) cps compared to the color violet (which is at the opposite end of our ability to differentiate energy as color) at 750 trillion (7.5×10^{14}) cps.

Its basis is energy, which is defined as the movement of an electron. The <u>rotational</u> movement of an electron - which vertically, as the y-axis, produces magnetism (space) and horizontally, as the x-axis, produces electricity (time) - this rotational movement of an electron (sinewave) is also the basis of a hologram. (see: Scientific Appendices)

Example
Cartesian Co-ordinate System

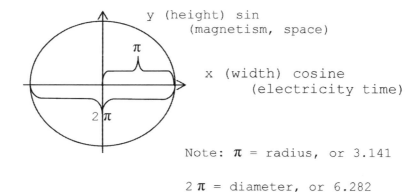

Note: π = radius, or 3.141

2π = diameter, or 6.282

An electron, as a "tendency to exist", is a point, when actualized or manifested, or a sinewave, when unactualized or field-like (see: Part I, Chapter Four: The Numerical Field Structure of Thought).

Chapter Two

Archetypes 1 through 4; Myths as science, religion, and fairytales

As presented in the last chapter, the twelve zodiacal signs represent metaphoric dramas from the thought/energy patterns (archetypes) of the collective unconscious as psychical expression in the three-dimensional realm.

When David John Oates discovered the complementary backward speech patterns, originally in the right-brain hemisphere, which he called Reverse Speech, containing the metaphoric aspect of the collective unconscious' archetypes, a physical basis was proven for Jung's concept of synchronicity and ESP; Bohm, Peat and Talbot's interconnectedness of reality as a whole; von Franz's concept of "matter" as being a mythical expression; and Seth's worldwide telepathic dream network.

The expansion of a person's consciousness interval from .95-1s to .94 to 1s or .94 to 1.1s, etc., which would allow them to directly experience the "paranormal" or unaccepted collective unconscious energy as objects, can lead to schizophrenia or manic-depression.

Whereas, the schizophrenic only gets doses of the holographic order, the manic-depressive jumps in with both feet leading to grandiose feelings of identification with something larger than himself and a need to lie to, manipulate, etc. those around him in order to explain the immense vistas that he experiences.

This ability to experience the paranormal can result from a malfunction on the reticular activating system (r.a.s.) or more dominant theta waves in the brain at any rate in order to keep oneself balanced when acknowledging both realities a proper framework for understanding is necessary.

Also, Marie von Franz, in <u>Psyche & Matter</u>, presents Jung's concept of science (and mathematics, which science is based on), religion and fairytales as being expressions of myths from the collective unconscious' archetypes.

In The Interpretation of Fairytales, von Franz describes how "fairy tales offer the simplest and purest expressions of the collective unconscious."[1] The Brothers Grimm compiled 211 of these fairytales in 1812, demonstrating archetypal dramas from the story of "The Frog Prince" to "The Beam" and their eternal appeal.

Joseph Campbell, in Transformations of Myth Through Time, refers to a Pueblo Indian myth, which is isomorphic with Jung's Father archetype: "And isn't this interesting? It is the wind, spiritus, the spirit, we got in Chief Seattle. That's an archetype, the recognition of breath as the breath of life."[2] And later again, in reference to Jung's Father archetype, Campbell states, "In most of the mythologies of the Indo-Europeans, the principal deities are those of the universal order."[3]

In Psyche and Matter, Marie von Franz clarifies and lists the Jungian component concepts of each of the four primary archetypes: Mother, Father, Union, and Self. (see: Part Four; Chapter One)

1) The Mother archetype "symbolically represents the mother, the grandmother, the step-mother," etc. It also symbolizes the concepts of "salvation, paradise, the church, heaven/hell," etc.
2) The Father archetype represents father and authority figures, the mind, air, spirit, energy, movement, duality, etc.
3) The archetype of Union represents structure, dynamics, periodicity, linear succession of images, any religious trinity, DNA and RNA.
4) The archetype of the Self represents the synthesis of the parts (*i.e.*, the probably I's into one individual) into the whole. Jung demonstrated that this archetype exhibited "dynamic, sequential, quaternary structures isomorphic to the field of natural numbers."[4]

In reference to science being a product of myth, von Franz states, "S. Sambursky in his outstanding book ("The Image of the Physical World in Antiquity") demonstrates in a detailed fashion that all basic themes of modern Western physics are derived from the intuitive primal symbolic images of Greek natural philosophy."[5]

She continues, "From these comes the idea of a single prime matter [for example: quest for Unified Field Theory], out of which the entire visible cosmos is somehow constituted, as well as the idea of a conservation of this prime matter [*i.e.*, The Law of Energy Conservation], in other words, the concept of a universal energy"[6] [*i.e.*, "Nun" in ancient Egypt, "nada" in India].

S. Sambursky relates, "The main contributors to scientific thinking were not the great scientists themselves, like Euclid, Archimedes, Apollonius and Hipparchus, but rather the founders or representatives of philosophical systems of thought men like Democritus, Plato, Aristotle, Epicurus and Chrysippus, and in late antiquity the Neo-Platonists."[7]

Marie von Franz further elucidates, "For example, we have the fiery pneuma of the Stoics or the logos-fire in the philosophy of Heraclitus. There also we find the idea of the transformability of material substances, [*i.e.*, alchemy] into one another (for example, in Aristotle)." She continues, "In the Stoic idea of the pneuma, we already have the basic intuition for the modern force field or a stationary wave."[8]

Explaining the Greek thought processes, Sambursky points out, "Greek scientific thinking elaborated in a qualitative, non-mathematical way two main patterns which became precursors of the basic trends in modern physical thought: continuum theory [already established by the zero paradoxes] and atomism."[9]

He continues, "The scientific world-picture of Aristotle, an all-embracing theory loosely related to experience and built on a few theoretical assumptions which were derived in part from earlier conceptions, became dominant in Greek and medieval thought."[10]

Elaborating further, he states, "In fact, it is one of the three major world views in the history of science, being followed by a long interval by that of Newton which has since been replaced by that of relativity and quantum physics."[11]

Giving an example of the origin of one of quantum mechanics principles, von Franz adds, "Also the idea of the [Heisenberg's] uncertainty principle [*i.e.*, a particle doesn't have both a position and momentum simultaneously - it's either/or] has its germ in the view of the Greek atomist Lencippus, who taught that atoms has a certain free will,"[12] [*i.e.*, an electron as a "tendency to exist"].

But, in her view, "Most interesting are the conceptions of space-time, for they all derive from the archetypal image of the omnipresence of a deity or the omnipresence of the divine pneuma."[13]

Archetypes contain not only mythical concepts for science, math and fairytales but also the frameworks for the world's religions.

The term "religio" in Latin is the base of the term religion. "Religio" means "to re-connect," and as such demonstrates the universal human need to be a part of an all-encompassing something, *i.e.*, the parts seeking the whole.

In Jane Roberts' Oversoul Seven and the Museum of Time, she comments, "Christianity represented the human psyche at a certain point, forming first inner patterns for development that then exteriorized as myth, drama, and history, with the Jewish culture of the Talmud presenting the psyche's direction."[14]

Roberts continues, "The traditional personified god concepts represented the mass psyche's one-ego development; the ego ruling the self as God ruled man, man dominant over the planet and other species, as God was dominant over man - as opposed to the idea of many gods or the growth of a more multi-focused self with greater nature identification."[15]

Marie von Franz offers "that in late antiquity the major part of what we call today the psyche was located outside the individual in the animated matter of the universe; it consisted of a multiplicity of colliding components, or of gods, star-divinity and demons, or of powers in the organs of the body, or in chemical substances."[16] She adds, "The monotheism of the Old Testament and the idea of Christ being the One Man required from other human beings an ethical decision in their confrontation with the varied inner demons and animal souls."[17]

In Psychology and Alchemy, Jung refers to the universality of the serpent myth in religion: "The serpent is Mercurius who as the fundamental substance [i.e., Mother archetype as it relates to origin] (hypostatica) forms himself in the water and swallows the nature to which he is joined. Matter is thus formed through illusion, which is necessarily that of the alchemist. This illusion might well be the very imaginatio possessed of 'information power.'"[18]

As Joseph Campbell elaborates in The Power of Myth, "Now, the biblical tradition is a socially oriented mythology. Nature is condemned."[19] Relating the myth to a more modern time, he continues, "In the nineteenth century, scholars thought of mythology and ritual as an attempt to control nature. But that is magic, not mythology or religion. Nature religions [i.e., Wicca] are not attempts to control nature but to help you put yourself in accord with it. But when nature is thought of as evil, you don't put yourself in accord with it, you control it, or try to, and hence the tension, the anxiety, the cutting down of forests, the annihilation of native people."[20]

Seeming to substantiate this view, Seth comments in The Individual and the Nature of Mass Events, "In various ways your religions have always implied your relationship with nature's source, even though they often divorced nature herself from any place of prime importance." And he continues, "In those terms, the great religions of your civilizations rise from myths that change their characters through the century even as mountains ranges rise and fall."[21]

Since religion is formalized myth, the same themes or dramas, as constellated archetypes, from the collective unconscious keep presenting themselves in the various world religions. As David Noss notes in Man's Religions, "Myths emerge going back to the beginning of things, thereby setting questions, concerning the origin of the world and the place of the community in it."[22]

Virgin births (i.e., Osirism, Christianity, Zoroastrianism, the Greek mystery cults), Creation and Flood myths, heaven/hell, resurrection or rebirth of a hero and the personification of good and evil are all common religious themes with only the characters and backgrounds changing.[23]

The similarity of these mythological themes in Osirism, Judaism, Zoroastrianism, the Greek Mystery cults of Attis, Dionysus, etc.,

Christianity, Hinduism, Taoism, Islam, the Goddess religions, Buddhism, Confucianism and the American religions of the Incas, Mayans, Olmecs, Aztecs, Eskimos and Native American religions substantiate a common origin – that of the collective unconscious or Framework 2. Reflecting on religion as myth, Jung in Man and His Symbols informs us, "[W]hile personal complexes never produce more than a personal bias, archetypes create myths, religions, and philosophies that influence and characterize whole nations and epochs of history."[24]

Continuing on, he adds, "We regard the personal complexes as compensations for one-sided or faulty attitudes of consciousness; in the same way, myths of a religious nature can be interpreted as a sort of mental therapy for the suffering and anxieties of mankind in general – hunger, war, disease, old age, death."... "The universal hero myth, for example, always refers to a powerful man or god-man who vanquishes evil in the form of dragons, serpents, monsters, demons, and so on, and who liberates his people from destruction and death."[25]

Expressing the idea of a common source in The Egyptian Mysteries, Lucie Lamy writes, "There is a fundamental notion, abstract yet vitally real, which colours all the myth, the morality and the life of the ancient Egyptians. This is Maât. Divine entities and human beings alike live by Maât, for Maât and with Maât."[26]

As Lamy explains, "Thus Maât does not judge: she is consciousness itself, and also the individual consciousness that each person carries in his heart, for this she is both the motivating force and the good of life. She is invoked on all occasions; she is omnipresent. Maât moves and directs existence, and Maât is its ultimate treasure."[27] These myths are the oldest known religious hieroglyphs and found in the Fifth and Sixth Dynasty royal burial chambers. They are known as the Pyramid Texts.

The ancient Egyptian concept of Maât is tantamount to the mathematitian George Cantor's concept of infinity and a common origin expressed by this Continuum Hypothesis:

$$2^{x_0} = x_1$$

It is also similar to the astro-physicists concept of a Big Bang or Christianity's concept of a god creating the universe out of nothing in six days and resting on the seventh, or the Hindi, Buddhist, or Native Americans religious concepts of something out of nothing by a divine being.

She also refers to the Heliopolitan myth as "represent[ing] the metaphysical phase of Creation, the enunciation of archetypes."[28] Referring again to the pyramid Texts, she relates, "In Egyptian terms, Origin corresponds to the Demiurge [*i.e.*, Plato's Doctrine of the World Soul], alone in the Nuni Mass the last and lowest term, corresponds to the primordial hell."[29]

Jill Purce in <u>The Mystic Spiral</u> notes that, "In Islam the breath is the 'Divine Exhalation,' the manifestation of the Creative, the feminine principle [*i.e.*, the Mother archetype representing origin] of the One, analogous with the Hindu goddess Sakti. Manifested through this creative breath are the Divine archetypes as names in the twenty-eight letters of the Arabic alphabet. The alternating breaths of 'continuous creation,' are the origin of the Sufi ritual, the <u>dhikr</u>."[30]

R.J. Stewart explains in <u>The Elements of Creation Myth</u>, "The foundations of creation mythology are anonymous and protean. Such primal myths are timeless, yet we recognize that they have been handed down to us in various forms from ancient times." He goes on to say, "In the vast mythic timeframe of Indian myth and religion for example, cosmological lifetimes are accounted, with the reiteration of new cycles occurring over periods of time that are on a stellar rather than a human scale."[31]

Stewart elucidates, "The primal subjects of creation myth, however, were tackled by the ancients in a number of ways: they fused myth, astronomy, cosmology, and poetic or mystical intuition in a synthesis that is often unacceptable to the modern intellect. It should be emphasized in this context that the viewpoint of the ancients was coherent, organic and holistic." He continues, "In other words, there was no compartmentalizing or rigid separation of myth, astronomy, cosmology, mystical intuition, magic or religion. This unification does not imply lack of discretion or an undeveloped state of mentation in our ancestors worldwide, but a way of thinking and living that resonated to cycles and values vastly different from our own."[32]

And, illustrating the basis of the universal need to connect with the One, he writes, "In orthodox religions, despite that accumulation of propaganda and style inevitable in any power structure, there is always an element of creation myth. Religions are founded upon many supports, but the deepest of all is often the creation of the worlds, even when it is thrust into the background of attention or corrupted through political maneuvering."[33]

In other words, man needs the sense of cohesion or grounding source that all religious myths, as originating from the collective unconscious provide for his conscious mind's day-to-day functioning.

Chapter Three

The Importance of ritual; fractal geometry; the Chaos Theory; dissipative structures

The importance of ritual (habit) is reflected in religion and myth because it is the grounding source of the psyche's expression in the three-dimensional realm. Ritual serves to create and maintain the illusion of density as matter, by and for the conscious mind. It serves as the basis of matter, which per Bohm is recurrence, and so doing lends coherency and cohesiveness for the conscious linear succession of archetypal images and dramas emotionally projected outward by the psyche through the senses from the world's collective unconscious.

As Jung notes in Man and His Symbols, "The narration or ritual repetition of sacred texts and ceremonies, and the worship of such a figure with dances, music, hymns, prayers, and sacrifices, grips the audience with numinous emotions (as if with magic spells) and exalt the individual to an identification with the hero."[1]

Jung alludes to repetition of the psyche's linear succession of images: "[A]ll the mythologized processes of nature, such as summer and winter, the phases of the moon, the rainy seasons, and so forth, are in no sense allegories of these objective occurrences; rather they are symbolic expressions of the inner, unconscious drama of the psyche which becomes accessible to man's consciousness by way of projection – that is, mirrored in the events of nature."[2] In Psychological Reflections, he adds, "The psyche creates reality every day."[3]

Elaine Pagels discusses the significance of rituals in everyday life in The Gnostic Gospels: "But it is not only the story of Christ that makes ordinary life sacred. The Orthodox Church gradually developed rituals to sanction major events of biological existence: the sharing of food, in the Eucharist; sexuality, in marriage; childbirth, in baptism; sickness in anointment; and death, in funerals."[4]

As David Noss relates in Man's Religions, "Religion provides a year-round schedule of rituals and activities which help to maintain community cohesion by filling the days and weeks with specific things to do."[5] Illustrating further the psyche's need for ritual, he adds, "First, there is a primary anxiety arising from crises or strains in the life of the individual or the community, and this calls forth rituals whose purpose is to provide restoration and reassurance."[6] Noss continues, "But once these rituals have been firmly established, with their mythical and institutional accompaniments, a secondary anxiety lest the rituals have <u>not</u> been promptly enough nor properly performed gives rise to further rituals of purification and expiation."[7]

In <u>The Archetypes and the Collective Unconscious</u>, Jung discusses the significance of ritual in relationship to religion: "The experience of the Mass is therefore a participation in the transcendence of life, which overcomes all bounds of space and time. It is a moment of eternity in time."[8]

Since we are constantly flashing "in-and-out-of existences" (see: Part One, Chapter Four; Numerical Field Structure of Thought, and the Appendices, Part C: Neurological Concepts - Maturana and Varela's "phase-locking" resonance concept), the conscious mind constantly seeks reassurance of the continuance of reality through ritual. <u>Literally</u>, we - and everything that we perceive - are being re-created or "re-born" in each instant. The concept of re-birth - either as the transmigration of the soul or the "heavenly ascension" of the soul - in myths and religions has its roots in ritual as recurrence.

Jung writes, "By the 'transcendence of life' I mean those aforementioned experiences of the initiate who takes part in a sacred rite which reveals to him the perpetual continuation of life through transformation and renewal."[9]

He continues to explain, "The transformation process takes place not within him but outside him, although he may become involved in it. The initiate who ritually enacts the slaying, dismemberment, and scattering of Osiris, and afterwards his resurrection in the green wheat, experience in this way the permanency and continuity of life, which outlasts all changes of form and, phoenix-like, continually rises anew from its own ashes. This participation in the ritual event gives rise, among other effects, to that hope of immortality which is characteristic of the Eleusinian mysteries."[10]

As Murry Hope expresses in <u>The Psychology of Ritual</u>, "How many structures across the length and breadth of this planet have been erected ostensibly for the performance of the Rite? Too many to include in a single tome, but for a start we could try Stonehenge, Karnac, the Potala at Llasa, the Parthenon, the temples of the East, and the churches and cathedrals of the West." She continues, "Even the sacred caves of the ancients and holy places of the Australian Aborigines and Amerindians merit consideration in this context."[11]

Hope adds another category of ritual, whereby "[m]usic is another avenue of artistic expression which certainly owes much to the Rite.[12],[13] The earliest recorded dance forms may be evidenced in shamanism; and anthropology and ethnology are generous with their material when it comes to the music and ritual movements of earlier races, much of which has survived to this day. The folk music of all countries also carries a thread of the Rite."[14]

Commenting on the historical influence of ritual, she states, "The Rite in its many forms has been in existence since man first organized himself into distinct groups and cultures. The Elders of the tribe, or those who exerted authority over the populace at large, were quick to realize both the coalescing effect of the public rite and its possibilities as a tool of central control. Supplementing her view, she adds, "The early priest-hoods, and those ecclesiastics that followed in their footsteps down the pages of history, were only too well aware of the power to be gained by subjecting the people to the kind of mass rites which either gave access to the racial collective unconscious, rendered the mind vulnerable to auto-suggestion, or simply encouraged the release of corporeal emotions."[15]

The mathematical, non-linear process corresponding to a feedback loop is called iteration - literally meaning "repetition". This concept is central to fractal geometry, the Chaos Theory and Prigogine's dissipative structures, which can be metaphorically viewed as the psyche's tools of expression.

Each process allows man to neurologically process and experience the numerically-coded, non-linear (circular), archetypal thought/energy patterns of the collective unconscious of Framework 2, which through the ritual of one moment following another, repeating themselves at various scales/resolutions (octaves) of the electromagnetic spectrum, in order to be interpreted by our 17 senses as matter.

As Deepak Chopra explains in <u>Unconditional Life</u>, "When the nervous system is intact, we may be said to have as many as seventeen senses, according to researchers on perception. We do not give names to most of these, and some are still disputable."[16]

He continues, "Under the sense of touch, for example, we include our response to heat, texture, pressure, the placement of our limbs, the weight of our bodies, and pain - all are things we 'feel'."[17]

Chopra explains how we create each conscious probable second of our unique reality: "If each person is constantly creating his own inner experience, placing innumerable interpretations on the raw data that the senses provide, that is strong grounds for not denying anyone his personal version of reality. A generation ago, the ruling assumption was that one reality - hard, scientific, materialistic - would do for all. Now we have to learn to cope with the state of many realities."[18]

In order to describe the complexity of nature's shapes, for example, a fern, lightning, a mountain, or a coastline, Benoit Mandelbrot developed a branch of mathematics that he coined as fractal geometry. Its basis is the dynamical systems theory, whose foundation is attributed to Poincare.

Mandelbrot demonstrated that nature's fractal shapes could be duplicated by repeating (iterating) a certain geometric operation again and again, producing these shapes at ever-decreasing scales of resolutions; consequently resulting in the property of self-similarity, which is the underlying principle of a hologram - the part contains the whole (see: Appendices, Part B: Mathematical Concepts).

As Mandelbrot points out in <u>The Fractal Geometry of Nature</u>, "Nature has played a joke on the mathematicians. The 19-century mathematicians may have been lacking in imagination, but Nature was not. The same pathological structures that the mathematicians invented to break loose from 19-century naturalism turn out to be inherent in familiar objects all around us."[19]

Commenting on the subjectivism of geometry, Michael Barnsley in <u>Fractals Everywhere</u> says, "Geometry is concerned with making our spatial intuitions objective. Classical geometry provides a first approximation to the structure of physical objects; it is the language that we use to communicate the designs of technological products and, very approximately, the forms of natural creations."[20]

Explaining further, he adds, "Fractal geometry is an extension of classical geometry. It can be used to make precise models of physical structures from ferns, to galaxies."[21]

An example of a geometric figure repeating itself on a descending scale is the H-fractal.

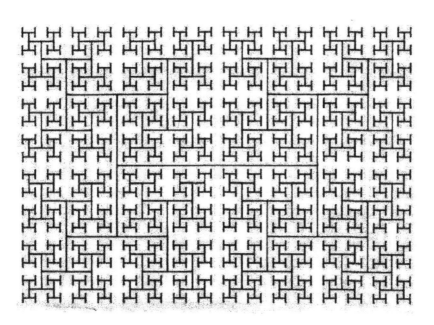

Ritual, or repetition, is central to Chaos Theory as well as to fractal geometry since they are both branches of dynamical systems theory. The term Chaos is actually a misnomer, because what appeared as chaotic systems actually showed a deeper level of order once non-linear mathematics was applied to it (see: Part Two: Chapter Four; Non-Linear Mathematical Organizers of Form).

Prigogine's theory of dissipative structures demonstrates how the chemical processes of a living organism are feedback loops, exhibiting self-similarity, self-actualizing and self-organizing properties. Properties which are inherent in dynamical systems (*i.e.*, the Father archetype concepts) far from equilibrium, being based on non-linear (circular) equations, (*i.e.*, numbers as archetypes of order) - the higher the degree of non-linearity (*i.e.*, $x2$, or $x3$, or $x4$ variables in the equation), the more complex the form (see: Appendices, Part A: Scientific Concepts, and Part Two, Chapter Four: Non-linear Mathematical Organizers of Form).

As Bohm has stated, "recurrence is the basis of matter" - meaning the endless repetition of energy/thought patterns that give a "form" continuity through "time".

So, consequently, when a sinewave is confined to a boundary system (*i.e.*, our .95s - 1s consciousness interval), the probability of an electron becomes an actuality - a point - and its thought/energy patterns become periodic. It is periodicity (repetition) which thus creates the illusion of the permanency of "objects".

In accordance with Bateson, Maturana and Varela's concepts of cognition being a process of self-referral, self-actualization and self-production, the American physicist David Bohm discusses his concept of creating a language experiment called the rheomode (from a Greek verb meaning "to follow") in his book <u>Wholeness and the Implicate Order</u> in order to present reality as a relationship or unity rather than fragmentation.

He observes that the current structure of the English language, *i.e.*, subject - verb - object, serves to fragment one's thought processes; but conversely, if we placed the emphasis of action on the root verb in our language rather than the subject, then reality's seamlessness or wholeness would become more apparent. For example, the Russian language places the verb before the subject resulting in circuitous thought and speech patterns, rather than the linear thought and speech patterns found in Western society. Consequently, one's sense of day-to-day events is broken into parts rather than experiencing an underlying sense of wholeness.

Bohm notes "that all knowledge is produced, displayed, communicated, transformed, and applied in <u>thought</u>. Thought considered in its <u>movement of becoming</u> (and not merely in its content of relatively well-defined images and ideas) <u>is</u> indeed the process in which knowledge has its actual and concrete existence."[22]

He continues, "What is the process of thought? Thought is, in essence, the active response of memory in every phase of life. We include in thought the intellectual, emotional, sensuous, muscular and physical responses of memory [obtained through structural coupling with the environment]. These are all aspects of one indissoluble process. To treat them separately makes for fragmentation and confusion."[23]

Chapter Four

The Numerical Field Structure of Thought
Cantor's Continuum Hypothesis: $2^{\aleph_0} = \aleph_1$

"This equation is a statement about the nature of infinity. A century and a third after Cantor first wrote it down, the equation – along with its properties and implications – remains the most enduring mystery in mathematics."[1]

George Cantor deeply believed in the concept of infinity – for him, its expression was mathematics – what he eventually coined as the transfinite numbers.

The real number line is comprised of rational numbers, which are positive and negative whole numbers (*i.e.*, 1, 2, 3… or -1, -2, -3…), positive and negative fractions (*i.e.*, 1/2, 1/3, 1/4… or -1/2, -1/3, -1/4…), and zero. It also consists of the irrational numbers, both algebraic and non-algebraic, or what is known as transcendental numbers. The irrational algebraic numbers, such as $\sqrt{2}$ (1.414…), $\sqrt{3}$ (1.732…), $\sqrt{5}$ (2.236…), etc., have unending, non-repeating decimals, but can be used as roots in polynomial equations; whereas the non-algebraic transcendental irrationals, such as π (3.141…) or e (2.718…), can't be used as roots in polynomial equations.

Cantor proved that even though the rational numbers were infinite, they could be counted or enumerated, but the non-algebraic irrationals were of a much higher order of infinity: they couldn't be counted – and that most numbers on the real number line were transcendental, *i.e.*, $\sqrt{2}^{\sqrt{3}}$, e^{π}, $\sqrt{5}^{\sqrt{7}}$, for which there wasn't a one-to-one correspondence.

Just as Bolzano proved that there were as many numbers between 0 and 1 as there is in the interval between 0 and 2; and thus demonstrating that the <u>length</u> of the line segment is irrelevant, Cantor proved that there were as many numbers on a given line segment as there were on a plane of two dimensions, or three-dimensional, or four-dimensional space, etc. He mathematically demonstrated that dimension is irrelevant as far as infinity goes; *i.e.*, continuous spaces have the same number of points ("power") as the real number line.

Cantor ascribed a name to his order of infinites, the transfinite numbers, and he assigned the first letter of the Hebrew alphabet, the aleph, ℵ, to each cardinal set. He envisioned a new beginning for mathematics - not just the <u>potential</u> infinity of the Greeks, *i.e.*, Zeno's paradoxes, but, rather the beginning of <u>actual</u> infinity.

The cardinality of a set merely means the number of elements in that posticular set; hence, for an infinite set such as Cantor's $\aleph_o$, it contains all of the rational numbers (*i.e.*, positive and negative whole numbers, fractions and zero), plus the algebraic irrational numbers (*i.e.*, $\sqrt{2}$, $\sqrt{3}$, etc., or any number which is not the result of a squared number, *i.e.*, 4, 9, 16, 25, etc.).

Then, his next lowest order of infinity, or $\aleph_1$, is the set of non-algebraic irrationals, or transcendentals, followed by the set of all functions.

He ran into a problem, though; the Axiom of Choice in Set Theory. He didn't know, and couldn't prove in the ensuing years, if there was an order of infinity between the $\aleph_o$ and $\aleph_1$. But what he had proved in the 1870s, and created modern set theory by doing it, was that for every set there was always a larger set: "the set of subsets of the original set."[2] This is called the "power" set. For example if a set contains {4, 5, 6, 7} then there are two possibilities for each element to be included or not included in a subset, so the "power" set would be 2^4 $\rightarrow$ elements / $\rightarrow$ possibilities = 16.

As a result, Cantor assumed that the cardinal number (*i.e.*, "power set") for the continuum of real numbers was $2^{\aleph_o}$ · # of elements / $\rightarrow$ possibilities. So $c = 2^{\aleph_o}$. But what he had hoped to prove was that $2^{\aleph_o} = \aleph_1$ $\rightarrow$. This Aleph represented the next higher infinite order of transcendental numbers. Unfortunately, when he died in 1918, unable to prove his continuum hypothesis, he was not aware that apparently it doesn't have a solution within the current system of mathematics.

The paradoxical problem that Cantor encountered in proving his continuum hypothesis was the Axiom of Choice in Set Theory, which states "that for every set A there is a choice function, f, such that for any non-empty subset B of A, f (B) is a member of B. The choice function assigns ('chooses') a member from each set A. The problem with the axiom of choice lies in the fact that there may be infinitely many sets B within A."[3]

This mathematical quandary along with the Axiom of Specification, which concludes with "nothing contains everything"[4], and "the Axiom of Powers, which leads to the prospect that there is always a larger and larger cardinal number set demonstrates a holographic view of reality. The ego-conscious mind is constantly seeking the meaning of "the part containing the whole".[5]

Significantly, the Greeks sought <u>potential</u> infinity in Zeno's paradoxes, which basically inferred that motion was impossible since space and time could be infinitely subdivided. For example, one could never leave a room; since every time a step was taken it was divided in half.

But this paradox was neatly and elegantly solved by the concept called a limit. Introduced by the Czechoslovakian priest, Bernard Bolzano, in the early 1800s and then rediscovered and introduced to the mathematical community by Karl Weierstrass in 1865, this property basically stated that <u>every infinite sequence in a subset of a space has a limit point within that space</u>.

The concept of a limit takes an <u>infinity of terms</u>; a sequence (*i.e.*, a set of numbers that are well-ordered, (1, 2, 3…)) or a series (1/2, 1/2 + 1/4, 1/2 + 1/4 + 1/8, 1/2 + 1/4 + 1/8 + 1/16…) and relates them to something finite as the limit.

A series is a collective sum of a set of numbers; hence the limit of the series is the sum total, or just one number.

For instance, The Golden Mean or 1.618… is the limit of the Fibonnaci' Series, (1, 1, 2, 3, 5, 8, 13…), where each term is the sum of the two previous terms. The Golden Mean is the result of dividing a line into the mean and the extreme, *i.e.*, This number as a limit is irrational and continues on but never reaches 2. The concept of a limit is to try to understand infinity within the finite of an imaginary illusionary concept called a "limit"

and incorporating it into a triangle 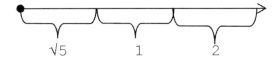 ; so that $1^2 + 2^2 = \sqrt{5}^2$, and, then dividing $\sqrt{5}$, + 1/2 = 1.618…

The Fibonnaci Series can be found in the logarithmic spiral of the conch seashell, the growth patterns of plants, the fetus of man and animals, etc.

The concept of a limit was extended by Richard Dedekind in 1858 to define irrational numbers as being the limit of rational numbers. For instance the $\sqrt{2}$ or 1.414… is the limit for all of the numbers and their decimal expansions between 0 and 1.414… And the converse is true, then, of the rational numbers being a limit for the irrational numbers.

Again, the concept of the infinite is brought within the domain of the boundaries of the conscious mind.

In 1850, Bernhard Riemann, a German mathematician, extended Bolzano's 1817 principle which proved that there were as many infinite points between 0 and 1 as between 0 and 2 to what is now called the Riemann sphere. (Shown below)

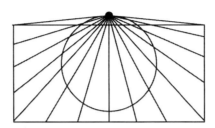

2-dimensional plane

He illustrated how the infinitely many points on the plane could demonstrate compactness; whereby it would be closed and bounded since all sequence of points would converge to a limit point.

The limit point contains the concept of both the negative and the positive infinity of the real number line, since all points on a curve - the sphere would be the model - tend to one point, or emanate from it. The limit point would be the north pole of the y-axis.

The "tendency to exist" known as an electron is also described as a point in an infinite-dimensional space. A line is an extension of that point containing an infinite number of versions, or expansions of that point into space. When confined within a system, that line revolves into a circle or sphere, with the rotating y-axis creating the properties of magnetism and space and the x-axis creating the properties of electricity and time (see: Appendices, Part A: Scientific Concepts).

The simplest atom is the Hydrogen atom - the first element on the periodic table. The universe is composed of 90% hydrogen. The hydrogen atom contains one proton, with a positive charge, in its nucleus and one orbiting electron, with a negative charge. The next element is Helium with 2 protons and 2 neutrons in the nucleus and 2 electrons orbiting in the first shell.

Out of the 200+ subatomic particles that physicists have discovered, the three most stable are the neutron, proton and electron. The neutrally charged neutron, though, can decay into a proton. And the proton can also decay into a neutral pion (which is comprised of or decay into, 2 photons) and a positron (which is a positive electron - its mirror opposite or antimatter). Just as these two elements can decay into an electron or its mirror opposite, they can also be created from an electron.

An electron rotates a million times within a billionth of a second, or a nanosecond. When the electron is confined within a boundary system, such as the conscious interval of .95s - 1s or the unconscious interval of 0.8s - 1.2s, it starts to rotate.

The rotation creates photons (light) as interactions at the boundaries when an electron becomes a positron. So a photon (light) is the result of an electron rotating and becoming its mirror opposite: a positron.

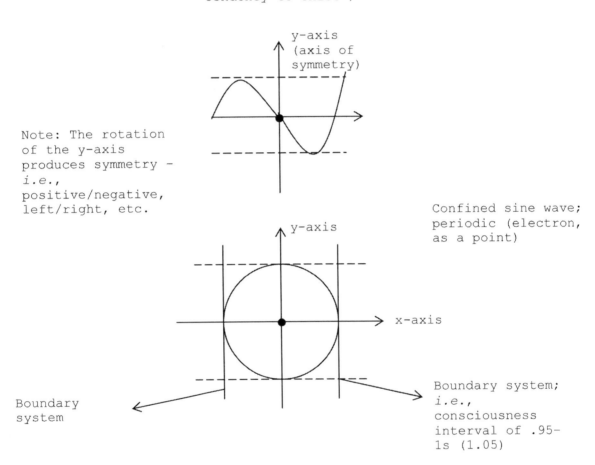

In his book, <u>Quantum Theory</u>, David Bohm states, "We have seen that the electromagnetic field can interact with matter only by means of indivisible processes in which a full quantum is either emitted or absorbed."[6] Continuing, he says, "If we wish to describe these processes in terms of the language of equivalent particles, we must then say that interactions between matter and light take place only by means of the emission and absorption of photons."[7]

Analogous to a number field in mathematics, which can be either ordered, as in the real numbers (*i.e.*, closed under all four operations of arithmetic, except division by zero) or not ordered, as in the complex numbers (*i.e.*, Real numbers on the x-axis and imaginary numbers on the y-axis -
→ real ⓐ + ⓑⓘ → imaginary - invented by Carl Gauss in 1799), the field of photons produced by the confinement of a one rotating thought/energy pattern, *i.e.*, electron, would be on the order of 2×10^{15} per second, or 2,000,000,000,000,000 photons.

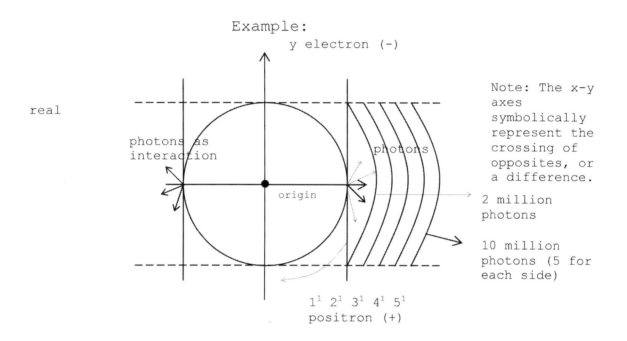

Example:

Note: The x-y axes symbolically represent the crossing of opposites, or a difference.

Within the first rotation, or 1 nanosecond (one billionth of sec) a million photons are radiated from each boundary for a total of 2 million photons, which travel one foot/nanosecond. For instance, within 5 nanoseconds, 10 million photons (light particles) would have radiated 5 feet, in one foot intervals, comprising a numerical thought structure energy field that then within one second would contain 2×10^{15} photons with the original 2 million photons being 186,000 miles away, and the last 2 million being only one foot away from the source; thus creating the illusion of space.

An average object contains 10^{24} particles, which would be atoms composed of ultimately electrons and their interactions (photons) produced by its mirror opposite: the positron within a confined system.

The system containing the probabilities for the unordered number field would be the 0.8 - 1.25, or 1.5 collective unconsciousness interval, while the ordered number field would be isomorphic with the consciousness interval of .95s - 1s, or 1.05.

Since E = MC² (energy ~ mass) and matter is 99.999% empty space, with the remaining .001% being the interaction (photons) between the electrons, and as every cubic centimeter of space has been mathematically calculated to contain more energy than all of the visible matter in the Universe according to John von Neumann in Wholeness and the Implicate Order, then the electromagnetic energy patterns which constitute the 60,000 thoughts per day per person, or 41+ thoughts per minute for that one person, multiplied by nearly 7 billion people and which exhibit the properties of rotating electrons (which is the basis for a hologram) are ultimately composed of sinewaves, which produce frequency as sound.

The confined sinewaves within a boundary system (*i.e.*, the consciousness interval of .95s - 1s, or 1.05) would be spherical in nature, reflect the concept of octaves (*i.e.*, the electromagnetic spectrum from 10 to 10^{24}) and possess the holographic property of the part containing the whole.

Sinewaves (unactualized electrons)(see: scientific concepts in the appendices), according to Fourier, underlie all waves, or all waves are a composite of sinewaves. Joseph Fourier would have appreciated the connection between music and prime numbers (archetypes of order) that Riemann's Hypothesis of 1859 demonstrated as being sinewaves.

Prime numbers such as 2, 3, 5, 7, 11, 13… are numbers which cannot be broken down any further (*i.e.*, they are only divisible by themselves or 1), nor are they the result of the multiplication of other numbers. So all whole numbers which aren't prime numbers are composite numbers; for example 4 as (2 x 2), or 6 as (2 x 3), or 8 as (4 x 4), or 9 as (3 x 3). This is the Fundamental Theorem of Arithmetic. The composite whole numbers which are built from multiplying primes together would then be seen as harmonic octaves of primes.

Gauss, who authenticated complex (imaginary) numbers, was intrigued in 1792, as a schoolboy at age 15, with logarithms. These are based on multiplication and addition. And he was also fascinated by the distribution of the prime numbers. He succeeded in devising an equation by using the transcendental number e (2.718281…) as the base of a logarithm in order to obtain a fairly accurate estimate for the number of primes from 1 to N as N/log (N).

Since Gauss concentrated on the patterns of the primes and didn't try to predict the location of the next one, he unraveled the harmonic link between the primes and logarithms.

From Euclid on, mathematicians have been striving to find a solution for the seemingly random distribution of the primes. Gauss espoused the prime/logarithm connection. Then Euler, who believed that prime numbers were at the base of musical harmony (remember: music is based on the $12\sqrt{2}$, which is the 1.05 consciousness interval), stumbled across a connection with the zeta function and primes.

The zeta function is harmonic. A function symbolically represents a physical relationship between coordinate points on a graph, whether the numbers representing the points are real or complex (partly real and partly imaginary). These points (numbers) can result in a shape, form or object.

The zeta function, $\zeta(s)$, as $_{2s}$zeta of "s", represents the infinite sum of a harmonic series (*i.e.*, numbers or fractions added together). $\zeta(s) = 1 = \frac{1}{1^s} + \frac{1}{2^s} + \frac{1}{3^s} \ldots$ Euler accidentally discovered that when he substituted 2 for S in the series, (*i.e.*, $1 = \frac{1}{2} + \frac{1}{4} + \frac{1}{9} \ldots$) that the limit for this series was $\frac{1}{6}\pi^2$.

Emboldened with his discovery, he saw a way to equate the harmonic aspects of the zeta function with prime numbers. Euler's zeta function:

This function equated multiplication with addition and highlighted a connection between the primes and the zeta function.

Euler also dabbled with inserting complex numbers into an ordinary function as exponents and, surprisingly, sinewaves were the result.

In 1859, Bernard Riemann built on Euler's sinewave connection and, consequently, improved on Guass' estimate for the distribution of the primes. Riemann utilized Euler's zeta function, but substituted the complex numbers into it as the exponent so that $\zeta(s) = \sum \frac{1}{n^2}$ became instead $\zeta(s) = \sum \frac{1}{n^z}$, where "z" is a complex variable. (See pg. 48)

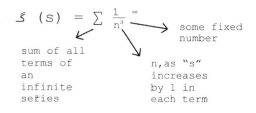

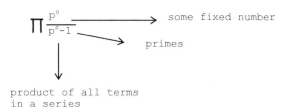

For example; $\sum 1 + \frac{1}{2^z} + \frac{1}{3^z} + \frac{1}{4^z} + \frac{1}{5^z} \ldots$ and "z" is of the form real # a + ib imaginary #. So, $1 + \frac{1}{2^{(a+ib)}} + \frac{1}{3^{(a+ib)}} + \frac{1}{4^{(a+ib)}} + \frac{1}{5^{(a+ib)}} 2^z \ldots 2$

What Riemann discovered when he charted, or graphed, his results were that where the equations equaled zero sinewaves were produced as the location sites of the prime numbers. In other words: prime = zeros = sinewaves. This was the basis of the musical beauty that Euler intuitively sought.

Riemann determined that the zeros were dependent upon "a" (in a + ib, as the real number element in the term) to be 1/2 or ($9 = \frac{1}{2}$). He called this byline the critical line and believed that all of the zeros (primes/sinewaves) would be on it. Unfortunately, his proof of this was not included in his 10-page paper, which was published in 1859, and no one has been able to prove it since.

R^1 (N) - $\sum \frac{1}{n^s}$ is Riemann's zeta function upon which he based his hypothesis. "R" gives you the number of primes up to "N" and the "s" exponent is substituted by the complex variable "z".

The Riemann zeros became tantamount to a Fourier Transform, which is based on sinewaves for the set of prime numbers. Hence, prime numbers, as archetypes of order, would display the holographic properties of sinewaves at the zeros.

One of Riemann's discoveries was that when he charted his zeta landscape onto a graph, it displayed the holographic properties of the part containing the whole when the value of the function equaled zero.

Consequently: "The sinewave is the sum total of the waveform (thoughtform)."

To summarize, "The sinewave (which is the basis of a hologram and is an unactualized electron [and a part of whole of All That Is], containing archetypal thought/energy patterns for the collective unconscious) is the sum total (or total sum of a series of numbers [archetypes of order] or fractions [representing the division of Unity] as one number, which would be the limit point. The limit point implies a bounded space, such as a sphere [which would produce spherical or 3-D waveforms], where all the numbers [archetypes of order] would tend to, or emanate from. The concept of a limit brings the infinite within the understanding of human consciousness) of the waveform (for example, all 3-D objects) (thoughtform)."

When a decision is made at the subconscious theta wave level of 5 - 8 cps in each unconscious 0.8 - 1.2s interval and the sinewave (electron (*i.e.*, containing all of the archetypal probabilities for the objects and events for the next <u>conscious</u> .95 - 1s interval)), collapses into a line (actualization) within the consciousness boundary system, the wave/particle, or energy/matter concept of duality, which according to Jung is an expression of the Father archetype, manifests as "matter".

This concept of a field (collective thought/energy hence) field of consciousness, would be the basis for lucid dreams, ESP, Jung's archetypes and synchronicity concept, Seth's "root assumptions" and "Spacious Present."

Jane Roberts' Seth terms these the units that underlie electromagnetic patterns as CU's or consciousness units.

In <u>The Unknown Reality</u>, Seth expounds on this concept: "When man realizes that he himself creates his personal and universal environment in concrete terms, then he can begin to create a private and universal environment much superior to the one that is the result of haphazard and unenlightened constructions."[8]

He continues, "All realities emerge from the psyche, and from the CU's (the units of consciousness) that compose it."[9]

In The Individual and the Nature of Mass Events, Seth expresses the concept of the "basic simultaneity of time" whereby the "Spacious Present holds all events side by side ready to be interpreted in cause-and-effect fashion by the organizational abilities of our more limited physical senses."[10]

Jung's concept of an archetype of Union assists in arranging the events in moment-by-moment, conscious linear succession along with the r.a.s. (reticular activating system) located at the base of the brain.

The events of each conscious moment, for instance a .95s - 1s interval, for every individual within this system are the result of an unconscious/subconscious decision utilizing the brain's theta waves at 5 - 8 cps. Consequently, the base resonant frequency for all reality phenomenon viewed within the conscious moment of approximately 7 billion people is the same. We all "blink on-and-off" nearly simultaneously and (for the most part) are unaware of being unconscious between the conscious intervals.

The spherical harmonic waveforms (*i.e.*, frequency as octaves interpreted differently by each of the 17 human senses), which are a three-dimensional extension of confined sinewaves within a boundary system, represent the natural vibrations of world phenomena.

The natural vibrations mean the base resonant frequency of 5 - 8 cps (matching the brain's theta waves at a subconscious level), which is the only frequency capable of entering a system, and only through the north pole of the y-axis. This would mean that the images/objects at this level would appear "ghost-like", *i.e.*, less dense to us, if we could perceive them due to the fact that they would only be composed of 10,000,000 (10^7) to 100,000,000 (10^8) photons and only be 5 feet to 50 feet away from the source of origin within 50 billionth of a second. This is the moment of actualization of an object within the human unconsciousness interval of .85-1.2 seconds and then viewed as a "solid" object during our consciousness interval of .95-1 second.

The north pole of the y-axis is analogous to the limit point on a Riemann sphere. The concept of a limit elegantly describes "the part containing the whole" by taking an infinity of terms - for example, a series of numbers representing archetypal concepts - and transforming them into the finite "matter" of the conscious moment, which would represent the sum total of the waveform (thoughtform).

Just as π (3.144...) is a ratio comparing the difference of the diameter to the circumference of a circle, which represents infinity, the square roots of 2, 3 and 5 represent a proportion, which acknowledges not only a difference, but also the equivalency of sameness within the difference.

The principle of the equivalency of sameness within difference is noted not only as the basis of a hologram, but also the superposition principle of quantum mechanics because the overtones of wave (harmonics), even though different from their base resonant frequency would be but different versions or aspects of that same wave as an archetypal concept.

Since algebraic irrational numbers have been mathematically proven to be the limits of rational numbers, and √2 as 1.414… is the limit for the rational numbers (*i.e.*, archetypes of order) between 0 and 1.414, constituting the crystallographic atomic structure, and √3 is the limit for the rational numbers between 1.414… and 1.713…, constituting the molecular structure, and √5 is the limit for rational numbers between 1.713 and 2.236…, constituting the cellular structure (see: Appendices, Part B: Mathematical Concepts), and √5 is incorporated in the mean-extreme line segments constituting a triangle as the Golden Mean, Ø, or 1.618… as the result of √5 + 1/2, then the amplitude or height (*i.e.*, north pole, as a limit point) of the triangle when squared (*i.e.*, actualized) represents in physics terms the "intensity" or the energy entering a system.

Example:
Atomic triangular structure based on the √2.

Molecular hexagonal structure based on the √3.

Cellular pentagonal structure based on the √5.

Consequently, the collective unconscious or Framework 2 contains within it all archetypal patterns (dramas as represented by the zodiac and displayed by the unconscious' Reverse Speech patterns) into which the personal psyche taps (similar to choosing a video to play in a VCR). The psyche emotionally projects an idea or concepts outward from the senses (according to Seth) as frequency (the repetitiously coded information as the number/coefficients of non-linear equations).

The frequencies meet and mingle as wave-front interference patterns within the numerical field structure of thought of other personal psyches.

These are actualized or manifested by the subconscious as a probable "I" (the "third eye" chakra or image maker) every time that a decision is made (for example, when the sinewave collapses) and the appropriate "phase-entanglement angle" occurs, so that, consequently, what we recognize as our personality is a linear succession of probable "I's".

In Hinduism, there is a belief that reality is being dreamed by a dreamer.

PART TWO

The Personal Unconscious

Chapter One

Bridge between idea and matter

Jung believed that a person's individual unconscious (subconscious) acts as a bridge between the collective unconscious and the conscious.

Jane Roberts' Seth mirrors this concept in <u>The Individual and the Nature of Mass Events</u>: "Now for a moment let us imagine that physical events occur in the same fashion that you choose those which flash upon the screen of your experience, and, as you do not know what happens in a television studio before you observe a program [the unconscious .8 - 1.2 interval], however, so you do not know what happens in the creative framework of reality before you experience physical events [in the conscious .95 - 1s interval], we will call that vast 'unconscious' mental and universal studio Framework 2."[1] Seth refers to the conscious interval where we experience actuality/events as Framework 1. "On a conscious level, and with your conscious reserves alone, you could not keep your body alive an hour."[2]

In <u>Dreams and Projection of Consciousness</u>, Seth comments further: "The so-called subconscious is a connective between mind and brain, between the inner and outer senses. Portions of it deal with camouflage patterns, with the personal past of the present personality with the inner memory. The greater portion of it are concerned with the inner world, and as data reaches it from the inner world, so can these portions of the subconscious reach far into the inner world itself…"[3]

Later in the book, Seth acknowledges the ego's (conscious mind's) distrust of the subconscious on the necessary grounds of the personality needing to be focused in three-dimensional reality for survival's sake. "You have here one of the main reasons why you must request the subconscious to enable you to recall dreams. The ego would see no reason for such a memory and on general principles attempts to repress them."[4]

Reflecting in <u>On the Nature of the Psyche</u>, Jung says, "If the unconscious can contain everything that is known to be a function of consciousness, then we are faced with the possibility that it too, like consciousness, is a subject, a sort of ego. This conclusion finds expression in the common and ever recurring use of the term 'subconsciousness'."[5] He adds further, "At the same time this hypothetical 'subconsciousness', which immediately becomes associated with a 'superconsciousness', brings out the real point of my argument: the fact, namely, that a second psychic system coexisting with consciousness -- no matter what qualities we suspect it of possessing -- is of absolutely revolutionary significance in that it could radically alter our view of the world."[6]

Also in Man and His Symbols, Jung stresses the importance that dream symbology has to the individual's personal unconscious (subconscious) in order to communicate only with the dreamer.

The body's seven to twelve chakras (Sanskrit for "wheel") are a product of the individual psyche's subconscious connective activity from the thought pattern energy field of the collective unconscious to the conscious mind's transformation of this energy into momentary objects.

The body emits a range of low frequency as well as receiving energy. The concept of chakras, or rotating energy patterns, is an ancient one dating back to early Egypt, India, Greece and Rome. The idea of an energy field surrounding a person finds expression also in Christian art as a luminous cloud around the whole body or a halo around the head.

Both the Hindu Bhagavad Geta and Upanishads mention the chakras and how they roughly correspond to certain physical organs, colors and elements. For example, the crown chakra (on the top of the head) corresponds to the color of purple, the pineal and pituitary glands and the mind. At the other end of the spectrum, the root chakra located at the base of the spine corresponds to the color red, the sexual organs and fire (as energy or dynamism).

C.W. Leadbeater in The Chakras describes the chakras as "[t]his divine energy which pours into each centre from without set up at right angles to itself (that is to say, in the surface of the ethnic double secondary forces in undulatory circular motion), just as a bar-magnet thrust into an induction coil produces a current of electricity which flows round the coil at right angles to the axis or direction of the magnet."[7]

Continuing, Leadbeater adds, "The primary force itself, having entered the vortex, radiates from it again at right angles, but in straight lines, as though the centre of the vortex were the hub of a wheel, and the radiations of the primary force its spokes."[8]

In 1908, Dr. Walter Kilner conceived of the idea that the human aura, or energy field, could be made visible if viewed through a piece of glass covered with a coal-tar dye called dicyanin.

After several hundred experiments, he published his findings in the January 6, 1912 "British Medical Journal". Although he met with much skepticism at the time, Dr. Kilner proceeded with his experiments. His later work, The Human Aura, published in 1920, met with more enthusiasm from "The Scientific American".

The human aura, or thought/energy pattern field, which is a result of the continually rotating chakras, can now be cheaply and effectively observed in real time on a computer screen or as photos by means of an aura camera (see: Part One, Chapter One).

From my own experiments with the aura camera, I observed a direct correspondence between the four primary colors (Red, Blue, Green and Yellow) and the four primary archetypes (Mother, Father, Union and Self) as they reflect a person's 60,000 thought per day, or 41+ per minute.

I would have a subject concentrate on the different aspects of the Mother archetype, such as a cave, the ocean, a forest, etc., and the color blue would show up on the computer screen in 'real time' or a photo.

The same results happened when a person was asked to focus on the image of themselves in a mirror (*i.e.*, the Self Archetype) and the color green would immediately come onto the screen from the left. The departing energy/thought always exited from the left side of a person.

Chapter Two

Image Maker

C.G. Jung viewed religion, science, fairytales and Mathematics as all expressions of myth, and as such originate in the collective unconscious as archetypal content clusters. The personal unconscious (subconscious) transforms them into images (in the unconscious 0.8 - 1.25 interval at the 5 - 8 cps theta wave level) for the conscious mind to view as objects in the .95s - .1s consciousness interval.

In Transformations of Myth Through Time, Joseph Campbell describes the importance of myth: "It coordinates the living person with the cycle of his own life, with the environment in which he's living and with the society which itself has already been integrated in the environment."[1]

Just as Jung observed, Campbell also noted "that throughout the mythologies and religious systems of the world, the same images, the same themes [*i.e.*, creation, death, resurrection ascension to heaven virgin births, etc.] are constantly recurring, appearing everywhere."[2] He remarks that the German anthropologist Adolf Bastian called them 'Elementary Ideas'.

Adding, Campbell says, "The main problem with symbols is that people tend to get lost in the symbol," and, "The whole world is of symbols. In Goethe's words, 'Alles Vergangliche ist mur ein Gleichne's.' ['Everything that is transitory is but a reference.'] But the reference isn't to anything. It's to what is called the world, sunya, and it's called the void because no thought can reach it."[3]

Then, in The Power of Myth, Campbell refers to the Paleolithic hunting scenes found in French caves - "Whatever the inward darkness may have been to which the shamans of those caves descended in their trances, the same must lie within ourselves, nightly visited in sleep"[4] - as being a mythic image from the unconscious finding expressions in modern day life as compelling memories of the hunt.

Echoing the universality of myth, R.J. Stewart, in The Elements of Creation Myth, says, "Myth does not seek to answer questions in the manner required by modern science, but is a perpetual, retelling, re-creation, of the great story of existence."[5]

Stewart adds, "The cosmology of the forest Indians is similar in a number of ways to that found in classical Greek, Roman, or Celtic myth. We may presume this to be a property of consciousness, and must certainly not fall into the trap of suggestion that there is any 'original' mythic sequence carried from place to place."[6]

The importance of symbols in myth is discussed in J.E. Cirlot's, A Dictionary of Symbols: "Jung stressed the traditional aspects: 'of the elements, two are active - fire and air, and two are passive - earth and water.' Hence the masculine, creative character of the first two, and the feminine, receptive and submissive nature of the second pair."[7]

Cirlot defines terms, concepts and objects in his dictionary such as "abandonment" and "zone" from a psychological standpoint by explaining the different levels and time periods of meaning by utilizing symbolizing agents and symbolic syntax. Highlighting Jung in On Psychic Energy, he specifically says: "'The psychological mechanism that transforms energy is the symbol.'"[8]

Seth, in The Nature of the Psyche: Its Human Expression, illuminates the concept of consciousness and symbols from a different aspect: "Consciousness forms symbols. It is not the other way around. Symbols are great exuberant playthings. You can build with them as you can with children's blocks", and, "You can learn from them, as once you piled alphabet blocks together in a stack at school."[9]

According to Jung in Man and His Symbols, "The symbol-producing function of our dreams is thus an attempt to bring the original mind of man into 'advanced' or differentiated consciousness, where it has never been before and where, therefore, it has never been subjected to critical self-reflection. For, in ages long past, that original mind was the whole of man's personality."[10]

Later in his book Jung gives a symbolic example: "Today, for instance, we talk of 'matter.' We describe its physical properties. We conduct laboratory experiments to demonstrate some of its aspects. But the word 'matter' remains a dry, inhuman, and purely intellectual concept, without any psychic significance for us."[11]

He further explains, "How different was the former image of matter - the Great Mother - that could encompass and express profound emotional meaning of Mother Earth. In the same way, what was the spirit is now identified with intellect and thus ceases to be the Father of all. It has degenerated to the limited ego-thoughts of man; the immense emotional energy expressed in the image of 'our Father' vanishes into the sand of an intellectual desert."[12]

In Egyptian Mysteries, Lucy Lamy cites many examples of symbols as expressions of myth in order to create worldview images for ancient Egyptians. The scarab was not only an insect, but as such represented metamorphoses or transformations of a person's consciousness.

Another example was the eye, which symbolized the liberation of divine light imprisoned in matter, and was also seen as the seat of the soul.

Lucy Lamy also mentions how the figure of Maât conveys the double meaning of individual and cosmic consciousness, and how the ancient Egyptians conveyed a unique sense of the simultaneity of time in their calendrical system by incorporating stellar, solar, lunar and seasonal cycles.

She points out how Shu is symbolic of space and how "ka" is "an abstract principle formerly translated as 'double', for it seemed inherent in every living thing."[13] Ka being symbolic of the concept of reciprocity, she says, "Yet prior to everything, appetite or attraction is needed, symbolized by the two appraised arms in a gesture of calling."[14] Attraction or desire, as emotion, is behind every conscious decision, which is needed in order to collapse a sinewave (into a line) and turn a probability into a three-dimensional actualized object.

Expounding on the concept of reciprocity in The Mystic Spiral, Jill Purce says, "The opposing solar and lunar currents symbolized by the serpents are the alternative forces of expansion and contradiction, manifested in the two halves of the Yin Yang symbol or the two halves of the double spiral or the world egg, and constituting, when joined, the spherical vortex."[15] As a confined sinewave within a boundary system (*i.e.*, our .95s - 1s consciousness interval) begins to rotate it forms a three-dimensional volume - the sphere.

A spiral is the involute of a sphere and the shape of DNA. It is the logarithmic (mathematical) expansion of number, constituting archetypes of order. Purce comments on the spiral as being a symbol: "It denotes eternity, since it may go on forever."[16]

In his book, The Symbolic Species, Terrence Deacon claims that the difference between humans and nonhumans lies in our process of thought-symbolic representation. Deacon explains, "The way that language represents objects, events, and relationships provides a uniquely powerful economy of reference. It offers a means for generating an essentially infinite variety of novel representations, and an unprecedented inferential engine for predicting events, organizing memories, and planning behaviors."[17]

"The notion of this universe, its heavens, hells, and everything within it, as a great dream dreamed by a single being in which all the dream characters are dreaming too, has in India enchanted and shaped the entire civilization,"[18] writes Joseph Campbell in The Mythic Image.

Echoing the dreamer motif, Seth in The Seth Material explains, "Desire, wish, and expectation rule all actions and are the basis for all realities. Within All That Is, therefore, the wish, desire, and expectation of creativity existed before all other actuality."[19]

He continues, "In other words, All That Is existed in a state of being, but without the means to find expression for its being. This was the state of agony of which I spoke."[20]

And, "The agony and the desire to create represented its proof of its own reality. The feelings, in other words, were adequate proof to All That Is that it was."[21]

Then, in further explanation, Seth continues, "At first, in your terms, all of probable reality existed as nebulous dreams (*i.e.*, the Hindu version) within the consciousness of All That Is. Later the unspecific nature of these 'dreams' grew more particular and vivid. The dreams became recognizable one from the other until they drew the conscious notice of All That Is. And with curiosity and yearning, All That Is paid more attention to its own dreams."[22]

In other words, our seemingly concrete reality of objects and events are the product of conscious energy being transformed from the collective unconscious by the personal unconscious (subconscious) as the image maker and viewed by our conscious mind's screen as solid objects and events.

Besides myths composed of symbols, mathematics (the basis of science) also originates in the unconscious and is an organizing factor of the subconscious' image producing ability for the conscious mind.

Pythagoras said, "All is Number," whereas Jung clarified this by differentiating number and other unconscious symbols as "archetypes of order which has become conscious." Marie von Franz in Number and Time goes on to explain, "This would mean that our idea of order possesses a preconscious aspect, or, to put it another way, it is based on an inborn unconscious psychic disposition in man."[23]

Hermann Weyl in Philosophy of Mathematics and Natural Science reminds us "that it is the function of mathematics to be at the service of the natural sciences."[24] And, "A conspicuous feature of all mathematics, which makes it so inaccessible to the layman, is the abundant use of symbols."[25]

He ends his chapter, "Number and Continuum, The Infinite", by saying, "If in summing up a brief phrase is called for that characterizes the life center of mathematics, one might well say: mathematics is the science of the infinite."[26]

So the totality or wholeness of all numbers (*i.e.*, 2, 3, etc. - all natural integers, fractions, rational, complex and imaginary numbers are divisions of the One into Many as the concept of multiplicity) implies, as with a hologram, that each part contains the whole.

The Jungian sense of number represents archetypes of order (*i.e.*, the linear succession of each person's conscious interval, .95s - 1s) which mathematically constructs segments of three-dimensional pictures of "reality".

Marie von Franz points out, "As a result of modern number theory, material numbers are nowadays considered in quite a different light; they are taken to be logical abstractions."[27] But she adds, "If we concede that material integers are true symbols in this sense, and this means acknowledging their origin in archetypes, then they must contain the psychic dynamism of the latter. In other words, they also possess the autonomy of an archetype."[28]

The basis of mathematics is set theory or, as mathematician Tobias Dantzig remarked in his book, <u>Number: The Language of Science</u>, "We derive this knowledge [counting] through a process which dominates all mathematics and which has received the name of <u>one-to-one correspondence</u>."[29] He continues, "It consists of assigning to every object of one collection an object of the other (*i.e.*, the field-like quality out of energy/thoughtforms [concepts] arranged as pixels on our visual cortex; in order to translate the symbolic content into forms and objects) the process being continued until one of the collections, or both, are exhausted."[30]

Another product of mathematics (number as an archetype of order) is music (see: Appendices, Part D: Musical Concepts). The musical notes are based on the $\sqrt[12]{2}$, which is the interval of 1.05, the same .95 - 1s interval as our span of consciousness. Music, as number, is isomorphic with the collective unconscious as relayed by Joscelyn Godwin in <u>Cosmic Music</u>: "Recent research shows that human hearing is not only attuned significantly to our familiar foundations of music (interval proportions, distinction of consonance and dissonance, twelvefold gradation, major - minor, etc.), but, most importantly, that the psychological and unconscious realm complements this disposition of the ear."[31]

She adds, "This unconscious realm <u>knows</u> something of the interval proportions, and takes a decisive part in the multilayered and complex process of musical hearing."[32]

Continuing further, Godwin clarifies, "Principally, however, this psychological disposition - and here we come to the crux of it - is capable of unconsciously correcting all deviations that occur (notably these of mistuning). Since the time of Euler, who discovered it, this property has been called 'correctional hearing,' and more recent studies in information theory have found that this unconscious compensation can account for up to 40 percent of a semitone [note]."[33]

Just as von Franz points out in <u>Number and Time</u> that the number two "plays a very important role in mathematics," and that "The mathematician Brouwer, like Plato, even looks on the concept of two-oneness as the root of mathematical thought,"[34] Arthur Benade in <u>Fundamentals of Musical Acoustics</u> describes the graphic result of one divided into two as, "for every octave one goes up the scale, the frequency doubles, and for every octave one goes down the frequency becomes half of its former value."[35]

Since music is an expression of math as number intervals (i.e. tones) and along with science, religion, and fairytales are expressions of the symbolic archetypes of the collective unconscious, when it is experienced during our conscious intervals it tends to reassure us that we are experiencing a cohesive framework for reality, hence the universal need for music.

Just as myth, mathematics and music are expressions of the collective unconscious, so are fairytales. "Fairy tales are the purest and simplest expression of collective unconscious psychic processes,"[36] writes Marie von Franz in The Interpretation of Fairytales. She explains that, even though fairytales have been around for several thousand years, their basic patterns, themes, motifs have remained the same.

The reason for this as she explains is, "An archetypal image is not only a thought pattern (as a thought pattern it is connected with every other thought pattern), it is also an emotional experience - the emotional experience of an individual."[37]

"Another well-known expression of the archetypes is myth and fairytale,"[38] writes Jung in The Archetypes and the Collective Unconscious. In one of the parts of that book entitled "The Phenomenology of the Spirit in Fairytales", Jung concludes, "When we consider the spirit in its archetypal form as it appears to us in fairytales and dreams, it presents a picture that differs strangely from the conscious idea of spirit, which is split up into so many meanings." Continuing, he adds, "Spirit was originally a spirit in human or animal form, a dominion that came upon man from without."[39]

Then he says, "True, the archetype of the spirit is capable of working for good as well as for evil, but it depends upon man's free - *i.e.*, conscious - decision whether the good also will be perverted into something satanic."[40]

Since fairytales, (symbolic archetypal thought patterns arising from the collective unconscious and projected outward from the personal unconscious [i.e. subconscious] as electromagnetic "potential" images, which are then viewed by the conscious mind as "solid" objects) resonate from the core of the psyche "soul", the second-by-second messages contained within them and viewed as a linear time sequence have the same result as music and religion which provide a cohesive and stable framework for the conscious mind to function within.

Jung viewed spirit and number as being isomorphic with the spontaneous principle of movement within the psyche, and this would be the Father archetype.

Since science is based on mathematics - which is due largely in part to George Cantor's work with set theory and its relationship to infinity, which is known as the continuum hypothesis - it became more relativistic, mimicking mathematics. "Before the advent of quantum theory, physicists thought of particles and fields as distinct entities,"[41] says Heinz Pagels in The Cosmic Code.

According to Pagels, "The dualisms of energy and matter, particle and field, were dissolved, and everything could be seen to be interacting quantum fields. There isn't anything to material reality except the transformation and organization of field quanta - that is all there is." He continues, "According to quantum theory, the intensity of the field at a point in space is interpreted as the statistical probability for finding its associated quanta."[42] From a psychological viewpoint (intensities) Jung defines these energic points (intensities) of the collective unconscious as archetypal clusters.

In their book, Science, Order, and Creativity, David Bohm and F. David Peat define science "as an attempt to understand the universe and humanity's relationship to nature"[43] and mathematics as "an especially significant example of the inter-weaving of intuitive reason and formal logic in the kind of process that has been described above."[44] Continuing, "In this connection, it is interesting to note that the mathematician von Neumann defined mathematics as the relationship of relationships."[45] As an example of the process of intuitive insight being the catalyst for scientific discoveries, Bohm mentions that "Einstein certainly appreciated mathematical beauty very keenly but did not actually begin from the mathematics, especially in his most creative period. Instead, he started with unspecifiable feelings and a succession of images out of which more detailed concepts eventually emerged."[46] "Relating back to" or religare is the Latin base for the concept of religion. Attempting to achieve a sense of security and orderliness regarding the world and relationships to it, man's conscious mind drew upon the archetypal thought clusters of the unconscious and devised an explanation. Gods and goddesses, "high gods", "material gods" (*i.e.*, the Jewish god Yahweh) and "lords of heaven" (*i.e.*, the Sumerians) appeared.

"Religion enables individuals to have moments of vision that give them insight into realities ordinarily not seen nor understood,"[47] offers John Noss in Man's Religions.

Jung acknowledges in Man and His Symbols, "But while personal complexes never produce more than a personal bias, archetypes create myths, religions, and philosophies that influence and characterize whole nations and epochs of history."[48] He continues, "We regard the personal complexes as compensations for one-sided or faulty attitudes of consciousness; in the same way, myths of a religious nature can be interpreted as a sort of mental therapy for the sufferings and anxieties of mankind in general - hunger, war, disease, old age, death."[49]

The emotional dividend of this kind of identification for the individual with the hero is an exalted sense of well-being and efficacy.

"Commenting on the changing face of archetypal clusters as they relate to religion," Joseph Campbell purports in The Mythic Image, "the recurrence of many of the best-loved themes of the older, pagan mythologies in legends of the Christian Savior was a recognized feature intentionally stressed in the earliest Christian centuries."[50] Elucidating further he says, "The meaning, for example, of the ass and ox in the Nativity scene would in the fourth century A.D. have been perfectly obvious to all, since these were the beasts symbolic in that century of the contending brothers, Seth and Osiris"[51] (from the Egyptian Osirian religion).

Chapter Three

The Senses as Channels for an Idea's Projection

The 60,000 thoughts per person per day, or 41+ per minute, (of which we may be <u>consciously</u> aware of a percentage of), are electromagnetic energy patterns within a field-like structure of which archetypes, representing numerically coded information and frequency, are projected outward from the psyche (soul) through the senses as emotion (energy) in order for the subconscious, which acts as an image maker, to mathematically transform (as in a Fourier series, *i.e.*, a series is the collective sum of a set of numbers 1/2, 1/2 + 1/4, 1/2 + 1/4 + 1/8...)[10] this symbolic information into objects and events for the conscious mind to view during the conscious interval of .95s - 1s.

Consequently, outer reality (with conscious second) becomes the direct replication of the soul's inner reality, and the drama that it is creating.

"The sinewave is the sum total of the waveform (thoughtform)" is the catalyst sentence which prompted this research and writing journey for me; and it also appears to be at the epicenter of the results, since it is what is being projected from the psyche (see: Part One, Chapter Four: The Numerical Field Structure of thought).

According to Webster's dictionary, "emotion" is a noun from the Latin emovere: stir up, psychical excitation, and <u>to move out of the psyche</u> are the meanings of it.

From a 1987 study done at the National Institute of Mental Health in Maryland by Dr. Candace Pert, we can understand that polypeptides, consisting of 60 to 70 large molecules, act as messengers between cells. And as Capra notes in <u>The Web of Life</u>, "By interlinking immune cells, glands, and brain cells, peptides form a psychosomatic network extending throughout the entire organism."[1] So, "Peptides are the biochemical manifestation of emotions; they play a crucial role in the coordinating activities of the immune system; they interlink and integrate mental, emotional, and biological activities."[2]

Peptides are known to produce emotions, as Capra points out: "this would mean that all sensory perceptions, all thoughts, and, in fact, all bodily functions are emotionally colored, because they all involve peptides." He continues, "Indeed, scientists have observed that the modal points of the central nervous system, which connect the sensory organs with the brain, are enriched with peptide receptors that filter and prioritize sensory perceptions. In other words, all our perceptions and thoughts are colored by emotion."[3]

From an endocrinology point of view, Deepak Chopra parallels the traditional healing practices of India, quantum physics and neurobiology in Quantum Healing: "The body is not a frozen sculpture but a river of information and energy that is constantly renewing itself. We are not physical machines that have learned how to think, we are actually these thoughts in a universal mind that have learned how to create the physical machine. The body is nothing but a field of ideas."[4]

In Unconditional Life, Chopra discusses the field of ideas, "the field where light and mind, nothing and everything, mingle as one."[5] He continues, "Before there can be a photon of light, there must be a field of light; before an individual electron, the field of electricity; before an isolated bar magnet the earth's magnetic field."[6]

The concept of a field is analogous with the concept of probability, which becomes an actuality, or point (*i.e.*, atomic and molecular structures) when the sinewave collapses (after a decision is made - implying emotion).

Referring to the background of the term "field" in India Chopra writes, "It is extremely intriguing that the word 'field,' which modern physicists use to describe the most fundamental forces in nature, was a divine word in ancient India. When Lord Krishna reveals his infinite greatness to the warrior Arjuna in the Bhagavad - Gita, he says, 'Know me as the field and as the knower of the field.'"[7] He explains further, "The Sanskrit word, kshetra… comes very close to what a physicist means when he says 'quantum field' or 'electromagnetic field'. These fields are infinite and all pervasive; without them, reality could not exist. Lord Krishna was making the same point about himself."[8]

And, from a psychical viewpoint, Seth explains how we project our thoughts into objects and events: "Thoughts and images are formed into physical reality and become physical fact. They are propelled chemically. A thought is energy. It begins to produce itself physically at the moment of its conception.[9]

"Mental enzymes are connected with the pineal gland. As you know them, body chemicals are physical, but they are the propellants of this thought-energy containing all the codified data necessary for translating any thought or image into physical actuality. They cause the body to reproduce the inner image. They are sparks so to speak, initiating the transformation."[10] This concept is echoed in Dr. Candace Pert's peptides as emotions research done at the National Institute of Health.

Seth adds, "Chemicals are released through the skin and pore systems, in an invisible but definite pseudophysical formation. The <u>intensity</u> of a thought or image largely determines the immediacy of its physical materialization. There is no object about you that you have not created. There is nothing about your own physical image that you have not made."[11] Remember, the height, intensity [i.e. emotion] amplitude of a wave is tantamount to the limit point of a sphere [i.e., the north pole of the "y" - axis], and is the only entry way of energy into a system and only at the base resonant frequency of 5 - 8 cps of the brain's theta waves.

He later comments, "Your physical senses, again, act almost like a biological alphabet, allowing you to organize and perceive certain kinds of information from which you form the events of your world and the contours of your reality."[12] (See: Part C Neurophysiological Concepts 4(b))

In the process of hypnotism, it has been discovered that the physical body reacts to an event every 1 1/2 seconds before the conscious mind is aware of the event happening, according to hypnotist Lindsey Brady. This is because the subconscious, as an image maker, has already mathematically constructed the event, during the 0.8 - 1.2s interval of unconsciousness, and then the conscious mind views the construction. And this is why we sometimes know what song is next to be played on the radio or automatically swerve around something in the road in order not to hit it.

"There is a certain periodic pattern of time in the activity of consciousness. One of these periodicities is 0.8 to 1.2 seconds and it interjects a rhythm into the observations and recognitions of music, singing and speech,"[13] writes Dr. Georg von Bekesy of the results of his forty years of psychological experiments in <u>Sensory Inhibition</u>.

He notes, "In hearing, and especially in speech and music, this separation of a continuous process [i.e., This could possibly be the reason that energy is viewed and measured as discrete little packages called "quanta"] into small discrete periods of time seems to be extremely important."[14]

Reflecting, von Bekesy adds, "Perhaps an even more interesting fact is that we are willing to make a fresh start after each lapse of consciousness."[15] (Remember: Maturana and Varela showed in their book, <u>The Embodied Mind</u> that there is a periodic rhythm of the brain's activity detectable in an electroencephalogram (EEG) of about .15 seconds and attributed to cortical alpha waves, and referred to in neuroscience and psychology as "perceptual framing.") And, from <u>Quantum Healing</u>, Chopra comments on, "The silent gap between thoughts, being tangible, still plays no part in modern psychology, which is oriented completely to the mind's contents or the brain's mechanics."[16] Continuing to explain, he adds, "The gap turns out to be the central player, however, if you are interested in what lies beyond thought. Every fraction of a second we are permitted a glimpse into another world, one that is inside us and yet obscurely out of reach."[17]

Chapter Four

Non-linear Mathematical Organizers of Form

Since math is the basis of science, Prigogine at first lacked a mathematical basis for his theory of complex living systems far from equilibrium.

But, with the advent of the acceptance of non-linear equations as viable solutions to an equation, he was able to develop his theory of dissipative structures.

A non-linear equation is one in which its variables are squared or raised to another power, *i.e.*, x^2, x^3, x^4, etc. The higher the raised power, the greater the degree of complexity of a system.

This is because each non-linear equation offers more than one solution, and each solution marks a bifurcation point (*i.e.*, the possibility of a system branching off and going in another direction).

Poincare, who developed the dynamical systems theory of mathematics, which utilizes non-linear equations in order to develop visual mathematical patterns and relationships, ushered in a new kind of geometry called topology.

"Topology is a geometry in which all lengths, angles and areas can be distorted at will. Thus, a triangle can be transformed continuously into a rectangle, the rectangle into a square, the square into a circle," remarks Capra in The Web of Life. And, explaining a little further, he adds, "Similarly a cube can be transformed into a cylinder, the cylinder into a cone, the cone into a sphere."[1]

So topology is a mathematics of relationships and patterns, which are invariant and do not change under transformation. "Another example of this, [is] that one cannot make a flat plate without a hole in it from the doughnut-shaped piece. The latter, incidentally, is called a torus. These characteristics - like having or not having a hole - are called topological invariants,"[2] writes Stephen Barr in Experiments in Topology.

A line is the projection of a point into space. This implies that the line is composed of an infinite number of aspects of the point (electron) and, within a bounded space (*i.e.*, the consciousness .95 - 1s interval), represents a closed interval of real numbers, which is compact and connected.

"Compactness and connectedness are topological properties,"[3] notes Chinn and Steenrod in their book <u>First Concepts of Topology</u>.

Prigogine's dissipative structures, Chaos Theory and fractal geometry all share the same mathematical base, which is dynamical systems theory, whose base is Poincare's topology.

Chaos Theory (used to predict the weather) (see: Appendices, Part B: Mathematical Concepts) and fractal geometry (used to describe nature's irregular shapes such as clouds, coastlines, etc.) (see: Appendices, Part B: Mathematical Concepts) both have a non-linear feedback-loop process called iteration (repeated multiplications) in common. Self-organization and self-similarity are the results of this repetitious process.

The holographic property of self-similarity, or "the part containing the whole" as patterns of order at ever-decreasing scales of resolution (*i.e.*, octaves), is exhibited by a non-linear (*i.e.*, an electron as a sinewave when it isn't actualized and as a point when it is actualized) feedback-loop process known as iteration. (see: Scientific Appendices)

As Bohm has noted, the basis of matter is recurrence. It is the repeated energy patterns, or iteration of points constituting an object, that give it a seeming permanence and density in time and space.

Consequently, iteration, at the microscopic level as the repetition of frequency (*i.e.*, numbers, as archetypes of order/concepts, representing the energy radiating [photons] from a rotating electron [See: Part One, Chapter Four: The Numerical Field Structure of Thought]) becomes isomorphic with the psychological need for ritual at the macroscopic level (see: Part One, Chapter Three: The Importance of Ritual). Ritual (habit), as reflected in religion and myth, supplies the necessary grounding source as repetition (*i.e.*, iteration of points) for the psyche to express the thought/energy concepts from the unconscious to the sub-conscious image-maker, whose final product is viewed by the conscious mind every .95s - 1s interval as "solid" matter/events.

Commenting on the mass hypnosis exerted by the conscious mind, from <u>Quantum Healing</u>, Chopra muses, "Normal reality is like a spell - a very necessary one, since we must live by habits, routines and codes that we take for granted. The problem arises when you can make the spell but not break it."[4] And, "Any sudden revelation of a deeper reality carries enormous power with it - one taste alone can make life undeniably worthwhile."[5]

In his book, <u>The Myth of Invariance: The Origin of the Gods, Mathematics and Music From the Rg Veda to Plato</u>, Ernest McClain proposes a "hypothesis that the 'lattice logic' [field-like structure], which de Nicholas perceives in the <u>Rg Veda</u>, was grounded on a proto-science of number and tone. The hymns describe the numbers poetically, distinguish 'sets' by classes of gods and demons, and portray tonal and arithmetical relations with graphic sexual and spatial metaphor. Vedic concerns were with those <u>invariances,</u> which became the focus of attention in Greek timing theory."[6]

As McClain explains, Autonio de Nicholas, who wrote <u>Four-Dimensional Man</u> in an attempt to retrieve the lost meaning of the ancient Hindu text the <u>Rg Veda</u>, discovered a "lattice logic" of thought consisting of four "languages." The languages of Non-Existence, Existence, Images and Sacrifice and the Embodied Vision in the <u>Rg Veda</u> express the primacy of sound (as frequency/number) and, when chanted (repetition/ritual), promote a sense of unity, continuity and "the well-formed instant."[7]

Rupert Sheldrake's biological hypothesis of formative causation posits that morphic resonance (*i.e.*, the structural interaction) between organisms, which produces the structure of future organisms from present organisms, "takes place on the basis of rhythmic patterns of activity."[8] He explains, "All organisms are structures of activity, and at every level of organization they undergo rhythmic oscillations, vibrations, periodic movements, or cycles."[9]

Sheldrake adds, "Because all post members of a species influence these fields, their influence is cumulative: it increases as the total number of members of the species grows."[10] He summarizes, "Morphogenetic fields are 'probability structures' in which the influence of the most common past types [*i.e.*, repetition of a form/iteration] combines to increase the probability that such types will occur again."[11]

PART THREE

The Conscious Mind

Chapter One

Consciousness as a process

Webster's Unabridged Dictionary defines consciousness as "the totality of one's thoughts, feelings, and impressions; mind."[1] And, just as electricity (time) and magnetism (space) (see: Scientific Appendices) are two different aspects of the result of the circular rotation of an electron, the Cartesian mind and matter split were seen as two different aspects of an organism by the neurophysiologists Maturana and Varela. Their systems theory of cognition called the Santiago Theory, and also the new concept of mental processes by the cybergeneticist Gregory Bateson in the late 1960s, presented the view that cognition or knowing was central to the process of life.

Bateson presented his theory that mind was the driving force determining the patterns and relationships of how a organism structured its form and that a physical brain wasn't necessary for a mind to exist (*e.g.*, a bacterium hasn't a brain yet is capable of perception, hence, cognition) in a 1969 paper on mental health in Hawaii.

The fundamental difference between Maturana and Varela's theories and that of Bateson's is one of epistemology, or the nature of knowledge. Bateson views reality as objective (*i.e.*, something that exists without an observer) and his computer model of the mind reflects an independently existing world, whereas Maturana and Varela's Santiago Theory is based upon a reality (*i.e.*, world) whereby the organism, through structural coupling with the environment, is bringing forth a world from a multitude of energy patterns as it perceives them through its neurophysiological apparatus. In conclusion, they assert that there is no independent world outside of the self-generating, self-referring and self-actualizing process of cognition.

Chapter Two

Rule, Boundary and Distinction Maker

The conscious mind is the rule, boundary and distinction maker. The conscious mind's boundary of .95s - 1s is the time interval that it views the thought/energy patterns (frequency) as objects which it has created through the human three-color channel visual system, *i.e.*, red → green, yellow → blue and black → white. These three-color channels of our visual system structure energy patterns into three-dimensional objects similar to the pixels of a computer screen or T.V. (see: Neruological Concepts). As the neurophysiological research team of Maturana and Varela noted in <u>The Embodied Mind</u>, color (frequency) is a distinction maker between what constitutes an object and its shape.

Following this same thought, psychologist and protégé of Jung Marie von Franz, in <u>Psyche and Matter</u>, notes that "[d]istinctness is <u>the</u> characteristic of order"[1] for the conscious mind, and that color as a quality determined that distinctness. She goes on further to add that "distinctness is an achievement of consciousness"[2] as opposed to the indistinctness of the archetypes in the collective unconscious.

Concurring with the importance of color (frequency/energy patterns) for the conscious mind in order to form objects, Francisco Varela concluded his research in <u>The Embodied Mind</u> that "it is impossible to separate the object sensed from its color because it is the color contrast itself that forms the object."[3]

Maturana and Varela also stress the fact that their research showed that color (as <u>repetitious</u> frequency patterns - repetition being an important factor of the conscious mind and determined by a sinewave confined to a boundary system, *i.e.*, the conscious interval of .95s - 1s) determines behavior, moods, habits, thoughts and actions.

So color (as thought/energy patterns in the frequency range of 429 [red] to 650 [blue] trillion cycles per second or 10^{14}), isomorphically as peptides, creates the body's network of biochemical manifestations of emotion. Dr. Candace Pert of the Mental Health Institute of Maryland in a 1980s study demonstrated that the entire group of sixty to seventy peptides linking the immune, limbic and endocrine systems into one network may constitute a universal language of emotions (see: Neurological Appendices).

The brain's filter, in order to screen out the thought/energy patterns (frequency) that are not accepted within this telepathically agreed upon three-dimensional reality, is the reticular activating system located at the base of the brain in the medulla oblongata. All incoming data from our 17 senses is filtered through this system before continuing on to various parts of the brain and then perceived in the .95s - 1s consciousness interval.

The conscious mind during this interval creates (actually views its creation) a sense of fragmentation from the whole or unity of which we are an intrinsic part by "languaging" (Maturana and Varela's term). Consequently, a sense of duality or plurality (many objects in a .95s - 1s image) and separateness from the whole is created - an illusion.

Only because of the difference between the conscious (.95s - 1s) and the unconscious intervals (.8 - 1.2s) do we appear to be separate and take form from the Unity of One.

As stated so eloquently in Sacred Geometry by R.A. Schwaller de Lubicz, "The Number One is only definable through the number two: it is multiplicity [plurality], which reveals unity." And as Sri Eurbindo relates in The Life Divine, "This does not mean that the One is plural, or can be limited or described as the sum of the many. On the contrary, it can contain the infinite many because it exceeds all limitation or description by multiplicity, and exceeds at the same time all limitation by finite, conceptual oneness."[4]

In religion this idea of oneness is found in Hinduism where the Divine One divided himself within himself (electromagnetic units/electrons as a field of waves) to form a self-created opposite - that which was total consciousness took form, and a universe or universes are consequently and simultaneously manifesting or actualizing.

In Lucy Lamy's Egyptian Mysteries, she notes that halving is the base of all Pharaonic mathematics:

> I am One that transforms into Two
> I am Two that transforms into Four
> I am Four that transforms into Eight
> After this I am One.
> (Coffin of Petamon, Cairo Museum)[5]

Duality and Plurality [objects], which is determined by the conscious interval as apparent separateness from the One, are explained as the active functional principles, the Neterocosmic or vital powers which find expression as the genesis of the world unfolds in Egyptian Mysteries.[6] Lamy further explains that in the Pyramid Texts, "the oldest known religious texts, from the 5th and 6th Dynasties that the Creator, Atum [which means All or Nothing] 'must project himself' or distinguish himself from the Nun, and thereby annihilate the Nun in its original inert state. 'Atum becomes.'"[7]

Since the function of the conscious mind is to apparently fragment the whole in order to perceive, then symbolism is necessary to bridge the gap between the conscious and unconscious intervals. As Jill Purce writes in <u>The Mystic Spiral</u>, "The function of symbolism is to go beyond the 'limitation of the fragment' and link the different 'parts' of the whole, or alternatively the worlds in which these parts manifest: these worlds are successive windings of the spiral."[8]

Continuing, she says, "This symbol, which is perpetually turning in on itself, expanding and contracting, has an interchangeable centre and circumference, and has neither beginning nor end: it will be referred to as the spherical vortex."[9] (Remember: a spiral is the involute of a sphere, which is a rotating three-dimensional circle [which is the result of the extension of a point into a line (diameter) within a confined space], within a boundary system.)

She further mentions, "It has been man's tendency to forget, in his enthusiasm for objective knowledge, that, ultimately, subject and object [Heisenberg's Uncertainty Principle] are one, and merely opposite ends of the same axis."[10]

Mirroring the concept that our conscious mind is by necessity a rule, boundary and distinction maker in order for us to experience a separateness from a psychological frequency realm, is an excerpt from <u>The Seth Material</u> by Jane Roberts: "All photons of <u>All That *Is*</u> are constantly changing, enfolding and unfolding. All That *Is*, seeking to know 'itself', constantly creates new versions of Itself for this seeking Itself is a creative activity and the core of all action[11]."

She further continues as Seth says, "Consciousness, seeking to know itself, therefore knows you. You, as a consciousness, seek to know yourself and become aware of yourself as a distinct individual portion of <u>All That *Is*</u>. You not only draw upon this overall energy but you do so automatically since your existence is dependent upon It."[9(17)]

Marie von Franz, in <u>Number and Time</u>, explains that even though Jung posited the collective unconscious as a field "isomorphic with the field of natural numbers,"[12] he saw it as being organized by what he called the archetype of the Self. She further explains that Jung viewed number as "an archetype of order that has become conscious,"[13] and that the conscious mind appears to exhibit a quaternary structure (*i.e.*, a double tetrahedron where one is right side up and the other [mirror opposite] is inverted).

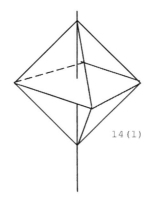

14(1)

Continuing, she adds, "Moreover, our field of consciousness is based on four fundamental functions: thought, intuition, sensation (function as perception), and feeling (function of evaluation). Any complete conscious realization takes place through the cooperation of these four functions."[1] The conscious mind's inte3rval of awareness is anywhere from .95 second to 1 second which is a ratio or comparison of differences (i.e. 1s/.95s=1.05sec as ratio). The sheer act of focusing on the conscious mind within boundaries produces the images that we view on our personal inner computer screen as moment-by-moment reality.

The conscious mind as a rule, boundary and distinction of reality is probed by Jean Piaget in <u>The Construction of Reality in the Child</u>. By studying hundreds of infants to eighteen months, Dr. Piaget comes to the conclusion that a child mathematically constructs reality's properties of space, time, causality and the permanence of objects. The latter he noted didn't take place until the child was at least a year old. He explains, "Perceptual images, not yet consolidated into objects or coordinated in a coherent space, seem to him to be governed by his desires and efforts, though these are not attributed to a self which is separate from the universe."[2]

Self-awareness arises (approximately at eighteen months) when the child's conscious mind starts to make the distinction between the whole and its parts, at which time objects become permanent and no longer disappear. Sensorimotorly, cause and effect would also arise as a result of the distinction of the relationships between object and subject and continues per Piaget until the eleventh or twelfth year.

In his conclusion he writes, "Of course, on the plane of action the child is no longer entirely dominated by the appearance of things, because through sensorimotor intelligence he has managed to construct a coherent practical universe by combining accommodation to objects with assimilation of objects to intercoordinated structures."[3]

Chapter Three

Language as Reality's Morphological Tool

The structure of language (within .95s - 1s) and the frequency of that sound which can be humanly apprehended (*i.e.*, 20 cps - 20,000 cps) become a morphological tool for reality. As Maturana and Varela demonstrate in The Embodied Mind, objects are linguistic distinctions, which can then have abstract concepts built on them. Also, Bateson notes that "a hierarchy of logical types emerges with human language."[1] Piaget gleans from his experiments those cognitive structures emerge from recurrent sensorimotor activities in children.

Bohm concurs in Wholeness and the Implicate Order that the structure of language acts as a fragmentor of reality and proposes that the concept of a rheomode (emphasis on root verbs) be introduced into language in order to unify the concept of reality for the conscious mind.

So, consciously and unconsciously (*i.e.*, David John Oates' [see: Part One, Chapter Two] reverse speech from the unconscious mind, whose metaphoric and archetypal content can be heard as a reverse background overlay of normal human speech), language structures every moment of conscious reality.

"Language actually structures your perception of objects,"[2] Seth comments in The Unknown Reality, (Vol. Two). "Words in a language function not only by defining what a specific object is, for example, but also by defining what it is not,"[3] he later adds. Continuing, Seth says, "A long time ago I said that language would be impossible were it not for its basis in telepathic communication and that communication is built up of microscopic images and sounds. These are translated into different languages."[4] (Note: this activity would have to take place in the 0.8 - 1.2s unconscious interval.) Lastly, he says, "Words, again, are related to the neurological structure, and languages follow that pattern."[5]

One of the implications of Maturana and Varela's Santiago Theory is that since the organisms of particular species have the same structure, then through structural coupling with the environment, they would bring forth a unique version of reality. Consequently, since humans are capable of abstract thought (based on "linguistic distinctions of distinctions"), then through languaging, we are capable of bringing forth a richly complex version of reality every conscious interval.

In Thought and Language (a study on the interrelationships of thought and speech), Lev Vygotsky analyzes Piaget's major focus as being a child's egocentrism, which he believes to be the result of identification with the unconscious until the subsequent socialization of the child after the ages of seven or eight. This socialization results then in the identification with the conscious mind. Critiquing further, Vygotsky adds that while Piaget focused on egocentric speech, he incorrectly saw it as static rather than an evolving process of thought and language, whereas Vygotsky deemed that it morphized into inner speech, and that only the aspect of vocalization diminished.

Linguistic and foreign policy dissident Naom Chomsky, writing on the "deep structure of language" as being based on the conscious fragmentation of subject - verb – object, parallels the work of Grinder and Bandler in The Structure of Magic. Both psychologists wrote the manual in 1975 in order to give other therapists the necessary tools and the ability to understand how humans structure their experiences through language systems. They identified three constraints which humans have in dealing with worldly phenomena: neurological, social and individual. So, "Language serves as a representational system for our experiences."[6]

They also discuss the three major modeling processes: generalization, deletion and distortion. It is in the modeling process of distortion that they uncovered the surface versus the structure of language.

Consequently, the conscious mind acting as a filtering system assists "human beings [to] create their linguistic models of the world, [as] they necessarily select and represent certain portions of the world and fail to select and present others."[7]

Further, they note, "Neurolinguistic programming teaches that language is more than communication -- it is also a means of perception and contains within it, codes and patterns of mental processes."[8]

In conclusion, they mention that the Deep Structure of language (from the unconscious [see: Part One, Chapter One regarding David John Oates' concept of Reverse Speech]) is the reference or source of the Surface Structure sentence. "The Deep Structure is the fullest linguistic representation of the world, but it is not the world itself. The Deep Structure itself is derived from a fuller and richer source."[9]

In continuance, "The reference structure for the Deep Structure is the sum total of all of the client's experiences of the world. The processes which specify what happens between the Deep Structure and the Surface are the three universal processes of human modeling, the rules of representation themselves: Generalization, Deletion, and Distortion."[10]

Finally echoing Maturana and Varela's concept of autopoiesis, Grinder and Bandler conclude, "Again, the way that the model each of us develops will differ from the world is in the choices (normally, not conscious) [choices imply emotions] which we make as we employ the three principles of modeling. This makes it possible for each of us to entertain a different model of the world and yet live in the same real world."[11] From linguists to neurophysiologists and from psychologists to physicists their research echoes the same refrain which is that language frequency as sound, structures what we consciously perceive of as a physical world.

Chapter Four

Reality as a Projected Hologram

In Jane Roberts' <u>Unknown Reality</u>, when she speaks as Seth, he comments that the human psyche (soul) propels ideas or thoughts as emotional energy (frequency or repetitious patterns) outward via the senses. (Remember: our bodies not only receive energy, but also emit a range of low frequency.)

Dr. David Bohm parallels this notion that our conscious reality, what he refers to as the Implicate Order, is the result of a deeper order in <u>Wholeness and the Implicate Order</u>. This deeper order is tantamount to Jung's collective unconscious. "Reality is projected from a higher dimension,"[1] he asserts.

He calls this enfolding and unfolding of the electromagnetic field motion a 'holomovement', which would differ from the static 'snapshot' context of a hologram.

He explains, "Our basic proposal was then that <u>what is</u>, is the holomovement, and that everything is to be explained in terms of forms derived from this holomovement."[2] Bohm continues, "Though the full set of laws governing its totality is unknown (and, indeed, probably unknowable) nevertheless these laws are assumed to be such that from them may be abstracted relatively autonomous or independent sub-totalities of movement (*e.g.*, fields, particles, etc.) having a certain recurrence and stability of their basic patterns of order and measure."[3]

In conclusion, Bohm states, "On the contrary, when one works in terms of the implicate order one begins with the undivided wholeness of the universe, and the task of science is to derive the parts through abstraction from the whole, explaining them as approximately separable, stable and recurrent [Note: Bohm has stated that the basis of matter, its stability, is the recurrence of energy patterns], but externally related elements making up relatively autonomous sub-totalities, which are to be described in terms of the explicate order [*i.e.*, everyday reality]."[4]

In another book of Bohm's, <u>The Special Theory of Relativity</u>, he says that "the transformation of 'matter' into 'energy' is just a change from one form of movement (inwardly, reflecting, to-and-from) into another form (*e.g.*, outward displacement through space),"[5] and that "the concepts of absolute space and time are based only on the continuation of certain modes of perceiving, conceiving, experiencing, etc., arising in the domain of everyday life, which are now habitual but which we once learned as children."[6] Meaning that, absolute space and time do not exist but are mental constructs.

Further he comments, "Indeed, as we have seen, the physical facts concerning space and time coordinates consists only of sets of <u>relationships</u> [invariant] between observed phenomena and instruments [Note: John von Neumann observed that instruments are only extensions of our senses], in which no absolute space and time is ever to be seen."[7]

Consequently, in his book he quotes Piaget and his work regarding children mathematically learning to construct reality from the energy flux. Bohm states, "The existing evidence shows that very young infants do not seem actually to have the notion of a permanent object. Rather, their behavior in relation to objects is such as to suggest that they regard them as coming into existence when they are first seen and going out of existence when they vanish from the field of perception. Only gradually does the infant build up the notion of an object that exists even when he does not perceive it."[8]

Coming from two diametrically opposed disciplines, Piaget a child psychologist, and Bohm a quantum physicist both agree that the reality of space, time, and obects is a learned mental construct.

Later in his book, Bohm comes to conclusion that "each person already has some sort of Euclidean [*i.e.*, geometrical - based on ratios/relationships] structure built into his bodily movements."[9] As a result, "The perceived picture is therefore not just an image or reflection of our momentary sense impressions, but rather it is the outcome of a complex process leading to an ever-changing (three-dimensional) <u>construction</u> which is present to our awareness in a kind of 'inner show'."[10]

Adding further to this concept, Bohm states, "This construction is based on the abstraction of what is invariant in the relationship between a set of movements produced actively by the percipient himself and the resulting changes in the totality of his sensual 'inputs'."[11]

Michael Talbot, in <u>The Holographic Universe</u>, discusses reality as a holographic image: "One of Bohm's most startling assertions is that the tangible reality of our everyday lives is really a kind of illusion, like a holographic image."[12] Talbot adds, "Underlying it is a deeper order of existence, a vast and more primary level of reality that gives birth to all the objects and appearances of our physical world in much the same way that a piece of holographic film gives birth to a hologram."[13]

The primary level of reality that Talbot is referring to is the same as Bohms holomovement, Jung's collective unconscious, the Egyptian "Nun" and the Hindu "Nada". In other words, a common source for all of the images that we in common day reality refer to as "objects".

The basis of a hologram is a sinewave, which is composed of the rotational movements of electrons. This movement (frequency) is perceived as sound by humans from the range of 20 cps to 20,000 cps. Consequently, the rotational movement of electrons within that frequency range as a sound beam can produce a holographic image so that a human can visually perceive that sound at 10^{14} or 450 - 750 trillion cycles per second by the conscious mind. This is achieved largely due to the fact that although all four brain wave clusters (alpha, beta, theta and delta) operate simultaneously, it is the beta state at 16 - 40 cps which dominates the mind during waking reality.

Mathematically, it is the dominant beta state which constructs "matter/objects" from the wholeness of the thought/energy patterns, and as such, is the reason for the wave/particle duality dilemma. Subatomic particles' "tendencies to exist" manifest as matter due to our conscious mind's beta waves at 16 - 40 cps.

In 1966, Dr. Karl Pribram published his first theories regarding the holographic nature of the brain due to wave inference patterns caused by the electrical impulses jumping from one synapse to another amidst the tightly packed neurons (brain cells). Talbot quotes Pribram on his discovery in The Holographic Universe: "The hologram was there all the time in the wave-front nature of brain-cell connectivity."[14]

Initially drawn by the mystery of how and where in the brain memory resides, Pribram began his search in 1946 as an assistant of Dr. Karl Laskley of the Yerkes Laboratory of Primate Biology. Due to experiments on rats, he realized that memories, motor skills, etc. weren't localized to a particular region but instead were distributed (as a field), throughout the entire brain.

Utilizing his twenty years of research along with his awareness of holography, it began to occur to him in the 1960s that the brain holographically constructs reality from the frequency analysis of the senses.

One of the major properties of a hologram is the concept of self-similarity. In other words, the part (*i.e.*, us and everything around us- the environment) contains the whole (*i.e.*, God, All That Is) at different resolutions/scales/levels.

Self-similarity is the underlying theme for the neurophysiological concept of autopoiesis, the mathematical concept of fractal geometry and the chemistry concept of the Chaos Theory.

Each person has 60,000 thoughts per day or 41+ thoughts per minute. It is my hypothesis that these thought/energy patterns are transformed into the colors of the auric field (electromagnetic energy - we both emit and receive energy), which continually surrounds a person. These thought/energy patterns are encoded into the four primary archetypes by the collective unconscious. As such they would reflect the four primary colors: Mother archetype (and all of the images and objects associated with this symbol, *i.e.*, matter, the ocean, the Mother figure, caves, etc.) as blue, Father archetype (and all of the images, objects and qualities associated with this symbol, *i.e.*, movement, duality, air, wind, father priest, professor, space and time) as red, Union as yellow and the Self archetype as green. These colors – frequencies – correspond also to the mammalian visual system and as such demonstrate how our conscious minds interpret the concepts/symbols from the unconscious and subconscious.

The subconscious is the image maker and functions basically at the theta wave level of 5 – 8 cps. It structures these color/number encoded concepts into images during the unconscious interval of 0.8 – 1.2s, then our conscious mind, which functions basically in beta, re-structures these images in a faster frequency of 16 – 40 cps and these resolutions appear as solid objects – matter.

One of the most important of our sensory organs for structuring objects, besides our visual system, is the ear. In 1953, Alfred Tomatis presented a paper to the French Academy of Sciences which detailed his findings that besides determining balance, coordination, verticality, muscle tone and the musculature of the eye, the inner ear (vestibular-cochlear system) acts as a relay system for all of the information (coded frequency) perceived by the other 16 senses.

In conclusion then, a confined sinewave (as the rotational movement of an electron, or a 'tendency to exist'), which would constitute the thought/energy patterns as archetypal concepts within the conscious boundary of .95s – 1s, becomes a spherical waveform (see: Nick Herbert's wave form family attributes from <u>Quantum Reality</u> in the App. Part A: Scientific Concepts).

These spherical waveforms (ultimately objects by the conscious mind) can only vibrate and hence only receive energy at the natural base resonant frequency of 5 – 8 cps, which happens to match our subconscious theta waves.

PART FOUR

Organizers of Form for the Conscious Mind

Chapter One

Number as frequency

In Number and Time, Marie von Franz points out that "when energy manifests itself in either psychic or physical dimensions, it is always 'numerically' structured, for example as 'waves' or as (psychic) rhythm."[1] And, "Natural numbers appear to represent the typical, universally recurring, common emotion patterns (archetypes) of both psychic and physical energy. Because the motion patterns (numbers) are identical for both forms of energy the human mind can on the whole, grasp the phenomenon of the outer world."[2]

For instance, Heinsenberg's mathematical model representing the energy transitions of an electron as it orbits around the nucleus is a matrix, or a rectangular array of numbers, so that the particle doesn't have a 'real' position described by a single number, but rather by the entire matrix of numbers.

The divinatory techniques such as the tarot cards, palmistry, Celtic rune stones, the African's bag of 'witch' bones, astrology, Chinese matrices or I Ching ("Legend says that many moons ago, the basic diagrams were revealed to a wise king through the markings on the back of a turtle, which crawled from a sacred river one day…a gift from the gods"[3], reports R.T. Kayser in I Ching), are all based on numbers.

Specifically, the movement of number, which is represented by the Father archetype, is also the definition of frequency. And frequency refers to the number of rotations of the electron.

According to Heinz Pagel in The Cosmic Code, the movement of number (frequency) is the basis for the entire logarithmic (*i.e.*, in an octave sense) electromagnetic spectrum from 10^1 to 10^{24}. And the basis for a hologram is the rotational movement of the number-coded sinewave.

The philosopher Rudolph Carnap comments in The Philosophical Foundations of Physics, "The facts of nature are concepts of numerical value."[4] This demonstrates how there could be a connection between the Jewish Kabbala ("in which the separate letters of the Hebrew alphabet are given a religious, moral, and mystical fantastic nature", explains Dr. Erich Bischoff in The Kabbala), the Hindu Rg Veda, also representing numerically coded information, and the Bible, as demonstrated in <u>The Signature of God</u> by Grant Jeffrey: "A careful examination of the names and numbers in the Bible's text reveals special mathematical designs and codes that are so complex no human or super-computer could have provided these features."[5]

Jeffrey adds, "Recently, Jewish computer scientists discovered a series of incredible messages encoded at equally spaced intervals hidden beneath the Hebrew text of the first five books of the Bible, the Torah."[6]

The primacy of number is demonstrated in ancient civilizations, such as Sumeria, Babylon, Egypt, China, India, Greece and also the Aztecs and Mayans through their pyramids and astonishing stellar calendars. In <u>Sacred Geometry</u>, Robert Lawler discusses the primacy of number in the Greek Pythagoras' viewpoint when he says, "All is arranged according to number," that "he was not thinking of numbers in the ordinary, enumerative sense," but rather as Plato viewed reality, as "pure essences or Archetypal Ideas" based on "the universal aspect of Number [being] analogous to the immobile, unmanifest, functional principle of its axis."[7]

In <u>Number and Time</u> and <u>Psyche and Matter</u> Marie von Franz demonstrates what she says Jung hinted at before his death, "that the natural numbers in fact do possess in exactly the same way in the world of psychic presentations all the qualities that they possess mathematically and they have in physics and in the hereditary code. Thus a real, absolute isomorphism is present."[8] Religion, science and fairytales, as expressions of myth from the unconscious, display triadic and quadripartite structure, *i.e.*, fairytales, folk tales, proverbs, traditional sayings, the four astrological elements of earth, air, water and fire and the four forces of the unified Field Theory are quadratic in structure, according to von Franz.

She notes the correspondence between the quadratic (4 bases) and triadic (the arrangement of the 4 bases into 64 triplets) structure of DNA and RNA and "Jung's hypothesis that number regulates both psyche and matter."[9] The elegance of DNA's quadratic and triadic structure is appreciated by its discoverers, Watson and Crick, in <u>The Double Helix</u> as they note that it represents "the perfect biological principle [which] is the self-replication of the gene."[10]

The quadratic functions of numbers representing "the One-Continuum's Model of Wholeness in all relatively closed structures of Human Consciousness and in the Body"[11] underlie color, sound, language and emotion (all various aspects of the electromagnetic spectrum as frequency) as the coded information within sinewaves.

The French mathematician Jean Fourier solved the mathematical problem of using differential equations, developed by Newton, to describe phenomenon. His "mathematical statement is that any periodic function [*i.e.*, A confined sinewave within a boundary system, such as our .95s – 1s consciousness interval] can be represented as a sum of sines and cosines – what is now called a Fourier series,"[1] writes Barbara Hubbard in The World According to Wavelets.

Fourier also showed that a sinewave underlies all waves. The Fourier Series and Transform explain how the conscious mind breaks down the mirror-image of an object or event, which the subconscious has constructed from the thought/energy patterns of the collective unconscious, and receives that information as frequency through the 17 senses and then reassembles that image/object/event for the conscious mind to view on the visual cortex. The Fourier Transform isomorphically breaks down the image, and consequently the Fourier Series reconstructs it in a linear manner for the conscious mind.

Hubbard comments on the sense of infinity contained in a sinewave function: "To define a function, one must know all its values: an infinity of numbers. A function, such as a wavelet or a signal, can be thought of as a single point [*i.e.*, electron] in an infinite-dimensional space."[2]

In Linus Pauling's The Nature of the Chemical Bond, he explains the "resonance" phenomenon between molecules as an interaction of a relationship pattern based on the quantum principle of ratio or comparison.

Periodicity (*i.e.*, repetition of patterns) is at the base of the evolution of the number concept from cardinal numbers to ordinal numbers, with the former based on the one-to-one correspondence principle (*i.e.*, matching) and the latter based on ordered succession (*i.e.*, both matching and ordering). As the mathematician Tobias Dantzig explains in Number: The Language of Science, "As man learns to rely more and more on his language, the sounds supercede the images for which they stood, and the originally concrete models take the abstract form of number words. Memory and habit [*i.e.*, ritual] lend concreteness to these abstract forms, and so mere words become measures of plurality."[3]

Consequently, number, as an archetype of order and also as periodic frequency, organizes forms for the conscious mind to view. The Swiss chemist Hans Jenny notes in Cymantics, "Numerical and symmetrical relationships can be demonstrated to disclose harmonic vibrations which conform strictly to laws in their structure, dynamics and pulsation. What is in effect a harmonic proto-phenomenon becomes visible in terms of pattern, movement and periodicity as a complex but unitary whole."[4]

In Jenny's experiments, he noticed that as the frequency increased (*i.e.*, the intensity of the sound), the form of the molecules became more and more complex (*i.e.*, tetra, penta and hexagonal forms with bilateral symmetry). (Remember: bilateral symmetry is a result of the rotation of the "y" – axis within a bounded space, and is tantamount to magnetism.)

Jenny discovered a triadic primal phenomenon of structure wave process and dynamics from his experiments using sound (*i.e.*, ratio) on chemicals. "The more one studies these things, the more one realizes that sound is the creative principle,"[5] he explains.

Jenny's triadic chemical phenomenon visibly demonstrates Jung's concept of the numbers, which "centers the symmetries and initiates linear [conscious] succession."

Qualities that numbers one through four exhibit as form or structure (actualization) which are listed in von Franz's Psyche and Matter- "the structure of the first four integers (Number and Time)" - include:

#1 Comprises wholeness, unity
#2 Divides, repeats and engenders symmetries;
#3 Centers the symmetries and initiates linear (time) succession and
#4 Acts as the stabilizer by turning back to the one as well as bringing forth observables by creating boundaries, rules, etc.[6]

Archetypal (images) qualities are represented by number.

#1 Archetype
MOTHER
Element-Hydrogen (H1)
Color-Blue
DNA Letter-A
Line-Horizontal
Shape-Circle
Chakra-Throat
Astrological Element-Water
Astrological Signs-Sagittarius, Aquarius, Capricorn
Brainwave-Delta (0-4 cps)
Frequency-6.00 to 6.50 x 10^{14}
Notes-G#, A, A#
Euler's Connectivity No. 1

#2 Archetype
FATHER
Element-Oxygen (O2)
Color-Red
DNA Letter-T
Line-Vertical
Shape-Square
Chakra-Root
Astrological Element-Fire
Astrological Signs-Pisces, Aries, Taurus
Brainwave-Beta (16-40 cps)
Frequency-4.29 to 4.92 x 10^{14}
Notes-C, C#, B
Euler's Connectivity No. 2

#3 Archetype
UNION
Element-Nitrogen (N3)
Color-Yellow
DNA Letter-C
Line-Jagged
Shape-Triangle
Chakra-Solar Plexus
Astrological Element-Air
Astrological Signs-Leo, Gemini, Cancer
Brainwave-Alpha (8-15 cps)
Frequency-5.08 to 5.26 x 10^{14}
Notes-D, D#, E
Euler's Connectivity No. 2

Science, religion, fairytales and language demonstrate triadic and quadratic structures

Science, religion fairytales and language are triadic and quadratic by structure

#4 Archetype
SELF
Element-Carbon (C4)
Color-Green
DNA Letter-G
Line-Peaked
Shape-Hexagon
Chakra-Heart
Astrological Element-Earth
Astrological Signs-Virgo, Libra, Scorpio
Brainwave-Theta (5-8 cps)
Frequency 5.26 to 6.0 x 10^{14}
Notes-F, F#, G
Euler's Connectivity No. 4

Number 1 constitutes the archetype of the Great Mother. On the personal physical level, it is symbolically represented as the mother, the grandmother, the step-mother, the wet nurse, the nanny, the ancestors, the goddess, the Virgin Mary and Sophia. It also symbolizes salvation, paradise, the church, baptismal font, the kingdom of God, heaven/hell, Easter, sea, land, non-flowing bodies of water, the moon, the tilled field, the garden, flower, boulder, tree, the spring hole, cave, mandala, oven, cow, hare and in general, the helpful animal, matter.[7] The dictionary definition of mother, from the Latin "mater", is womb, origin, source. Actually, the word "matrix" is the root for mater, matter and mother.

On the psychological level, this archetype reflects:

1) "Whatever is kindly, sheltering, bearing growth, fostering, fertility bringing, nourishment providing.
2) Places of transformation and rebirth (the concept of religion is implicit in the above concept).
3) That which is secret, hidden, dark.
4) The world of the dead.
5) That which devours, seduces, poisons, arouses fear.
6) That which is inescapable for example, fate.
7) The unconscious aspect (ninety-five percent of our being) of the human mind.
8) In Chinese cosmology, the yin principle."[8]
    On the symbolic level (octaves of energy manifested as various expressions):

Archetype One is represented by:

1) <u>Element</u>: Hydrogen (H1)
2) <u>Color</u>: Blue
3) <u>Frequency</u>: 6.00 to 6.50 X 10^{14}
4) <u>Line</u>: Horizontal
5) <u>Shape</u>: Circle
6) <u>Chakra</u>: One of the body's vortexes of energy; (a vortex is a spiral, which is the involute of a sphere and a sphere is a three dimensional circle) throat
7) <u>Astrological element</u>: Water
8) <u>Astrological signs</u>: Sagittarius, Capricorn, Aquarius
9) <u>DNA letter</u>: A
10) <u>Brain wave</u>: Delta (0 to 4 cps)
11) <u>Musical Notes</u>: G#, A, A#; and
12) <u>Euler's connectivity #1</u>: topology represents the fact that all of the regular polyhedrons can be continuously deformed into a

sphere, which is the three-dimensional expression of the circle. The circle is the two-dimensional expression of the line (which is an infinity of points) and a point is a particle in an infinite-dimensional space.

Number 2 constitutes the archetype of the Father. On the personal level, this archetype represents:

1) "Father, professor, priest, authority figure, king, etc.
2) The mind as the active, winged, moving, alive, stimulating, provocative, arousing, inspiring, dynamic element of the psyche, that which produces enthusiasm and inspiration; an ordering factor for example, number as an archetype of order)
3) Sun gods
4) Yang, the creative dynamic principle of the Tao (in Chinese cosmology this is the secret law that governs the cosmos - "cosmos" actually means order from chaos and chaos is interpreted as such by the conscious mind)"[9]
5) The number 2, which is the concept of duality (*i.e.*, the division of the one). Duality is the concept behind the object and the perceiver (fragmentation). On the symbolic level, this archetypal image (package of concepts) is represented by number (as a linearly, ordering factor) and by color (which as frequency is interpreted by the conscious mind as a differential response to the octaves [spirals] of the electromagnetic spectrum). By doing so, it creates dimensions, hence seeming boundaries/distinctions which are interpreted as objects by sound, which is the vibrational (oscillatory/rhythmic) movement of electrons, and by energy, as the quantized (actualized) bits of consciousness by the conscious mind, which is five percent of our being.

"The mythological associations of the Father archetype manifest as:

1) Moving air, wind, spirit, breath (in astrology, the three air signs of Gemini, Libra and Aquarius are masculine and the three fire signs, Aries, Leo and Sagittarius, are masculine concepts)
2) That which provokes possession, desire
3) Ghosts
4) Pneuma (Greek term for spirit)
5) The psyche (soul, for which the actual definition is breath, spirit)
6) Sprites, spirits, demons, angels, the helpful old man
7) The concept of time"[10] (which is the inversion of frequency). In December, 1999, the author experienced an episode in a sunlit area and, at the time, was certain of the feeling of being present in

ancient Athens. During such episode, time stopped literally (her watch ceasing its function) and the disorientation of the experience lasted two days. As mentioned in Psyche and Matter, the concept of time would be based on the concept of numerically structures rhythms (*i.e.*, oscillations/vibrations); and

8) The concept of space where the actualizations of energy are manifest.

Archetype Two is represented by:

1) Element: Oxygen (O^2)
2) Color: Red
3) Frequency: 4.29 to 4.92 X 10^{14}
4) Line: Vertical
5) Shape: Square (It is squaring, otherwise raising to another octave, of the probability wave that physicists can measure. It is really the squaring of the amplitude (which is another term for sound) that gives the wave shape its physical meaning. Hence, according to the quantum theory, it is the intensity of the energy field (as a point in space) which is interpreted as a statistical probability for finding associated quanta (particles). The square is the result of the crossing "+" of the vertical (masculine concept) line with the horizontal (feminine concept) line. The line, since ancient times, has represented matter. The "crossing" also represents the mathematical concept of addition
6) Chakra: Root (base of spine)
7) Astrological element: Fire
8) Astrological signs: Pisces, Aries and Taurus
9) DNA letter: T
10) Brain wave: Beta (16 to 40 cps)
11) Musical Notes: C, C#, B; and
12) Euler's connectivity #2, which is represented in topology (the branch of math dealing with invariant patterns) by the heplahedron. It can be deformed into a simple closed surface (the Roman surface). Its rectangular coordinates are $y^2 z^2 + z^2 x^2 + x^2 y^2 + xyz = $ zero. Finally, it is a surface of the fourth order.

"Archetype Number 3 constitutes the archetype of Union as represented by mythological associations:

1) The triadic form of the underworld divinities (for example, three witches, three hermits) and three locations (sun, moon and night wind)

2) The triadic structures of gods in Hinduism (Brahma, Vishnu and Siva) and in Christianity (the Father, the Son and the Holy Spirit)
3) The three-fold unity of structure, dynamics and periodicity, which Hans Jenny discovered as the basis of Cymantics empirical research for oscillation and wave phenomena
4) From a formal mathematical viewpoint, the number three is the first odd prime number
5) Jung gives a psychological description of the quality of three in "Psychology and Religion": "Every tension of opposites culminates in a release out of which comes the third. In the third, the tension is resolved and the lost unity is restored"; and
6) Three centers the symmetries (multiplicities) and initiates linear succession."[11]

Archetype Three is symbolically represented by the following:

1) Element: Nitrogen (N^2)
[*12] 2) Color: Yellow
*3) Frequency: 5.08 to 5.26×10^{14}
*4) Line: Jagged
*5) Shape: Triangle
*6) Chakra: Solar plexus
7) Astrological element: Air
8) Astrological signs: Leo, Gemini and Cancer
9) DNA letter: C
10) Brain wave: Alpha (8 to 15 cps)
11) Musical Notes: D, D#, E
12) Euler's connectivity #3, which in topology is represented by the prismatic block which can be continuously deformed into a torus, which is a circle with a hole in it (doughnut).

On the physical level:

1) The physical structure of DNA and RNA is quadratic (four bases consisting of the nucleotides of adenine ("A"), thiamine("T"), quinine ("G") and cytosine ("C"), and triadic, whereby the four nucleotides combine into groups of three and become messengers of the genetic code(information for structuring purposes)).
2) The concept of plurality and multiplicity; whereby, the one is expressed as the many. Implicit in this concept is the idea that the whole is contained within the parts (for example, the hologram).

"Archetype Number Four constitutes the archetype of the Self. On the physical level:

1) Four is the first square number
2) It represents the first two triangular numbers (one and three) and thus, heralds the law of sequences $S = T^1 + T^2$
3) The famous Pythagorean tetractys consists of the sum of $1 + 2 + 3 + 4 = 10$
4) It constitutes a boundary aspect reflected in many languages, which possess a trial and quaternal case beyond the dual."[1]
5) Mankind's attempts at synthesis of the parts into the whole reflect a quaternary structure, for example four to eight points on a compass; four corners of the world; out of the 92 naturally occurring elements only four make up 96% of living matter, *i.e.*, H_1, O_2, N_3 and C_4 (with their respective valences numbered one to four); the four forces of the unified field theory (the strong and the weak forces, electromagnetism and gravity); and the four bases of the genetic code (DNA and RNA)
6) Jung demonstrated that the archetype of the self exhibited dynamic sequential quaternary structures, which isomorphically correspond to the field of natural numbers. This field, whose excited points correspond to the archetypes and which Jung called the "field" of the collective unconscious, is organized by a higher energy center which Jung called the archetype of the self
7) The physicist Ernst Anrich stressed essentially that physical reality is connected with numbers as a whole oneness. The chemists P.J. Jensen and Maria Goeppe Mayer discovered the proportional "magic" numbers of the atomic structures which exhibit the qualitative property of creating proportional order within the atom. Hans Jenny, the Swiss chemist, demonstrated the same structuring ability of number in his 1960s molecular sound experiments. Include Carnap's information on the structure of nature that mirrors numerical values.

The symbolic expressions of the number four archetype of the self include:

1) <u>Element</u>: Carbon (C^4)
2) <u>Color</u>: Green
3) <u>Frequency</u>: 5.26 to 6.0×10^{14}
4) <u>Line</u>: Peaked
5) <u>Shape</u>: Hexagon
6) <u>Chakra</u>: Heart
7) <u>Astrological element</u>: Earth

8) <u>Astrological signs</u>: Virgo, Libra and Scorpio
9) <u>DNA letter</u>: G
10) <u>Brain wave</u>: Theta (5 to 8 cps)
11) <u>Musical Notes</u>: F, F#, G.

The contiguity of the archetypes and the number fields are evidently displayed in mandalas ("Jung says: 'The mandala symbolizes, by its central point, the ultimate unity of all archetypes as well as of the multiplicity of the phenomenal world, and is therefore the empirical equivalent of the metaphysical concept of the <u>unus mundus</u>.'"[2]), matrices and the Babylonian and Mayan religions, which accorded numbers to gods.

The philosopher and physician William James proposed a "transmarginal field," or a field-like arrangement of archetypes of the collective unconscious analogous to a matrix (a rectangular array of numbers). He also defined what he called a "stream of consciousness" as "all the thoughts, emotions, desires, and impressions that swirled through the mind."[3]

Chapter Two

Color as frequency and number

All visible light (10^{14}) is differentiated into ranges of frequency (rotational archetypal number patterns) known as color. The four primary colors of red, green, yellow and blue are utilized by our brains in order to create a three-channel circuitry, which produces the illusion of distinctions and boundaries, and creates objects and dimensions.

The opponent process theory says that since the pair of hues are "mutually exclusive or antagonistic" (see: Part C: Neurological Concepts - How color creates dimension), it explains the mammalian brain's three-color channel visual system, whereby the red-green, blue-yellow and white-black determine the number of dimensions into which we differentiate frequency; hence, three channels equals three dimensions.

Some species, such as birds, have four or five color channels for their visual system, and consequently, their reality is in four or five dimensions, as noted in The Embodied Mind. (see: Neurophysiological appendices)

Varela also proposes that color (*i.e.*, frequency or the rotational number/archetype patterns) is a "fragmentor, segmenter, and distinction-maker which determines frequency into the appropriate wave length for human perception to create objects"[1] from an energy domain.

He also comments on a 1969 article entitled "Basic Color Terms" by Brent Berlin and Paul Kay, which concludes by proclaiming that "the eleven basic color categories are pan-human perceptual universals" (*i.e.*, archetypes).

Hence, color, which is rotational archetypal number patterns as energy frequency, also represents thoughts and emotions. And, as emotion, it is manifested throughout the body's network as peptides, which determine mood, behaviors and habits (*i.e.*, this is the underlying reason why the colors that you dress in, decorate your house in, surround yourself with not only cause your moods, but can alter or change them).

In order to demonstrate the correspondence between number, color, archetypes, matter/energy and frequency (which is also known as the inversion of time) as being ratios, or octave relationships of pattern, there is a chart at the back of the book.

This chart delineates the correlations between planets, angles, astrological signs, color, musical intervals and note frequency, senses, molecular structure, the bonding length of the electron shells' sublevels, the binding strength of the neutrons and protons and chakras as harmonic intervals (numerical ratios) of the electromagnetic spectrum. And, to a smaller degree, the same correspondence information is shown on the front cover.

As previously mentioned in Part Three, Chapter Four, the chakra, color energy surrounding an individual in their aura-camera photos, demonstrated a connection between the four primary archetypal thought concepts (*i.e.*, the Mother Archetype/origin/blue; the Father archetype/dynamism, movement/red; the Union archetype/linear thought process/yellow; and the Self archetype/self/green) and color.

The colors coming in on the left-hand side are generated by the "wholeness concept"-dominated right-brain hemisphere. And, of course, as the thought(s) were leaving from the right-side, they demonstrated as color correlation to the linearly-oriented left-brain hemisphere.

In <u>Wavelets</u>, Hubbard describes mathematically, by utilizing the Fourier Transform, how an image (*i.e.*, photo, or object) can be broken up into the frequencies (*i.e.*, number/co-efficients) that compose it and, conversely, how the Fourier Series is used to give the original image (object) back as a "sum of layers."

She comments, "For each layer, only a very small number of coefficients in each basis were required to represent the layer."[2]

Consequently, all conscious images (*i.e.*, object-event) can be the sum of the thought/energy patterns from the collective unconscious by the personal unconscious/subconscious image-maker and then the subsequent de-composition of that subconscious mirror-image by the conscious mind's Fourier series ability to break down that mirror-image, receive those images (thought/energy patterns) through the 17 senses, process them and then again sum up the layers (*i.e.*, Fourier Transform) on the visual cortex as objectified, linear successive images.

(Note: In June of 2000, I was still trying to find the connection between colors, archetypes, emotions, numbers and the unconscious and conscious intervals.) While experimenting with the aura camera and by asking individuals to visualize themselves in a cave or by the ocean (*i.e.*, Mother archetypal thought concepts of origin, etc.) in order to see if the color blue would show up in their auras, I transposed (*i.e.*, mentally just popped into his mind for a nanosecond) with my nephew Alex, (who was 16 years old at the time) in order to see (feel) if he was in a cave in his mind. I felt that he was and took the picture. We waited a minute or so for it to develop – it's just regular Kodak film – and, then peeled back the cover.

I handed it to him – without really looking at it. He said, "This isn't me – it's you." Well, more accurately, it was Alex – with blue in his aura and me in front of him. My image was all white, and it was me probably half an hour to an hour prior to that time when I had my head cocked to one side with the phone on my shoulder, talking to someone. I mention this [Note: That photo is in this book] because it is empirical proof of the soul and the linear-succession of images that we create for this reality.

I was literally caught on film because I <u>had become</u> Alex for a split second, and my energy combined with his to produce the photo.

In order for the aura camera to take your picture, you have to be <u>in front</u> of the camera (I was behind it and the tripod) and your <u>hands</u> have to be on the 2 sensor boxes, which feed your electrical energy through the computer that the aura camera is hooked up to.)

As David Bohm so eloquently explains in <u>The Special Theory of Relativity</u>, the physical facts of space and time coordinates consist "only of sets of <u>relationships</u> between observed phenomena and instruments, in which no absolute space and time is ever to be seen."[3]

And, as he argues, "This means that both in the field of physics <u>and</u> in that of everyday experience, it may be necessary to set aside the notions of absolute space and time, if we are to understand what has been discovered in broader domains."[4]

Chapter Three

Sound/Language

The brain has four brain waves (beta, 16 - 40 cps; alpha, 8 - 15 cps; delta, 0 - 4 cps; and theta 5 - 8 cps) operating simultaneously as clusters. It is the beta waves which dominate in the conscious-waking state, although the other three are still present, but are in the background of each conscious second.

Sound is an aspect of the <u>movement</u> of energy (*i.e.*, numbered thought patterns). And the <u>sound</u> of the brain's theta waves at 5 - 8 cps (which is also the natural base resonant frequency of all earthly phenomenon, *i.e.*, macroscopic objects/events, during the unconscious 0.8 - 1.2s interval, when the subconscious image-maker operating primarily at the 5 - 8 cps theta wave level [*i.e.*, collectively and cooperatively and telepathically with all other species]) creates this three-dimensional reality for the conscious mind to view in the .95s - 1s interval.

Therefore, the "collective" sound (10^7 - 10^8) of the brain's theta wave at 5 - 8 cps helps to form and maintain an object's "seeming" permanency in time.

Human speech and hearing also help to maintain the brain's beta-wave (16 - 40 cps) illusion of solid reality. The human range of hearing is from 18 - 20,000 cps, with speech being at 80 cps to 10 cps. The sound of vowels is below 1000 cps and consonants are above.

All of the 17 human senses are octave (logarithmic) expressions of the electromagnetic spectrum which ranges from 10^1 to 10^{24}. We perceive the different frequencies as sight, sound, smell, taste, touch, etc. in the conscious interval - but they are all expressions of "root agreements" for this system.

The molecular experiments by the Swiss chemist Hans Jenny utilized sound in order to structure the energy of atoms into particular molecular configurations.

Specifically, he focused frequencies ranging from 160 cps - 600 cps and discovered that the higher the frequency, the more complex the form. He revealed by his experiments that the pattern of relationships (configurations) within the molecular structure could change the form from a solid to a liquid to a gas depending upon the sound projected toward it.

Jenny demonstrated in Cymantics correspondence between sound, as vibration, and the regularity of form, spatial configuration, chronological sequence, symmetry and topology. He accomplished this by utilizing a simple sinusoidal tone in a liquid in order to create complex periodic vibrations, so that a musical tone becomes a "visible" figure.

Consequently, when Jenny increased the tone, or intensity of the frequency, he was, in effect, squaring the height (amplitude or intensity) of the wave and actualizing the probability wave of an event.

Jenny explains how the use of harmonic effects result in regular polyhedron, *i.e.*, hexagonal, pentagonal, tetragonal and triagonal, molecular forms: "On looking at these formations one can properly speak of symmetrical diagrams, displaying mathematical order; but these are not merely diagrams, they are concrete reality."[1]

The reason for this "concrete" reality, he proposes: "[A] particularly interesting feature of these experiments is the quantitative intensification [*i.e.*, squaring of the amplitude of the probability wave] and structuration which brings forth qualitative phenomena (tetra, penta, hexagonal forms)."[2]

In Bohm's Wholeness and the Implicate Order, he demonstrates how the sentence structure of language (*i.e.*, the arrangement of sound) into "subject - verb - object" play an important role of how our conscious minds fragment the whole of reality into aggregate parts.

He comments, "In the previous chapter it has been pointed out that our thought is fragmented, mainly by our taking it for an image or model of 'what the world is'. The divisions in thought are thus given disproportionate importance, as if they were a widespread and pervasive structure of independently existent actual breaks in 'what is,' rather than merely convenient features of description and analysis."[3]

He views the "subject - verb - object" mode of language, as "a pervasive structure, leading in the whole of life to a function of thought tending to divide things into separate entities, such entities being conceived of as essentially fixed and static in their nature."[4]

He adds, "When this view is carried to its limit, one arrives at the prevailing scientific world view, in which everything is regarded as ultimately constituted out of a set of basic particles of fixed nature."[5] Instead, Bohm proposes a new conditioning habit for sentence structure; he calls it a rheomode. "Suddenly to invent a whole new language implying a radically different structure of thought is, however, clearly not practicable. What can be done is provisionally and experimentally to introduce a new mode of language."[6] So, the rheomode concept would place the emphasis on the flowing movement of a verb.

Collaborating in the 1970s, the neuroscientists Maturana and Varela set out to verbally, and then mathematically, describe Maturana's hypothesis "that the 'circular organization' of the nervous system is the basic organization of all living systems."

His hypothesis was based on his experiments with color, which then led him and Varela to define a concept which they called autopoiesis: a self-making, self-referring, circular pattern of organization whereby an organism cognitively interacts with its environment, thus intertwining self-awareness and language (*i.e.*, sound), or as Maturana points out, "Communication is not a transmission of information but rather a coordination of behavior among living organisms through mutual structural coupling."[7]

Consequently, the coordination of behaviors between the same members of a species, whether they are birds, bees, cats or humans, and between all 1.6 billion species worldwide, results in the creation of forms through structural coupling and languaging. "In language, we coordinate our behavior and together in language, we bring forth our world,"[8] explains Maturana. More explicitly, Maturana and Varela add, "The world everyone sees is not the world, but a world which we bring forth with others."[9]

"Language [*i.e.*, Number/frequency interpreted as sound patterns, which are non-linear relationships, and the result of a collapsed sinewave function within the .95s - 1s consciousness boundary, which represents the 1.05 interval, π/3, a 60°, 3:4, and ∠, upon which all music, language, and DNA are based] actually structures [*i.e.*, forms patterns] your perceptions of objects,"[10] notes Seth in The Unknown Reality.

Then, in Maturana's view, the world of objects that we bring forth through the process of structural coupling becomes linguistic distinctions, which then the abstract concepts, ("linguistic distinctions of distinctions") of height, size, etc. further define. Maturana's work with the morphology of color applies here, since it is the mammalian three-channel, opponent-process visual system which distinguishes energy patterns into three-dimensional objects.

Referring to man's ability of organizing informational patterns by utilizing language, Heinz Pagels, in The Cosmic Code states, "We have responded to the pattern of the whole world, a set of atomic sensations, by the creation of language. Indeed, symbolic representation is our highest organizational capability."[11]

The linguist Noam Chomsky asserts that the "deep structures" of language reflect the conscious mind's interpretation of the unconscious mind's contents; whereby the "surface structure of the sentence corresponds only to sound", "the deep structure, a formal structure that relates directly not to the sound but to the meaning."[12] (see: Neurophysiological and Musical Concepts)

The use of sound frequency, as language, for structuring objects from the energy flux domain is based on the 1.05 conscious interval of .95s/1s. This ratio (incidentally the Greek term "logos" means both word and ratio or proportion) is mentioned in <u>Sacred Geometry</u>: "St. John wrote of the relative moment or original scission, 'In the beginning was the Word.'"[13]

Reiterating the concept of Reverse Speech as explained in Part One, Chapter One, it was discovered by David John Oates and is the metaphoric expression of the unconscious mind utilizing the right brain hemisphere as backward (complementary) speech patterns underlying the forward speech patterns from the conscious mind's left brain hemisphere. In his book, <u>Reverse Speech</u>, he notes that 95% of our being is unconscious: "Reverse speech can be heard if human speech is recorded and played backwards. Once every five or ten seconds, very clear and precise phrases occur."[14]

He notes, "Language develops in reverse before it develops forward. If we are to play a tape recording of 'baby talk' backward, we would find words and simple <u>forward</u> phrases in the gibberish - as early as four months - before the baby has 'officially' learned how to talk forward."[15] And Alfred Tomatis discovered that our first sense to develop <u>in vitro</u> at 4 1/2 months is hearing. So, in other words, the fetus is already becoming acquainted with the collective unconscious' metaphoric contents.

In further explanation, "Any thought that is on the person's mind has the potential to appear in speech reversals. These thoughts include all activities in all regions of the mind, ninety-five percent of which are below consciousness. Thus, Reverse Speech can describe unconscious motivations, desires, and thoughts."[16]

Oates noted a structural metaphor, 'Whirlwind', as representing the energies, concepts, feelings and perceptions of the collective unconscious, which would be too difficult to put into words. This structural metaphor would parallel William James' "transmarginal field" of consciousness, which fluctuates in and out of the collective unconscious and personal unconscious (subconscious) as information streams.

Oates also noted in his experiments that the more emotional or agitated a person's dialogue was, the more frequently the metaphoric reversals appeared in backward speech.

"Spoken language is formed by a series of rapidly fluctuating sounds that the brain recognizes as intelligible information,"[17] comments Oates.

In the late 1970s, researchers John Grinder and Richard Bandler developed a framework encompassing, communication, behavior and thought. NLP, or Neurolinguistic Programming, "addresses how the brain internally codes, organizes and processes experiences with pictures, sounds, words and feelings."[18]

In their book, "<u>The Structure of Magic</u>, (see: Part Three, Chapter Three), they synthesize that "Neurolinguistic Programming teaches that language is more than communication - it is also a means of perception and contains within it, codes and patterns of mental processes,"[19] and that it is a compilation of cybernetics, psychology, neurology, linguistics and communication and systems thinking.

And, in concurrence, Seth states in <u>The Unknown Reality</u>, "Language actually structures your perception of objects."[20]

Chapter Four

Emotion

According to the Mental Health Institute of Maryland study done by Dr. Candace Pert in the 1980s, large chains of macromolecules called polypeptides are the biochemical manifestations of emotion, and, as with color, both determine and alter behavior, moods, and actions (see: Part One, Chapter Three).

Capra, in The Web of Life, summarizes Pert's study: "Indeed, scientists have observed that the modal points of the central nervous system which connect the sensory organs with the brain are enriched with peptide receptors that filter and prioritize sensory perceptions."[1]

He continues, "In other words, all our perceptions and thoughts are colored by emotions. This, of course, is our common experience."[2]

Consequently, emotion (manifested as peptides) can be isomorphically construed to be the equivalent to color as frequency whose expressions are number, sound, magnetism and time.

As magnetism, which is the vertical (y-axis) or vortex rotational movement of the collapsed sinewave within a boundary system resulting in an electron, emotion would be isomorphic with the alteration and creation of "space" and representative of "time" along the "x"-axis.

Seth comments in The Unknown Reality that "All being is an emotional manifestation of energy." (see: Scientific and Neurophysiological Appendices) And these emotions "propel ideas outward through the sensory channels."[3] These ides, or thought/energy forms as frequency, which the human body emits at low levels is attested to in the Institute of Maryland Reports by John-Hopkins University.

In order for a probability wave to be actualized, the amplitude/height (intensity) has to be squared (multiplied by itself or a crossing of the vertical with the horizontal as differences (*i.e.*, "†"). "Intensity" is a quality which needs quantitative attributes (squaring) in order to be physically actualized.

Consequently, desire, as an "intense" emotion, collapses the sinewave function, and a probability becomes a three-dimensional actuality. The dictionary definition of emotion is based on a Latin noun "to move out of the psyche."

According to Oates in <u>Reverse Speech</u>, "Over ninety percent of all language in Reverse Speech is metaphoric in nature."… "Metaphors, words that are, symbolic or pictorial, increase in frequency the more emotional dialogue becomes." He continues, "They represent emotions and thought processes from deeper regions of the mind."[4]

In his book, Oates refers to his encounter with Jung's concept of, "'the collective Unconscious,' which states that buried deep within the psyche can be found an inherent storehouse that contains the entire spiritual and cultural heritage of humanity's development."[5]

Jung discovered "in the psyche that there exist 'complexes' (a word well known by now) that are <u>emotionally</u> intensified content clusters that form associations around a nuclear element (archetype - a universally recurring theme) and tend to draw ever more material to themselves." So wrote Marie von Franz in <u>Psyche and Matter</u>.[6]

These "content clusters", or archetypes, are magnetic and consequently associative because they are <u>rotating</u> energy patterns. And, as a confined sinewave within a boundary system (*i.e.*, our unconscious and conscious intervals), the rotation produces periodicity which is "recurrence:[10] the basis of the stability of matter,"[35] according to Bohm.

Therefore, language, whether it be forward or backward speech, represents emotional choices, which a human makes as the "sum total of his worldly experiences" and is represented as the "deep structure" of forward speech for the conscious mind, or as the metaphoric expression of the collective unconscious as backward speech.

Conclusion

"In other words, there is no exteriorization of nature; everything is the mental, spiritual, and psychic manifestation of All That Is". The universe is a three-dimensional emotional projection through the senses at 5-8cps. This is the same frequency as the human brain's theta waves and the base resonate frequency of all worldly phenomenon. So that all worldly phenomenon is a holographic projection viewed on our visual cortex.

This phenomenal world springs into being or actualization written the first 5 billionth of a second during our .95-1s consciousness interval in accordance with inner models. These models are part of collective unconscious archetypal thought/frequency patterns. The patterns represent the 60,000 thoughts per day per person.

Thus, the infinite versions of the sinewave function are collapsed when a decision is made by the individual conscious at 5 billionth of a second. Actualization of what appears to be all worldly phenomenon during this conscious interval is starting to be built-up on individual visual cortexes at 5-8cps.

Consequently, physical forms are the linear, time-oriented succession of 150 images or resolutions being built up on our visual cortex. These images as archetypes then return to the overall energy of All That Is.

Seth, the "non-physical 'energy personality essence'"[1] for whom author Jane Roberts speaks as while she's in a trance, could have been referring to the hologram [note: in ancient India, the Hindus had a term for this reality being an allusion: it was "maya"] or holomovement, that a rotating circle (representing two octaves, so that the interval which is one octave represents the radius as π (Pi), or 3.141, which corresponds to a 2:1 [radius to diameter] ratio [as represented by the √2, which defines a square, and is also the diagonal of the square with sides of "1"], a 90 degree angle and the intervals of 1.414). The intervals √3 as 1.73 and √5 as 2.24 are latently implied, or nested within the √2, as is ^{12}√2 as the intervals of 1.05 [which is what all the earth 1.6 billion species' DNA is based on, as is human language and human music along with bird's song], and represents the crystallographic multiples of π, as they correspond to atomic and molecular structures. The √2 represents the Principle of Alternation ["everything alternates towards its opposite"], which is the crossing of opposites, resulting in the attractive forces of magnetism and electricity as in water, H_2O [2 Hydrogen atoms and 1 Oxygen atom], and also the seven-fold axial system [axis of symmetry] of crystal lattices [whose atoms are represented crystallographically as a regular system of points], representing archetypal forms generated by a confined sinewave resulting in spherical harmonic waveforms.

"The sinewave is the sum total of the wave form (thought form)." The sinewave is a formal, numerical relationship that is also a non-periodic (its vibrations are arbitrary), single, harmonic partial, containing only one frequency component (the octave sense is not strong with pure tones), which underlies all other waveforms that are generated by a rotating circle (the ratio of the circumference to the diameter equals π (Pi) which is the interval of 3.141 [or one octave (radius), or 22/7, or 3 1/7], by which the circle is defined) and when confined (as in the interaction [resonance] or "the crossing of opposites" [which produces an angle, whereby "energies are controlled, specified, and modified"[2] by initiating from duality (as a "seeming" difference from All That Is), the principle of alternation (frequency), the √2 (Note: The ancient Egyptians portrayed this "crossing of opposites," etc. as the mouth of Re; this generative principle was the symbol for the supreme creator, Atum-Re), and the Taoist Yin and Yang female/male concepts]), the y-axis being perpendicular, as magnetism is to electricity [at right, 90° angles], to the x-axis, for example the division of a circle as unity electron patterns (probabilities), which are then by their nature quantified, discrete, discontinuous and periodic bits of movement [energy] as spherical, harmonic (octave) waveforms. These possess both kinetic and potential energy, and can then only vibrate at certain periodic (repetitious patterns [iterations], which constitute recurrence as the basis for the molecular stability necessary for our 1.05 intervals-based 17 senses to be able to apprehend frequency as an object), natural frequencies, or a narrow bandwidth of frequency. This bandwidth for all worldly phenomenon is 1 1/2 - 2 octaves (a circle), or 5 - 8cps.

Vibration, as movement, is the basis of the electromagnetic spectrum and is the result of the interaction, or confinement of a sinewave to the boundary of a spherical surface, or "the crossing of opposites", which produces the holographic and dual aspects of electricity and magnetism. These are perpendicular (at right, 90° to each other) interactions, whose height/amplitude/hypotenuse are the √2 (the square root is a proportion, and as such is the comparison of equivalent ratios, which measure differences so that a proportion simultaneously and paradoxically represents the holographic property of sameness within difference; for example, the part containing the whole [note: the atomic valence structure of carbon - all earthly organisms are carbon based - is tetrahedral and reflects the √2 and 90° electron bond angles of the "p" orbitals]), or the interval of 1.414 (which defines the shape or form of a square) as the crossing of opposite, equal line lengths as arms of the atomic structure of carbon, which are at 90° right angles to each other, and also as the multiplication (symbolized by the cross), or any number (as "an archetype of order", concept, or thought pattern) by itself is a square. Logarithms, such as the musical scale ($12\sqrt{2}$ defines the musical notes) or our perceptual senses of sight, hearing, touch, taste, smell, etc., are the result of squaring (crossing) a number (*i.e.*, $^{12}\sqrt{2}$ = 1.05 when multiplied by itself 12 times equals the $\sqrt{2}$, or 1.414 [an archetype of order]) - multiplying it by itself - then, continually multiplying (*i.e.* crossing) that result by the original number ("an archetype of order").

Consequently our sensorial experience (*i.e.*, moment-by-moment or image frame-by-frame built up on the visual cortex combined with the appropriately matching smell, touch, taste, and sound sensation, etc.) is an "octave", or harmonic experience of holographic aspects, based upon the natural resonant frequency, 5 - 8cps, and then produces an axis of symmetry (the "y"-axis, *i.e.* magnetism/space) for the waveform.

These spherical, harmonic waveforms that are produced by the confinement (interaction) of a sinewave to a surface (*i.e.* a boundary, such as our conscious, .95s - 1s interval of 1.05, or our unconscious, 0.8s - 1.2s interval of 1.5), symbolically represent interacting thought/energy patterns within the conceptual frame work of opposites in order to produce duality (for example, the earth is a sphere); and they possess an axis of symmetry similar to that of the earth's 23.5° degree axis (which designates the four seasons),and are marked by north and south poles. According to Quantum Theory, confined waveforms have quantified (same as, discrete, discontinuous or periodic), dynamic attributes (note: as mentioned earlier from Sacred Geometry, dynamic quantities result from the asymmetrical divisions [such as the hypotenuse of a right triangle and/or the diagonal of a square resulting in a square root] of unity [as represented by the #1 Mother Archetype]; for example, 1: $\sqrt{2}$, which is the proportion for growth: psychological as well as physical), such as position, momentum and external spin, which are contextual and depend upon the manner of measurement (note: an electron, as an elementary particle, does have innate or static attributes, such as mass, charge and internal spin about the axis of symmetry). From a physics aspect, Heisenberg's Uncertainty Principle applies here, because it states that a particle does not possess both position and momentum simultaneously (note: Sambursky, in The Physical World of Late Antiquity, concluded that all key modern scientific concepts originated from Greek natural philosophy [for example; atoms, matter, space, time, energy, the unified field theory, and mathematics as the language of science]). David Bohm, in Quantum Theory (pg. 147), concurred that "actually, many of the ancient Greeks were unable to grasp the idea of continuous motion, as those who have studied Zeno's paradoxes will know." One of the most famous of these paradoxes concerns an arrow in flight. Since at each instant of time the arrow is occupying a definite position, it cannot at the same time be moving (this is the Uncertainty Principle's unconscious base).

Consequently, all particles composing an object (from an electron, to an atom, to a molecule, to a cell, etc.) have an axis of symmetry which determines their internal spin, and that acts as both a channel for energy (note: energy can only be absorbed into a system through the north pole of the "y"-axis - and, only at the natural resonant base frequency) and its focal point for the exchange (interaction - "crossing of opposites") of that energy (i.e. the rotational moment of informational patterns) between the center (for example, the origin, which is the intersection of the "x" and "y" axis of a circle, and its symmetrical divisor - the diameter) and the outside (for example, the perimeter of a circle is its circumference, so that the comparison of difference - the ratio - of the divisor or diameter to the perimeter or circumference [c/d = π] is defined by π [π, 22/7, 3 1/7, or 3.14]) of the motion.

Motion involves a change of position (a dynamic, quantified, periodic attribute defined by the #2 Father Archetype, whose qualities include dynamism, ordering [as in number, frequency, and time], duality [defined by the √2 as the Principle of Alternation or Yin and Yang], creativity, movement, and energy) and is generally expressed as a function of time (i.e. the "x-axis"/electricity), which is the same as the phase or angle of the wave, and is determined by a ratio (interaction, or "crossing of opposites") of two whole numbers. (Note: in the case of earthly phenomenon these two whole numbers are 2 [represented by the #2 Father Archetypal concept of conflict], and 3 [represented by the #3 Archetype of Union resulting in an outcome]. This orthogonality of repetitious, relational, informational thought patterns, as standing waves [the #2 Father Archetype represents the frequency 4.29 to 4.92 x 10^{14}, which is the color "red" and the #3 Archetype of Union represents the frequency 5.08 to 5.26 x 10^{14}, which is the color "yellow" as the ratio 2:3], creates the unconscious [0.8s - 1.2s] interval of 1.5 or π/2, where our psyches agree and decide upon [the site or measurement where the sinewave collapses, and a possibility becomes a probability] the information that will be physically manifested as objects/events in the next conscious interval of [.95s - 1 second], 1.05 or π/3.)

Therefore, a rotating circle, as an archetypal thoughtform, creates a sinewave (a formal, numerical relationship which is the basis of a hologram), which, when confined, vibrates periodically only within a narrow bandwidth of frequency/rotation (the natural resonant frequency), defined by the √2 and resulting in a repetitious, circular pattern of numerically coded information; for example, a wave signal, which has an axis of symmetry similar to our spine's function as the human axis of symmetry, and both of which create a cortex of energy analogous with a "y"-axis.

As mentioned earlier, the basis of energy, albeit the entire electromagnetic spectrum, is movement or motion caused by interaction. (This is the basis for the recurrence found in nature, which gives the molecular structure of matter its stability. This resonance phenomenon, or the interaction of electrons within an atom and between atoms (photons), is based on the quantum mechanical principle of differences having a common base; for example, a ratio. In the case of all worldly phenomena this ratio is 2:3, the interval of 1.5, the angle of 90° degrees, √2, the atomic structure C:G, the perfect fifth, and √3 as a formative principle that defines a triangular and hexagonal structure as 60° for molecular structures). The confinement of a sinewave to a spherical surface (defined by the ratio of π (pi), and the interval of 3.141) results in periodic frequencies having the holographic properties of self-actualization and non-linearity (as in the sense of an octave), creating as its aspects: electricity and magnetism (represented by interaction at right, 90° angles to each other); sound, which is the movement of the circular, repetitious, numerically coded patterns within the human perceptual hearing range of 18cps - 20,000cps ($10^1 - 10^4$); and visible light, which is the circular, repetitious, numerically coded patterns within the human visual range of 429 trillion cps - 750 trillion cps, 10^{14}. In other words, the entire electromagnetic spectrum, from 10^1 (power and telephone frequency) to 10^{24} (gamma ray frequency), is harmonically based on the logarithmic scale of 10 and is arranged in octaves. (Note: "The musical octave is based on a tone, whose vibrational frequency is in an exact ratio of 2:1 with another tone.") A scale of eight natural tonal divisions from C to C' is called an octave. For example, water as H_2O represents a 2:1 ratio and occurs on earth as a solid [ice], liquid [water], and gas [steam]. Similarly, hydrogen and carbon both have a tetrahedral atomic valence structure, whose bonds [arms] are at right, 90° degree angles to each other and this then corresponds to the √2. The human body is composed of 70-90% water [with the remainder mostly being carbon], as H_2O [a 2:1 ratio or an octave, $1/2$ of a circle, or π (3.141)], which receives and divides the sunlight [photons] by utilizing the crystalline, √3 molecular structure [which finds its stability in recurrence, or the repetitious wave patterns] of the water in our cells into √5, pentagonal cellular structures. So, the two atoms of hydrogen and one atom of oxygen represent a 2:1 ratio, or an octave. As an octave, it represents π, or 3.141, and reflects the division of the One [unity] into two [duality]. Or, more precisely, the archetypal form of a circle, which is defined by the proportion of the √2 whose asymmetrical divisor is the diagonal, which then becomes the root of the next square. From the 12√2 is manifested the ratio of π/3, or the interval of 1.05, which defines not only the musical notes [semitones], but also language and our perceptual senses, but also our conscious interval of .95s - 1s, or confinement of a sinewave to a surface.

Just as there is a narrow, finite range of frequencies that vibrate as a result of a confined (interacting) sinewave to a surface so that they're called spherical, harmonic waveforms, and they have an axis of symmetry resulting in the bilateral symmetry of molecular structure (which was demonstrated by Hans Jenny's Chemical experiment Cymatics) that produces a particle's intrinsic spin (a static attribute) and an external (dynamic) spin as it rotates and creates space, there is also a finite amount of crystallographic groups of motion according to Hilbert in Geometry and the Imagination. The discrete, discontinuous, periodic, or quantized nature of energy (as a result of the √2), translates into a regular, geometrically arranged system of points; for example, the atoms of all of the 92 naturally occurring elements (of which 96% can be reduced down to only four elements: hydrogen, oxygen, nitrogen, and carbon).

This system of points defines the atomic (√2) and molecular (√3) structure of cells or crystallographic classes of motion in space (Hilbert refers to them as the five regular polyhedron; for example, the tetrahedron, the octahedron, the icosahedrons, the cube and the dodecahedron, or, as they were known in antiquity, as the five Platonic Solids, all of which can be deformed to a sphere [topology] as they represent the elements of the periodic table).

In his book, Geometry and the Imagination, Hilbert mathematically proved that there cannot be any rotations (of that waveform's axis of symmetry) through angles, which are the result or the comparison of two whole numbers as a ratio (interaction), other than the multiples of π (3.141), 2 π/3(2.1), π/2, and (1.6; + π/3 (1.05) for the crystallographic atomic, molecular and cellular structures of earth's carbon-based organisms. (Note: in Plato's Timaeus the concept of reality as being the result of a revolving model of simultaneous, mathematical forms [sinewaves/thoughtforms] from the body of ideas [collective unconscious] arranged in a linear, temporal succession by the demiurge finds a parallel with the earth's (π), carbon-based structures.)

Just as π, 3.141, defines a circle (and a confined sinewave by a boundary, such as the conscious and unconscious intervals, which generates a circular holographic pattern), it also represents the radius, as an octave and, consequently, 2 π, 6.282, which represents the diameter as two octaves. So that 2 π/3 (2.1) represents C#' as an octave above the fundamental tone of C, and also the √5 (2.24) and the angle of 45°, which defines both DNA's (this includes all earthly 1.6 billion species which have the same DNA, and only the bases are different) (see:

Neurophysiological Appendices) pentagonal, cellular structure, and also the earth's dodecahedron electromagnetic grid system; for example, the major ley lines.

Another multiple of π, through which the crystallographic molecular structures manifest, is π/2 (1.6 or the golden mean, also Φ "phi"), which with the √3 results in a 60° angle defining a hexagon consisting of six equilateral triangles and manifesting as carbon's molecular structure. The interval of 1.5 also represents all earthly organisms' DNA structure and our lapse of consciousness from 0.8 – 1.2s and language (which Varela and Maturana demonstrated that we use to "structurally couple" [co-create] with our environment).

The lapse of consciousness interval is produced by the ratio (or the interaction of the two whole numbers) 2:3, which is the ratio of 1.5 (3₅2). This ratio of 1.5 represents our 0.8-1.2 unconscious span of time (1.2₅.8). Our unconscious span of time occurs alternately between our .95s-1s conscious span of time. The ratio of our conscious interval of time is 1.05 (1₅.95). These unconscious and conscious intervals are produced by the discrete discontinuous quantized and periodic nature of energy as produced by the √2 (note: all mass is an equivalent aspect of energy, *e.g.*, $E=MC^2$). This interval of 1.5 would be the same for all carbon-based earthly organisms that share the same DNA. Consequently, due to the periodic nature of energy, all worldly phenomenoa would blink on-and-off together (*i.e.*, materialize/manifest/actualize and dematerialize/non-manifest/deactualize) since the angle (phase/time) of the wave is the same over the entire sphere centered on the origin at any given time per Ditchburn's <u>Light</u> and as waves whose phases (*e.g.* height/amplitude/intensity/hypotenuse) would match (or square, which to multiply something by itself, or to cross opposites, *e.g.* magnetism and electricity, which are two seemingly different aspects of the same thing at right, 90° angles to each other manifested by the √2), or amplify, the result would be the apparent actualization or manifestation of an object (the "intensity" [*e.g.*, the squaring of the height or amplitude of a wave] of a feeling [*e.g.* emotions are at the 5 – 8cps theta brain wave frequency, which is also this reality's base resonant frequency]).

This interval of unconsciousness (1.5) would be the basis for the interconnectedness and telepathic agreement between all worldly phenomena whose natural base resonant frequencies vibrate within a narrow bandwidth of 5 – 8cps, or meters. This natural resonant frequency range coincides with our human theta (5 – 8cps) brain wave clusters.

In 1982, Dr. Alain Aspect conclusively demonstrated, in an experiment at the University of Paris, Bell's Theorem (itself a mathematical proof on non-locality and the interconnectedness of existence) of the non-locality concept of quantum mechanics, that electrons, or other sub-atomic probabilities (expressed as particles), possess the ability to instantaneously transfer information in a web-like (non-linear) or holographic manner.

And since rotating electrons constitute a sinewave, which is the basis simultaneously of magnetism and a hologram, and they consequently produce the aspects of sound and light, depending upon the frame of reference, and are the basis for electricity and magnetism, then, since all earthly phenomenon are composed of these same rotating electrons, which display telepathy - the instantaneous transfer of information - as one of their holographic properties, and we as humans are composed of the same electrons, then at the collective unconscious (1.5 intervals) level there would be the telepathic root agreements of matter, energy, space, time and cause and effect, in accordance with the ratio of 2:3 and the resultant intervals of 1.5 (0.8 - 1.2s) and π/3, or 1.05 (.95 - 1s), as the unconscious and conscious intervals, respectively.

The last multiple of Pi (π) correlating to the crystallographic atomic structures is π/3, or the interval of 1.05, which is the $^{12}\sqrt{2}$ that defines the 12 semitones (notes) of an octave, or musical scale. This interval also corresponds to the ratio of 18:19, which is the basis of the human canon (for painting, sculpting, drawing, etc.), and it also closely resembles the syntonic comma of 80:81 (1.012), the comma ratio of 531441:524288 (1.013), and the ancient Hindu comma of 49:50 (1.02) that is found in the 10,000 hymns of the Rg Veda.

From a subatomic to a microscopic to a macroscopic level, all of the interacting conscious energy/thought (sinewave) patterns that result in actualized particles, which compose atoms, molecules, cells, tissues and then ultimately macroscopic forms, e.g. objects, have at each pattern level an axis of symmetry for that structure.

At the macroscopic level of our physical bodies, our spines constitute an axis of symmetry and act as a conduit for the energy (as part of All That Is) from the psyche (manifesting as π [Pi], the 2:1 ratio, √2, the intervals of 1.414 and the right angle of 90°) in order to propel the archetypal,[1] conscious - energy thought patterns from the matrix (which would represent a 2:1 ratio, π, √2, a 90° degree angle, one octave, the radius of a circle, 1.414 as the interval, the Principle of Alternation, [as frequency, vibration or oscillation], duality [as the "crossing of opposites," i.e. a wave or Yin and Yang], as represented by the #1 Mother Archetype [matrix] and the #2 Father Archetype, [energy, dynamism, movement, and creativity]), of the collective unconscious as energy (waves) through the seven chakras, which are isomorphic with the seven semitones (notes) of an octave, and they also correlate to the seven-fold axial system of crystal lattices and the seven-fold transevering axis of the yantras of the ancient Hindu hymns of the Rg Veda: F,C,G,D,A,E, and B.

The seven chakras (known as "wheels" in Sanskrit in the Rg Veda, whose 12 spokes symbolically represent divisions of the $12\sqrt{2}$ into the

12 semitones of the musical scale, which isomorphically relates to the differential logarithmic aspect of our 17 different senses), which can now be physically demonstrated by the aura camera, are rotating energy vortices located at the intervals along our spine (just in front of the vertebrae), and correlate to the major body organs. In addition to these, there are also chakras in the hands and feet.

These energy vortices are the source for the human body's aura-energy field (which represents the archetypal contents before the senses translate that frequency information into what appears to be a solid form, e.g., our body), which has been documented for over 5,000 years and been known by various names over the centuries: prana, karnaeem, chi and Illiaster, consisting of seven major levels or layers of energy and represented by the colors of red through violet, which are determined by their appropriate frequency.

The psyche's human subconscious (Jung's personal unconscious) functions as image-maker and utilizes the brow chakra (known in ancient times as "the third eye") in order to translate the 60,000 thought/energy waves (41^+ per minute per day per human) from the archetypal contents of the collective unconscious as they interface with the energy waves from other psyches similarly focused within this same framework in order to form wave-front interference patterns, which either add (as do those in-phase [e.g. with the same angle/time], which square and then actualize into objects [note: the non-linear structure of the inner ear matches (squares) the incoming frequency information with the sound frequencies arising from the ear itself per the Husmann Theory of Conscious published by Heinrich Husmann in 1953]) or cancel (as do those waves not-in-phase), by metaphorically utilizing the mathematical Fourier Transform process, into the natural resonant frequencies of spherical harmonics, which are produced by a confined (interacting) sinewave (thought/energy patterns) to a surface. These periodic vibrations represent all worldly phenomena; for example, humans, plants, animals, minerals, rocks, the ocean and the earth itself -- all animate <u>and</u> inanimate, within the narrow range of 5 - 8cps, or $10^7 - 10^8$ meters in wavelength, or $1\frac{1}{2}$ - 2 octaves (which represent a circle, or 2 π), that also correspond to the human brain waves of theta (5 - 8cps).

This, then, is the "magnetic glue" level of telepathic root agreements for matter, energy, space, time and cause and effect, by which the earth's 1.6 billion species cooperatively form, and what we consciously perceive to be as our corner of the universe.

The periodic lapse of consciousness, represented by the interval of 1.5 common to all earthly organisms sharing the same DNA, constitutes the temporal, linear time-frame, in which every bit of consciousness from a protozoa to a human builds up its own perceptually unique version of reality, which is then consciously perceived in the next second, etc.

For humans, after the energy from the psyche is channeled in through the crown, then down the spine and emotionally (at the 5 - 8cps theta wave frequency) propelled "outward" through the chakras in telepathic accordance with all other species at a 2:3 ratio, then these sinewaveforms (thoughtforms) are apprehended by our 17 different senses and metaphorically broken down and analyzed by Fourier analysis into frequency based on the $^{12}\sqrt{2}$, with its 1.414 intervals broken up into "the wheels' 12 spokes or divisions", of 1.05 correlating to π/3. (Note: these differential logarithmic divisions represent colors, notes, plants, astrological signs, organs, personality traits, etc., to our senses.)

This "incoming", numerically coded frequency, depending upon which perceptual sense that it is slotted for, is mathematically translated back into waves and transmitted throughout the body's nervous system to the brain via the inner ear – the cochlear – overtones (as waves) that arise as a result of the nonlinear (spiral-like) structure of the ear matching or squaring the amplitude/intensity of those same incoming waves, and, in essence, actualizing, or concretizing what will ultimately be the frequency construction of a one-second image, after the periodic 1.5 intervals lapse-of-consciousness.

The squaring ("crossing of opposites", *e.g.* as in the attractive force of gravity) of the waves that are transmitted throughout the body, including the frequency information from the retina through the optic nerve, that are then sent to the brain via the reticular activating system (filter) every $1/100^{th}$ of a second and then dispatched to the visual cortex (for example, where it takes 150 resolutions [only 60 images are needed for a T.V. image on screen per second] or scalings to construct an image (this implies the process of a scaling function, and in this case it is the √5, or "phi" as 1.618…), which are then "funneled" or "localized" outward, as described by von Békésy in his 40 years of experiments, in order to form a conscious one second of three-dimensional reality as a holographic projection).

So, in other words, we cooperatively help create (each individualized version is unique) the holographic projection of this thoughtform reality.

<u>THE END</u>

APPENDICES

PART A

Scientific Concepts

●

A particle (electron) as a point in an infinite-dimensional space

●⟶

A line (an infinite number of versions of a point) as an extension of a point (particle) in space

∿∿∿

A wave as an abstract mathematical concept representing the *probability* of finding a particle in various places and with various properties

A particle, such as an electron, is contained in one place when it is actualized, but it is described as a wave (field) when it is uncontained (not observed within the consciousness interval of .95 – 1s) as a probability. A wave has height amplitude, frequency (as number of rotations of an archetypal thought pattern), time/period (which is the inversion of the frequency, phase (angle) and wavelength. The "wavelength

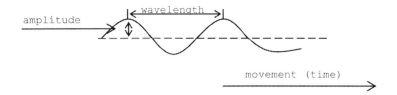

is the shortest distance at which a wave pattern repeats itself".[1] And, according to Jane Roberts' Seth, "Concepts [archetypes/numbers] fit together in patterns [waves]."[2]

A sinewave (electron) is non-periodic when uncontained (*i.e.*, not observed - still in the collective unconscious realm of 0.8 - 1.25), but periodic (thought patterns as points, *i.e.*, atoms repeating themselves) within a boundary system (*i.e.*, out conscious mind operating from .95 - 1s intervals).

Fourier's Theorem states that any periodic wave can be represented as a unique sum of sinewaves having the appropriate amplitude, frequency and phase. Furthermore, the frequencies of the component waves are related in a simple way: they are all whole number multiples of a single frequency, which is the base (first) resonant (interacting) frequency (number of rotations of archetypal thought patterns) of an object.

For example, all 17 of our human senses represent the whole number multiples of a basic concept (from the unconscious), which we subconsciously construct and then observe during our conscious, (.95 - 1s) moment. Consequently, what we deem as physical objects are all constructed at the subconscious, theta wave level of 5 - 8 cps and are variations on a theme.

Another term for the sinewave is momentum.[3],[4] The momentum or movement/vibrations of a string (line) is two-dimensional, but when that momentum (sinewave/thought field) is contained within a boundary system (the consciousness interval of 1.05, or .95 - 1s), then what was a circle (two-dimensional) becomes a sphere (three-dimensional), and the resultant vibrations of that sphere (*i.e.*, electron, atom, molecule, cell, object, earth) become known as spherical harmonics, all of which are composed of the same base resonant frequency.

So a point (particle/electron) extends into space as a line containing infinite versions or divisions of itself and confronts a boundary system, then starts to rotate. And within that confined region the two-dimensional circle becomes a three-dimensional sphere.

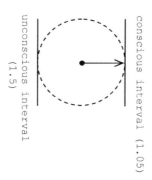

In 1932, the famous mathematician and inventor of the digital computer John von Newmann reluctantly came to the conclusion that human consciousness is the site at which the sinewave function collapses in his presentation entitled "The Theory of Measurement", or as it is also known as the "Problem of Measurement."[5] A wave function contains three dimensions for each particle that it represents, so that an average object (for example, a chair, table or human) contains 10^{24} atoms which means that upon collapse, or actualization, in human three-dimensional reality the 10^{72} possibilities ($10^{24 \times 3} = 10^{72}$, or a 1 with 72 zeros after it) of that thought/energy pattern reduce to one event (object) within one human's .95 - 1s consciousness interval, and the rest of the 10^{72} possibilities either continue per Schrödinger's wave equation or become actualized in parallel realms per the Many Worlds Theory.

<u>How</u> and <u>where</u> the sinewave collapses into a system particle/object is what is called the "Problem of Measurement".

In 1925, Werner Heisenberg mathematically determined that at the subatomic level we (experimenters) can't observe an electron, etc., without changing it. This is known as Heisenberg's Uncertainty Principle, whereby both the position and momentum of a particle can't be measured simultaneously. The wave/particle duality is an aspect of this concept such that an electron can only be observed as either a wave (field/momentum) or particle (position) but not both simultaneously.

The ancient Hindu's <u>Upanishad</u> sums up this three-dimensional reality's seemingly paradoxical properties by saying, "Whether we know it or not, all things take on their existence from that which perceives them."[6] So the subatomic realm appears as a web of interconnected parts of a unified whole. The human conscious beta state, 16 - 40 cps, creates objects, *i.e.*, beds, chairs, humans - animate and inanimate matter - out of the energy-conscious information domain.

Heisenberg's Uncertainty Principle provides a loophole for the energy conservation law, which says that something can't be created out of nothing. The loophole is basically that the lower the mass of the particle, *i.e.*, electron-positron pairs, the more likely it is to create them out of nothing - a vacuum. So consequently, as Bohm notes, there is a virtual sea of electrons waiting to be actualized (into objects), which is what our conscious beta state (.95 - 1s) mind does by putting energy-conscious awareness into the system (the wave function).

In David Bohm's Wholeness and the Implicate Order, he explains that there is a shortest wavelength possible, 10^{-33} cm (physical experiments have only gotten to 10^{-17} cm), which would contribute to the zero-point energy of space and be the virtual sea of electrons (electron-positron pairs). Consequently, what is called empty space by our senses contains an immense background of possible/probable actualized matter (*i.e.*, $E = MC^2$).

In Jane Roberts' Seth books the same concept is explained as "patterns-out-of-focus" due to our neurological bias, which is determined by our consciousness interval of only .95 - 1s. Again, the same concept is addressed in The Dancing Wu Li Masters by citing the example of a whirling propeller blade which creates a solid image when it is in motion (our 17 senses interpret the rapid motion of the thought/energy patterns as one solid object/image during the consciousness interval of .95 - 1s) and the example of a 2 x 4 stud which appears solid but is composed of fibers, cells, molecules, atoms and subatomic particles.

In 1900 Max Planck demonstrated mathematically and experimentally that energy was discrete (in little bits), or quantized, and that it was emitted or absorbed in packets, whose size (*i.e.*, the lower the frequency, such as red, the smaller the amount of energy) was determined by the frequency multiplied by Planck's constant, which is a number that never changes: $h = 6.63 \times 10^{27}$ erg-sec.

So together, Planck with his concept of quantized or discrete energy (remember: $E=MC^2$, where energy *is* matter, and matter *is* energy simultaneously - but, not to our conscious [.95 - 1s] mind, because neurologically we are incapable of apprehending matter as energy), and Werner Heisenberg with his Uncertainty loophole, which allows for energy/matter to be created out of nothing, *i.e.*, electron-positron (anti-electron) pairs supply the implicit conclusion that the reason *why* energy is discrete and appears and disappears out of seeming empty space is our conscious (.95 - 1s)/unconscious (0.8 - 1.2s) intervals interpret it as such, and also *why* there appears to be fragmentation (*i.e.*, objects - you and me for instance) of the whole, or All That Is.

Paul Dirac in the 1920s supplied the mathematical theory which introduced the electron-positron pairs (Heisenburg's loophole), predicting matter and its mirror opposite - anti-matter - by showing both positive (resulting in positrons) and negative (resulting in electrons) solutions to the equations.

Also in the 1920s, Bohr and Heisenberg developed the Copenhagen Interpretation of Quantum Mechanics, which essentially demonstrated the interconnectedness of reality by dividing the physical world into observed (*i.e.*, objects)/observing systems, whereby they learned that the observed systems (objects) couldn't be measured for both position and momentum simultaneously by the observing systems (*i.e.*, experiments) without interfering with the probability patterns that constituted the form of the object.

Indeed, it was shown that subatomic particles such as electrons/positrons do not independently exist at a definite place and time, but rather show "tendencies to exist" and "tendencies to occur", which led Niels Bohr to comment that the "wave function is a complete description of reality".

Contrary to the Copenhagen Interpretation is the Many Worlds Interpretation of Quantum Mechanics by Hugh Everett, John Wheeler and Neill Graham. Whereas consciousness (the observing system, *i.e.*, experimenter) is central to the collapse of the sinewave function (represented by the observed system, *i.e.*, object) to the Copenhagen Interpretation, in the Everett-Wheeler-Graham Many Worlds Theory consciousness isn't necessary due to the proposal that the wave function isn't just a mathematical description but a <u>real</u> thing, whereby all of the endless possibilities of events generated by the Schrödinger wave equation do actualize as infinite branches of reality because the wave function doesn't have to collapse, but instead splits. So basically, the Copenhagen Interpretation says that only one of the possibilities contained in a wave function (*i.e.*, event or .95 - 1s of conscious reality) actualize and the other versions of an event don't, compared to the Many Worlds Theory where <u>all</u> of the possibilities of an event occur, just as soon as we observe it, but we are unable to physically ever apprehend the other branches of that particular second of reality. In other words, each "I" believes that its particular version of reality is the entirety of reality.

This sense of wholeness or unbroken unity of reality is further explored by Bell's Theorem and later proven by the Clausen-Freedman Experiment (1972) at the Lawrence Berkeley Laboratory. John Stewart Bell, an Irish physicist working at CERN in 1964, mathematically proved that reality is non-local, which means that information can be passed between particles such as electrons faster than the speed of light. Bell's Theorem was empirically proven by John Claussen in 1972 at the Lawrence Berkeley Laboratory.

This instantaneous transfer of information (*i.e.*, telepathy) was again proven in 1982 by Dr. Alain Aspects at the University of Paris. The fact that thought travels faster than the speed of light (186,000 miles/sec), is everywhere simultaneously and is the reason for the superluminal connections of reality demonstrates a background for Jung's collective unconscious. This would then constitute the thought/energy pattern pool, with the necessary space/time unconscious root agreements, which all potential humans would have access to in the unconscious interval of 0.8 - 1.2s, so that the resultant objects in our conscious interval of .95 - 1s would all appear to be the same (*i.e.*, we all agree that a table is a table, a rock is a rock, etc., due to our r.a.s., reticular activating system, which screens out information that doesn't fit into this 3-D reality).

The basis for this quantum connectedness is rooted in the mathematical concept of "phase entanglement". Phase is another term for angle, which is the "crossing of opposites",

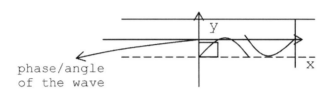

and the "crossing of opposites" is an <u>interaction</u>. Phase entanglement merely means that when the waves for the possible/probably electrons meet (before the electrons as "tendencies to exist" actualize into particles) and then go their separate ways, even though the amplitude/height becomes different, the angle/phase always remains the same; hence, the background reason for the instantaneous transfer of information.

In 1925, Erwin Schrödinger proposed that electrons were actually standing waves, which are stationary patterns of movement. Then, as a consequence of Schrödinger's equation, physicist Wolfgang William Ahestrian discovered that an electron with a particular set of properties (quantum numbers) excluded another electron with similar properties from forming. This became known as Pauli's Exclusion Principle.

Pauli's Exclusion Principle was cited as being one of the basic principles underlying chemistry in Lewis Pauling's 1939 <u>The Nature of the Chemical Bond</u>. In his book, Pauling explains that the exclusion principle provides the reason for the arrangement of elements in the periodic table.

Every element differs from the next by only one electron.

Pauling also mentions that the stability of an atom or molecule is due to the energy exchange (resonance) between electrons, and that the fundamental principle of quantum mechanics, which underlies this important concept of resonance (energy exchange), is the comparison of one system to another, *i.e.*, a ratio b/a. (Note: remember only when something appears different can it be perceived, *i.e.*, actualized.)

Resonance is harmonic (as a result of confinement within a boundary, *i.e.*, the consciousness interval of .95 - 1s), which means that the oscillations (frequency repetition of thought patterns within a certain "time" interval) are in octaves. Our 17 senses perceive these patterns as an image, a sound, a taste, a smell, a touch, etc., combined and experienced within .95 - 1s.

In the 1960s and the 1970s the Swiss Chemist Hans Jenny experimented with frequency (manifested as sound) on the molecules of particular liquids, such as a mixture of salt and water, determining that vibration prompted the mixture to "clump" together in a circle. In his book, Cymantics, Jenny notes, "Throughout the animal and vegetable kingdom Nature creates in rhythms, periods, cycles, frequencies, reduplications, serial phenomena, sequences, etc."[7]

He focused sound in the 100 - 600 cps range at molecules in order to determine what liquid structure would result from it. Consequently, he noticed the correlation between increased frequency (*i.e.*, from 160 to 600 cps) and increased pattern complexity and symmetry.

Basically describing one of the properties of a hologram, Jenny asserted, "In the vibrational field it can be shown that every part is, in the true sense, implicated in the whole."

This concept of holographic self-similarity and self-organization is found in Ilya Prigogine's theory of dissipative structures, whereby he proved that these properties were inherent in systems far from equilibrium (moving, dynamic systems). And a system far from equilibrium is based on the mathematical concept of non-linearity. A non-linear equation is one with squared, x^2, or raised powers, x^3, such as a circle, $x^2 + y^2 = 1$. A spiral form (helix), which is based on an algorithm (*i.e.*, octaves of the original element), is also non-linear. Our DNA is in a spiral or helix shape and based $\sqrt{5}$.

Both Jenny and Prigogine observed how increased energy (frequency) resulted in structures of increased complexity. But in the 1960s, Prigogine went on to demonstrate mathematically how these structures utilized the thermodynamic concept of dissipation (waste) in an open system to become a more complex and orderly structure.

He proved that dissipative structures, as a result of being in an open system (*i.e.*, a non-linear self-reinforcing, feedback network), were to be considered alive.

Starting at the opposite end of the spectrum from Prigogine and Jenny's occupation with structure, Chilean neuroscientist Humberto Maturana, in collaboration with French neuroscientist Francisco Varela, concentrated on the organization of that structure.

In the 1970s, they produced a theory and mathematical model for the circular, self-reproducing, self-referring, self-organizing concept of living organizations which they coined "autopoiesis" (self-making) in order to explain human consciousness.

In their book, The Embodied Mind, Maturana and Varela discuss a concept whereby the behavior of a living system is determined by its structure. They termed this concept "structural coupling" and explained how a living structure interacts and is determined by its environment.

Extending the concept of autopoiesis in relationship to the Earth is the Gaia theory by the microbiologists Lynn Margulis and James Lovelock. Their theory shows nature as being a complexity of self-regulating, self-referring, self-producing networks of energy pattern relationships.

Echoing this idea of rhythmic patterns of activity resulting in networks of information to create the structures of organisms is the hypothesis of formative causation (morphic resonance) by the English biologist Rupert Sheldrake.

In the late 1980s, Sheldrake published his book entitled The Presence of the Past (Morphic Resonance and the Habits of Nature). In it, he presents his case for his theory of formative causation by morphogenetic fields. Fields, whether they be gravitational, electromagnetic or that of the strong or weak nuclear forces, are non-material realms of influence that surround us.

He postulates in his book that the morphogenetic fields that structure forms are based on evolution. It means the most essential features of the fields evolved and that organisms inherit them from ancestors. So memory being inherent in the morphogenetic fields of all organisms, which are built upon "transcendent mathematical realities", is the basis for Sheldrake's hypothesis of formative causation.

He explains that the memory aspect works due to a kind of resonance-morphic resonance, which is based on similarity and does not depend on space or time. But the memory of how an organism should structure its form would be action at a distance and independent of both time and space.

Later in his book, Sheldrake draws a parallel with Jung's collective unconscious as possibly being the source of an organisms' memory structuring ability.

Part B

Mathematical Concepts

1) Mathematics is described as the language of science, which, besides having - along with religion, fairytales and language - triadic and quadratic structures, is part of the self archetypal thought patterns of the collective unconsciousness per Jung; in other words, the translation of phenomena into numbers (frequency).

   a) A point is represented (i) on a line by a single number, (ii) on a plane by two numbers (its two coordinates, *i.e.*, x, y), and (iii) a point in three-dimensional space by its three numbers (coordinates, x, y and z). This is the Cartesian coordinate system upon which classical physics is based. Physics

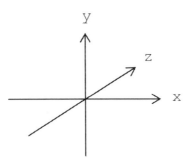

(and science) are predicated upon the assumption of the objective existence of reality; there are objects independent of the observer.

   b) Geometry is concerned with a system of points that form a figure and can be continued congruent to itself and extended into space. The atoms and/or molecules of a structure such as carbon, whose four arms point toward the four corners of a regular tetrahedron, have the atom at its center:

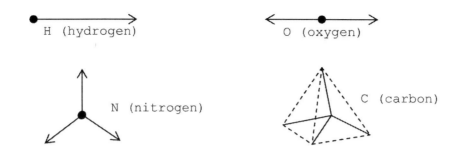

(i) "Geometry" means "measure of the earth" and is the study of spatial order through the measurement and relationships of forms."[1] Weyl mentions in <u>Philosophy of Mathematics and Natural Science</u> that "the only decisive feature of all measurements is, it seems, symbolic representation. Measurement permits things (relative to the assumed measuring basis) to be presented conceptually, by means of symbols."[2]

(ii) For Plato, reality consisted of pure forms or archetypal ideas. Originally, the Greek word for "idea" also meant "form", *i.e.*, thoughtform.

(iii) Pythagoras was the first credited with establishing the relationship between number ratios and sound frequencies. But, as Lucy Lamy mentions in <u>Egyptian Mysteries</u>, the Egyptians, with whom Pythagoras studied, were familiar with and used these number ratios for music long before Pythagoras. This is the relationship upon which Kepler eventually based the current diatonic musical scale. For example, 3/4 = the musical fourth; 2/3 = the musical fifth; 1 = the fundamental and 2 = the octave. The rectangle of 3:4 is the ratio of two numbers (numbers, as they qualitatively represent concepts), which creates an angle and demonstrates "the function of leverage; the principle that <u>energies are controlled, specified and modified through the effects of angulation.</u>"[3]

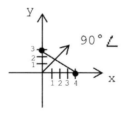

As an example, a bridle becomes the symbol for this archetypal activity. The angles in the bonding patterns of molecules determine whether the substance is a solid, liquid or gas. An angle of 60 degrees has quite different structural and energetic properties than do 90 degree or 45 degree angles.

"The ancient astronomers designated the movement and position of celestial bodies through angular rotation. And today the new science of heliobiology verifies that the angular position of the moon and planets does affect electromagnetic and cosmic radiations which impact with the Earth and, in turn, these field fluctuations affect many biological processes."[4]

(iv) The square roots of two, three and five (also known as the Golden Properties of Phi) exhibit properties that are metaphors for generative, formative and dynamic, principles, which explains how forms appear and change into other forms. This is the transformation of forms, the branch of geometry called topology which deals with invariants.

(aa) "The square root of 2 is the geometric function which represents the universal metaphor or root; the root (of a plant, tree, etc.) grows by the constant division of its square shape. It is a metaphor for the principle of integration and transformation. It is a symbol of sacrifice in nature for example like a mother to uplift. Its efforts are not for its own benefit but to uplift the plant in its movement toward light."[5] The square root of two represents the generative process and is a paradox because it simultaneously divides the first square into 1/2 (its diagonal), but that division becomes the root of the second square, and so forth, which is the result of the squaring of the circle.

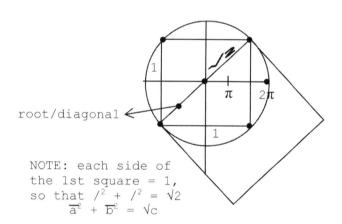

"Like the vegetal root, the root of two contains the power of nature which destroys in order to progress (it servers the initial square)."[6,7] The paradox is expressed by the fact that the same line unit is both the root and diagonal (sameness and difference concepts in one unit).

(bb) The square root of three symbolizes the formative process by appearing in two major geometric configurations. The first is the *Vesica Picis* (literally meaning a bladder filled with air that then takes the form of a fish [Pisces]). This was a major symbol for Christian mysticism in the Middle Ages. It was constructed by drawing two equal circles so that the center of each lies in the circumference of the other and is also the diagonal of a cube.

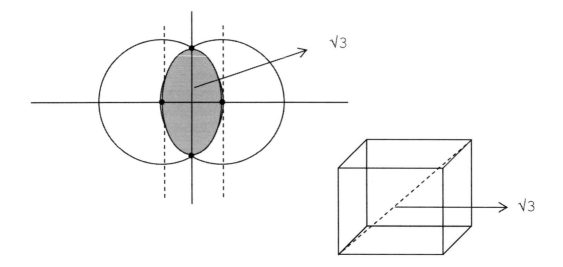

The overlapping circles symbolize unity becoming dual (similar to a cell dividing), and it also forms a fish-shaped central area, which is symbolic reference to Christ as a fish - a universal function which joins together heaven and earth, creator and creation. Geometrically, *Vesica* is the form generator (principle) behind all of the regular polygons to which Euler applied his connectivity number one by utilizing the formula V - E + F (vertices minus edges plus faces equal a certain number). The human molecular structure is based on the regular polyhedron (polygons). The plan of the Chapel of St. Mary at Glastonbury is based on the square root of three.

(cc) The square root of five symbolizes the regenerative principle and is the proportion upon which the Golden Mean (or proportion), is based.

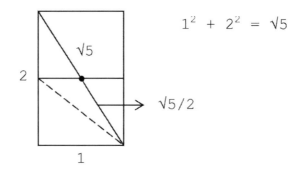

The double squares with a basis of one and a side of two has a diagonal equal to the square root of five so that the semi-diagonal of a single square equals the square root of five divided by two.

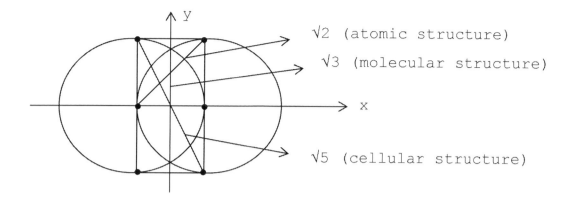

(dd) The square root of two, three and five all demonstrate proportional relationships between two ratios (numbers as concepts)[8]. A ratio constitutes a measure of difference and is based on angulation, which demonstrates the principle of leverage whereby energies are manifested, controlled and specified. The ratio as a "difference" is that to which our sensory facilities respond. So our reality becomes an intricately woven differential response of our 17 senses as they correspond to a range of frequencies from the electromagnetic spectrum. A proportion means one element is to a second element (as a is to b), as that second element is to a third element (b is to c). The perceiver (b) himself forms the equivalency or identity between observed differences (a and c). The differences (objects) are formed by the human visual system and are responses to frequency changes. The Golden Mean is an asymmetrical division of a line (into mean and extreme ratios) or unity (circle), *i.e.*, a is to b as b is to (a + b).

It symbolizes inequality (differences), without which there would be no perceptual universe. It also symbolizes dynamism (movement) - a cosmic creative dance. Poincare demonstrated that dynamical systems are non-integratable, such as the flux of the frequency domain that we call reality. An integratable system conveys a static, deterministic world. He demonstrated mathematically that our world system is non-integratable (fluid and dynamic). He also identified the reason for it: "the existence of resonances between the degrees of freedom."[9] "There is frequency that corresponds to each mode of motion."[10] And, as Linus Pauling in The Nature of the Chemical Bond observes, "Resonances are the interactions (the exchange of electrons) between the atoms and molecules which forms the structural bonding of chemicals."[11] Prigogine adds, "Resonances appear each time a field frequency Wk is equal (in height [amplitude] or phase) to the oscillator frequency W1."[12]

(ee) The Golden Mean spiral is a logarithmic expansion based on the principle of the square roots of two, three and five. The logarithmic spiral (which is the involute of a circle and also forms the basis of the double helix [the structure for DNA and RNA]) is found to be superimposed on the fetus of man and animals and is present in the growth patterns of many plants, including the conch shell."[13] The square roots of two, three and five governed the archetype of ancient Greece (*i.e.*, the Parthenon), whose principle elements, the circle and the square, were the result of the act of self-division. These same dynamic principles, including the Golden Mean or phi (1.618…) and also pi (3.141…), were also discovered in the First Dynasty (3,200 B.C.) royal Egyptian tombs as mentioned in Lucy Lamy's Egyptian Mysteries. The numbers generated by the logarithmic spiral are recognized in biology as the Fibonacci Series, which is generated by the Greek symbol Phi, *i.e.*, 1+1=2, 1+2=3, 2+3=5, 3+5=8, 5+8=13, etc. That series was discovered by a thirteenth century Italian mathematician and governs "the laws involved with the multiple reflections of light through mirrors as well as the rhythmic laws of gains and losses in the radiation of energy. The Fibonacci Series perfectly delineates the breeding patterns of rabbits as a symbol of fecundity."[14] Just as the square root of two is demonstrated in the structure of the roots of plants, the square root of five as the Golden Mean, Phi, is demonstrated in the structure of the branches of plants, trees and flowers (*i.e.*, the number of petals).[15]

2) Topology, which is a branch of geometry, represents relationships of unchangeable or invariant patterns of numbers (*i.e.*, concepts isomorphic with form). *Topos* (topology) means position or situation in Greek. In physics, a particle (a tendency to exist) does not have both momentum and position simultaneously.

a) In topology, we are concerned with geometrical facts that do not even involve the concepts of a straight line or plane but only the continuous connectedness. The concept of topological connectedness as being isomorphic is consistent with the concept of quantum connectedness, *i.e.*, 'sea of energy' or the 'sea of electrons', or 'phase entanglement' between the points of a figure. A figure can be distorted at will but will not torn or cemented (because invariant relationships are involved).[16]

b) The simplest surface is the two dimensional plane. The simplest curves are the plane curves and, of these, the simplest in a straight line. A straight line is defined as the shortest path between two points (point=particles~electrons, atoms or molecules). The next simplest curve is the circle.

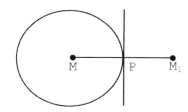

(i) The topological figures generated from a straight line: circle, ellipse, hyperbola, parabola, circular cylinder, square, triangle, rectangle, all of which are two-dimensional forms.

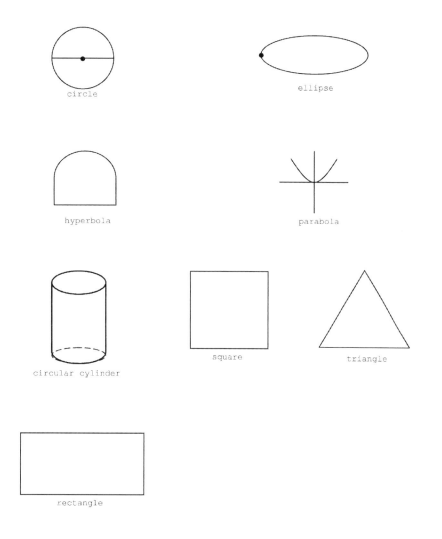

The circular cylinder is the simplest curved surface obtained from a straight line and a circle and its surface revolutions (based upon the square root of five) form drinking glasses, bottles, etc. The spiral, which is the involute of a circle, is the concrete (manifested/actualized) form of an octave and represents the simultaneous interwovenness of interior and exterior. Also, the spiral constitutes an image of continuity between fundamental polarities, *i.e.*, the duality of existence, yin and yang, male and female, cosmic principles (creative and dynamic).

(ii) The topological figures generated from a sphere are based on the square root of three. The Earth's electromagnetic grid system is dodecahedron and icosahedron.

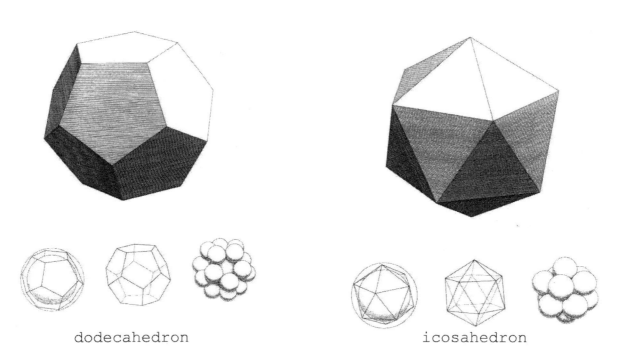

dodecahedron					icosahedron

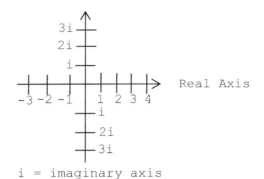

i = imaginary axis

$z \rightarrow z^2 + c$
$1^i \rightarrow 1^{i2} + 2^i = 3^i$
$3^i \rightarrow 3^{i2} + 2^i = 11^i$
$11^i \rightarrow 11^{i2} + 2^i = 123^i$

These are the coordinate points that would be mapped and *then when connected* would form a fractal shape

Its frequency is based on the square root of five, the Golden Mean,
  (aa) All simple or regular polyhedrons - tetrahedron (triangles form faces), octahedron (triangles form faces),

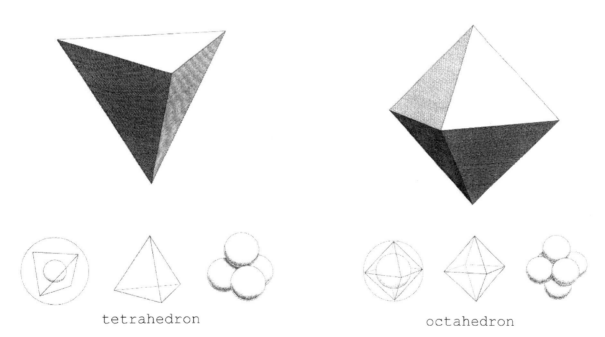

tetrahedron   octahedron

isocahedron (triangles form faces), cube (hexahedron, square forms faces), dodecahedron (pentagons form faces) - can be continuously deformed into spheres (based on the invariant relationships between their vertices, edges and faces equaling topology). V = vertices, E = edges, F = faces. The formula for connectivity is $V - E + F = n$.
  (bb) The invariant number (concept) relationships were put into a formula by Euler and called Euler's Connectivity numbers. Include a brief biographical sketch of Euler and what a prolific mathematician he was.

(cc) Therefore, the connectivity number of a sphere is the number one.

(iii) The topological figures generated from the Roman surface are heptahedrons (seven-sided figure which has four triangles and three squares as faces). The connectivity number is number two. It is an equation of the fourth order whose rectangular coordinates are $y^2 z^2 + z^2 x^2 + x^2 y^2 - xyz = 0$.

(iv) The topological figure generated from a torus (basically, a donut shape): prismatic block (squares and trapezoids form the faces). Its connectivity number is the number three.

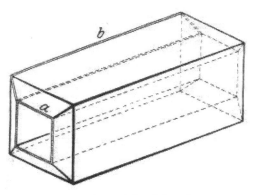

prismatic block

3) Fractal geometry is an extension of classical geometry. Its author is the French mathematician Benoit Mandelbrot. He invented fractal geometry to describe the irregular shapes of natural phenomena such as clouds, ferns, mountains, lightning, branches, etc. He observed that the characteristic patterns found in the "fractal" shapes repeated themselves at descending scales, so that at any scale (resolution), the shape was similar to the whole. This "self-similarity" is a property of a hologram, whereby the part contains the whole and the principle behind the part containing the whole is a property of a sinewave. The concept of "self-similarity" is a link between fractal geometry, the Chaos Theory and the theory of autopoiesis. Mandelbrot illustrated the feature of fractal shapes by posing the question: "How long is the coast of Britain?" He pointed out that since the measured length can be indefinitely extended by going to smaller and smaller scales, there is no clear answer, although it is possible to designate a number between one and two to characterize the jaggedness. Britain's coast is 1.58 and the Norwegian coast is 1.7, which depicts even more jaggedness. The mathematical procedure for constructing these fractal shapes is iteration – the repetition of a certain geometric operation again and again in the complex plane. This could be the reason behind an image being flashed approximately one hundred and fifty times onto the visual cortex (once every one hundredth of a second) before it is consciously acknowledged. The reason is that the composite image of

an object is a result of repetitive fractal patterns (frequency). For the image of the object to appear dense (as matter), it needs the factor of being the sum of layers upon layers of certain frequencies in order for there to be resolution corresponding to our physical receptors. The mapping (determining thousands of coordinate points from the Julia set equation of z to $z^2 + c$, where z is a complex variable [in the imaginary axis] and c is a complex constant) of a mathematical fractal set by Mandlebrot led to actualization of complex fractal shapes of spirals, seahorses, whirlpools and spiral-armed galaxies, whereby the multitude of shapes were repeated at ever-finer scales (octaves). In <u>The Web of Life</u>, Capra draws the analogy between the LSD psychedelic "mind manifesting" art of the 1960s and the similar shapes drawn from the mapping of coordinate points in the complex plane so that the resultant forms demonstrate "that the fractal patterns [actually the frequency of certain coefficients of sinewaves] which are inherent mental processes amplified or catalyzed by the LSD."[17]

The Mandelbrot set

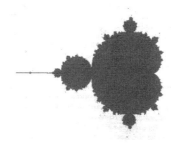

Delving into level after level of the Mandelbrot set

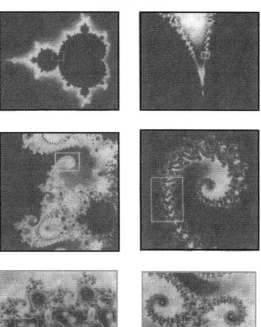

4) Chaos Theory (which, along with fractal geometry, is a branch of dynamical systems theory developed by Poincare and based on nonlinear equations, which means that some of the variables are squared or raised in power, *i.e.*, x^2) and the resultant theory of Ilya Prigogine's dissipative structures are being linked to fractal geometry by the principle of iteration (repetition, *i.e.*, frequency). Chaos Theory and dissipative structures also have in common the features of self-organization and self-reinforcing feedback processes. The mathematics of dissipative structures describes the processes that the forms follow as they evolve simple to complex patterns, *i.e.*, an amoeba to a whole. As Prigogine mentions in his book, From Being to Becoming, "Chaos gives rise to order", because when a system (chemically) reaches a critical point, *i.e.*, a bifurcation point, the system acts as a whole despite the shortness of the chemical interactions. The importance of Prigogine's work is commented on in The Holographic Paradigm: "So I [Ken Wilber] think Prigogine's work is very important not because I can then say he has proven the laws of psychological or spiritual transformation but because he has demonstrated that the transformation process itself extends all of the way down the hierarchy to the lowest levels."[18] And, as Bohm mentions in The Holographic Paradigm, "One of the basic features of matter is recurrence or even with greater regularity, periodicity - the very structure of the holomovement is recurrence."[19]

An elegant example of recursion is demonstrated by the fractability of the fern whose tree, branch, leaf and leaf tip all have the same self-embodied shape. Prigogine proved that dissipative structures were non-integratable and were thus dynamic systems. He utilized Poincare's mathematics in order to show that "there is a frequency that corresponds to each mode of motion."[20] The non-linear equations that he used called "reaction-diffusion equations" referred to thermodynamic systems (chemical reactions) that were far from equilibrium (the motionless state); hence, he named them dissipative structures. These chemical instabilities require the presence of catalytic loops (feedback loops), which bring the system back to the point of instability, which is then called the bifurcation point. At this juncture, the (chemical) system can break down or evolve to a more complex form. This choice is probabilistic and non-deterministic, but depends on the previous structural history. "Living structure, as we shall see, is always a record of previous development."[21]

As Prigogine proved, dissipative structures display order amidst chaos. Deterministic equations apply to the dissipative structures only until they reach the bifurcation, or point of instability, at which time random (probabilistic) fluctuations are the deciding factor. "Thus, self-organizing, the spontaneous emergence of order, results from combined effects of non-equilibrium, irreversibility, feedback loops and instability."[22] Just as Prigogine showed in his studies that chemical instabilities will not automatically appear far from equilibrium but require the repetition (iteration) of self-amplifying feedback or catalytic loops, so did the meteorologist Edward Lorenz demonstrate that the atmosphere's fluid system was also explainable through the iteration of the Chaos Theory. Both Prigogine's dissipative (chemical) structures and Lorenz' weather model are a result of the topological mathematics of Poincare. A "chaotic" system may appear disordered but actually demonstrates a higher degree of order based on the quality and pattern inherent in the nonlinear equations used to describe the system.

In the 1960s, Lorenz (as well as Prigogine) used deterministic equations to simulate a weather model with three coupled nonlinear equations, only to find that the result of what would later to be named the "Lorenz Attractor" was to be a "phase portrait" whose trajectory it was impossible to predict. The "portrait" was painted in "phase space" by the random movements of a "few oscillations of increasing amplitude [i.e., octaves] around one point, followed by a few oscillations around a second point, then suddenly moving back again to oscillate around the first point and so on."[23] So the Chaos Theory (developed to explain weather patterns) describing chemical reactions and autopoiesis (the theory of cognition whereby an organism undergoes continued structural changes while maintaining its network pattern of organization) and fractal geometry have a common basis in that they are extensions of topology, which is a branch of geometry.

5) Sinewaves are the basis of all of the above and are the link between the geometry of form and human thought. A sinewave (which Fourier proved) underlies all other waves and, conversely, is a unique sum of sinewaves. Remember that an image (form) is a wave actualized in time and is the sum of the coefficients (numbers/frequency). So an image is a result of the other side of the "wave" coin - frequency. And frequency means repetition of a pattern (iteration) at the various levels (movement, which is the basis of the entire electromagnetic spectrum). The source of electric and magnetic fields is moving electrically charged particles [electrons], and these can be either positively or negatively charged.

A sinewave would be a metaphorical tool of explanation for the "material" (thought patterns) manifestation into three dimensions of the all-inclusive psychological realm of All That Is. Sinewaves are non-periodic, single harmonic partial (meaning that they contain only one frequency - no octaves or partials), pure tones. They underlie prime numbers per Riemann's Hypothesis, music, mathematics, science, language (as sound), etc. In fact, they underlie the entire electromagnetic spectrum; consequently, all of the world phenomena. Since thought displays e/m properties, it too is composed of sinewaves. The shape of a sinewave is designated by the part of a graph in the interval $[0, 2\pi]$.

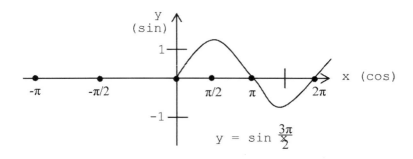

The term "function", as it applies to the sinewave function, refers to a relationship correspondence or interrelation between the x and y coordinates on the Cartesian Graph. A function gives a rule for changing an arbitrary number into something else; the function $f(x) = x^2$ says to square any number x: if x = 2, then f(x) = 4.

It was in 1807 that Jean Fourier, born near Paris, France, demonstrated that virtually any periodic function (and also nonperiodic functions, which have to decrease fast enough at infinity so that coefficients of all possible frequencies have to be computed) can be expressed as a sum or a series of sines and/or cosines. This summation is called a Fourier series and it concerns only those sines and cosines that are integer multiples (in other words, harmonic octaves) of the base frequency: for example, sin 2πK, sin 2π2K, sin π3K, and so forth. The Fourier Transform is the mathematical procedure that breaks up or analyzes a wave function into its component frequencies. Remember that frequency is tantamount to the pixels on a computer screen which builds up an image for the eye to perceive. The new function is called the Fourier Transform (or, if the function is periodic, the Fourier series) of the original function. This procedure can be reversed by reconstructing the function from the transform (or series) and is the Fourier synthesis of the waveform.

A sinewave is generated from a circle and has a period of 2π. The attributes or components of a wave also describe the shape: amplitude, period and phase. The amplitude represents the height of the wave; it is also the hypotenuse of the triangle formed by the coordinates, or coefficients.

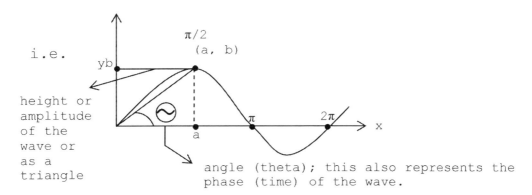

When the amplitude (height) is squared (the intensity), a probability becomes an actuality. Also, when the particular wave function represents a frequency perceived by our ears, the amplitude represents sound.

The period of a sinewave is the time (interval) between amplitude peaks. The reciprocal of T=I/T, which gives the number of peaks per second, and is the frequency of the sinewave, f=I/T.

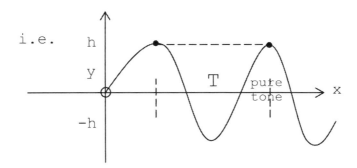

Frequencies used to be called cycles per second (cps, or revolutions of a circle), but now are called Hertz (honoring the physicist Heinrich Hertz, 1857-1894). For example, a sinewave with a frequency (repetition of the standing wave pattern) of 440Hz (abbreviation for Hertz) has a period of:

T = 1/440 = .0022727 seconds

Conversely, a sinewave with a period of 1/1000 or 0.001 second will have a frequency of:

f = 1/0.001 = 1,000 Hz (cps)

The phase of a sinewave is the angle created by the hypotenuse (amplitude). Two sinewaves can have the same frequency and amplitude but have different phases (angles) by crossing the horizontal x-axis at different times. This would be a cosinewave, which is a sinewave with a different phase. Remember: in <u>Sacred Geometry</u>, angulation represents the principle of leverage whereby energies are controlled, actualized and specified.

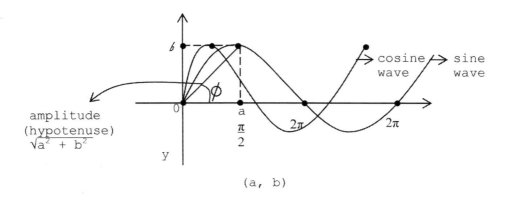

The sinewave is a circular (trigonometric) function. A function is a correspondence or relationship of numbers/points. There are six trigonometric functions: sine, cosine, tangent, cotangent, secant and cosecant.

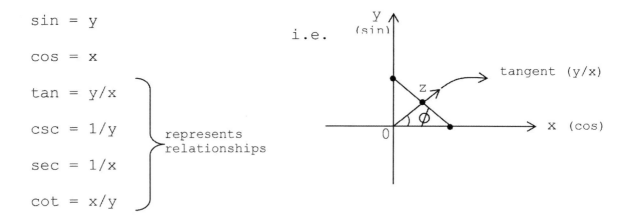

So the concept of a sinewave is based on circular or self-actualizing network of numbers as frequency (which means repetition of those numbers within a prescribed "time" interval/period). Those numbers ("archetypes of order", as Jung described them) represent concepts, ideas, thoughts, feelings, beliefs. Just as any wave can be written as a unique sum of sinewaves (Fourier's Theorem), and if waves compose all objects, then all objects can be written as a unique sum of sinewaves (numbers/frequency representing idea/thought packages). Consequently, "the sinewave [as function or relationship of numbers/archetypal concepts] is the sum total [the total sum of an infinite series of numbers within a bounded system, *i.e.*, lim 1→2] of the waveform [thoughtform]."

Just as the movement of a circle generates a sinewave, which is an unconfined wave and vibrates as it pleases, a sphere (a three dimensional circle) generates the natural vibrations or waveforms called spherical harmonics, which are confined waves whose vibrations are restricted to the surface of a sphere. Conversely, just as an unconfined sinewave vibrates as it pleases, a confined wave vibrates only at certain resonant frequencies, hence the reason for the narrow range or bandwidth of frequencies necessary to shape world phenomena. This encompasses every object in the earthly realm (including the Earth) whose frequency used to be 7.8 cps and is now 8.6 cps.

Spherical harmonic waveforms are a three-dimensional extension of sinewaves. They represent the natural vibrations of world phenomena, *i.e.*, the Earth, its occupants, its magnetic field. Snowflakes to atomic nuclei are a result of the vibrations of the confined spherical waveforms. The fact that humans and all world phenomena have a natural resonant frequency which is within a small bandwidth (about 1.5 octaves) is the result of the confinement (and confinement of a particle causes movement) of the electron, which produces the interactions called the natural resonant frequencies. The definition of magnetism is the movement of electrons and the movement of electrons is the basis of a hologram. The sinewave is the basis of a hologram. The movement of an electron caused by confinement produces "standing waves". These wave patterns occur in a confined, finite region:

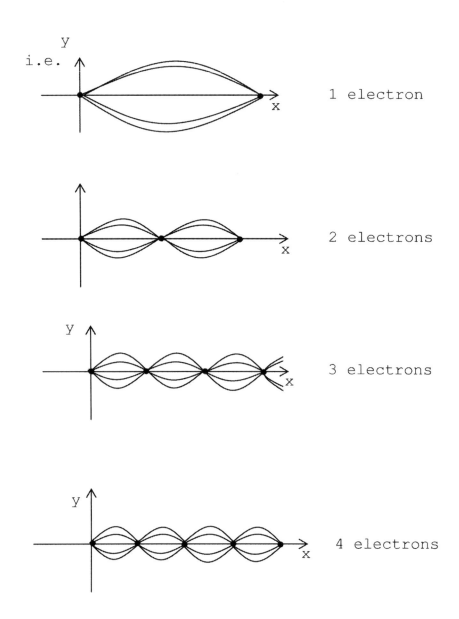

In an atom, the electrons have to be arranged so that "their ends meet". For example, they then can form patterns known as "standing waves". These patterns appear whenever waves are confined to a finite area like the surface of a sphere. "Confinement" is the result of the interaction between the nucleus' attractive electric force to the electrons and their violent reaction to the reduction of the bound state. This reaction causes movement.

The constraint on vibratory states (*i.e.*, the base resonant frequency of 5 - 8 cps/theta waves) translates into a universal code of integers for perceiving world phenomena. This is the waveform attribute connection, whereby, as mentioned in Heinz Pagels' The Cosmic Code, a waveform is attributed to every physical attribute of an object (*i.e.*, that which determines how electrons form the structure of a chair so that we recognize the pattern of movement as a chair), such as how the structure of a violin is formed (second-after-second).

When a sinewave (thought pattern) is confined to the surface of a sphere it becomes a spherical harmonic waveform. The concept of harmonics is illustrated in the fact that the fundamental frequency can be heard and is a part of any resultant octaves. The concept of harmonics is demonstrated by the range of frequencies, 10^1 to 10^{24}, of the electromagnetic spectrum where the fundamental frequency can be heard and is a part of any resultant octave. The human perspective of reality is also harmonic due to the fact that our senses apprehend and analyze various octaves (sight, sound, taste, touch, smell, etc.) of the electromagnetic spectrum, which is itself an expression of an ultra high frequency.

The concept of a hologram is based on the "part containing the whole" and also a sinewave as it becomes a spherical waveform. The result of the confinement of the sinewave to the surface of a sphere is a "standing wave" electron pattern and the motion that results from the confinement (which is the interaction between the electrons and the nucleus). Motion, as has been noted before, is the basis of the entire electromagnetic spectrum, so the circular movement (frequencies) of the thought patterns (sinewaves) creates the camouflage of this system. Seth notes, "reality is circular in manner."[1] He also mentions in the same book, "Action is an idea in motion."[2]

According to R.W. Ditchburn, dynamical, non-integratable systems (per Poincare) are such because of the "existence of resonances between the degrees of freedom."[3] Spherical waveform systems are dynamic and contain both kinetic and potential energy simultaneously, whereas a sinewave contains only one or the other. Spherical elastic waves possess both types of energy because the medium is moving (kinetic) and it is a state of strain (potential). The idea in motion being the thought patterns or packages (as represented by that mythical creature, the sinewave) and the action are represented by the various energy levels of the e/m spectrum from 10^1 to 10^{24}.

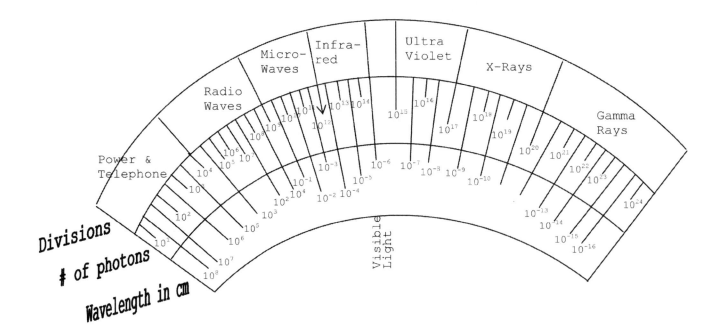

At every level, "it is always interaction which is important," as Seth notes in <u>Dreams and Projections of Consciousness</u>.[4] "It is held today that all 4 <u>interactions</u> (the 4 forces of the unified field theory as represented by the electromagnetism, the strong and the weak nuclear force and gravity) become unified as one <u>universal interaction</u> at ultra high energies,"[5] and "that this realm [universe] is an asymmetrical remnant of a symmetric beginning."[6]

The interactions (resulting in movement or patterns of "standing wave electrons") are manifested "between electrons and atomic nuclei and are thus the basis of all solids, liquids and the gases and also of all living organisms and of the biological processes associated with them."[7] This movement is the result of the confinement of a particle to a small region of space; the smaller the region of confinements the faster the particle moves around (in a circular manner). If we substitute the concept of focus for space (which is a relative term, dependent upon the neurophysical structure of the organism), then the movement of the sinewave thought pattern becomes a property of psychological focus. So that the confined spherical harmonic waveform "vibrates only at certain resonant frequencies."[8]

The natural resonant frequencies produced create phenomena (the Earth and all inhabitants), which vibrate within a narrow bandwidth of frequency. The wavelength of our collective hologram is 10^8 to 10^7 nanometers. These conclusions demonstrate the interconnectedness of all world phenomena and the basis for a telepathic agreement via the collective unconscious.

The equation "$E = A/r \sin(wt-kr) = A/r \sin \Theta...$" from R.W. Ditchburn "represents a spherical wave since at any time the phase is the same over the whole of any sphere centered on the origin."[9] "[T]he phase existing on any sphere of a radius r^0 is transferred to a larger sphere of radius $(r^0 + bt^0)$ after a time t^0 and, therefore, the expression represents a spherical wave diverging from the origin."[10] Remember that the "phase" means the angle of the hypotenuse (represented by the amplitude of the length of the vector defined by the points a, b on the coordinate system).

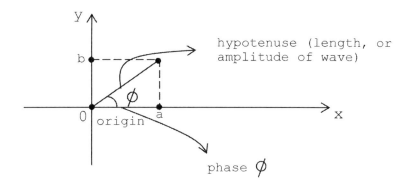

The phase determines where the wave crosses the horizontal x-axis and also the time of "actualization or manifestation of the 'smeared' electron standing wave into a particle" frequency and ultimately into a "solid" object. Consequently, the phase (angle/time), as quoted form the physicist Ditchburn, would be the same for the entire sphere (world phenomena), meaning that the Earth and all inhabitants, as well as having the same natural resonant frequencies, would oscillate (blink on and off together) at the same rate and this oscillation would be the basis for our .8 to 1.2s lapse of consciousness, which is the ratio 1.5 (2:3, the perfect fifth) or π/2. It corresponds to 60° and √3.

Part C

Neurological Concepts

1) <u>How color generates dimension</u>: The differential response of the human visual system to the frequency of the e/m spectrum called color determines dimension. The human color vision is trichromatic, meaning our visual system is comprised of three types of photoreceptors cross-connected to three color channels. Consequently, three dimensions are needed to represent the kinds of color distinction that we can make. The theory that originally proposed the three color channels is called the opponent-process theory by Leo Hurvich and Dorthea Jameson in 1957. It is accepted dogma that the "channels correspond in some way to the complex cross-connections among retinal cells and post retinal neuronal ensembles."[1]

The opponent-process theory proposed that there are three color channels: one channel is achromatic (black and white) and involves the photoreceptors in the retina, called rods, which signal differences in brightness (these are involved in night vision); the other two channels are chromatic (red-green and yellow-blue) and involve the photoreceptors which are less sensitive to light, called cones, which signal differences in the hues. Together the rods and cones account for seventy percent of the body's receptors since there are one hundred twenty-five million rod cells and six million cone cells. Red, green, yellow and blue are the four fundamental colors or hues from which the approximate 50,000 binary hues are formed, *e.g.*, reddish-blues (purple), reddish-yellows (oranges), greenish-yellow (chartreuse), etc.

The retina cone cells, which, like the rod cells, process visual information signals either in vertical or horizontal pathways, absorb the 10^{14} frequency of the visible light spectrum (or 560, 530 and 440 nanometers in wavelength) in a mosaic pattern. These three cones analyze and differentiate the incoming frequency into two mutually exclusive or opponent pairs which constitute the two chromatic channels. The process of the intermingling of the three types of cones result in the long wave (L), middle wave (M) and short wave (S) receptors. "Excitatory and inhibitory processes in post-retinal cells enable the signals from these receptors to be added and or subtractively compared."[2] And, as discussed in Sacred Geometry, the reason for the necessity of these periodic oscillations, for example lateral inhibition, might be found in an unlikely source. "The answer is simply that with equality, there is no difference, and without difference, there is no perceptual universe."[3] So the human visual system is based on the interactions of its parts (the rods and cones), resulting in an eventual image being built upon the cells of the visual cortex in the brain. Also, the visual system constitutes the difference between the signals from the L and M receptors generated by the red-green channel, and the difference between the sum of the signals from the L and M receptors and the S receptors, which generates the yellow-green channel.

The integration process called lateral inhibition results from the signal processing of sinewave coded information (frequency) of the vertical and horizontal pathways of the rods and cones. "When a rod or cone stimulates a horizontal cell, the horizontal cell stimulates nearby receptors but inhibits more distant receptors and bipolar cells that are not illuminated, making the light spot appear lighter and the dark surroundings even darker."[4] This process sharpens edges and enhances contrast in the image, which determines dimension so that our "color coded world is brought forth by complex processes of the structural coupling." "The colors we see must be located not in a pregiven world but rather in the perceived world brought forth from our structural coupling."[5]

The authors (Varela, Thompson and Rosch) go on to say that "indeed, it is fair to say that the neurological processes underlying human color perception are rather peculiar to the primate group."[6] As explained in Wavelets, "mammalian vision systems always use filters that are oriented in two dimensions."[7] These are the high and low pass filters in the wavelet transform. They are represented by the differential frequency response of the L - M color channel receptors (low pass) and the difference between the sum of the frequency from the L - M receptors and the S receptors (high pass). "The visual neurons are also narrowly tuned to orientation," says psychologist David Field of Cornell University.[8] "The role of the Wavelets is played by the receptive fields: the patterns of light that provoke a reaction from the neurons of the primary visual cortex, at the back of the brain. These receptive fields vary in size and are oriented at different angles, different neurons responding to different receptive fields. Just as a signal in signal processing can be decomposed into wavelets of different sizes, what we look at can be decomposed into different receptive fields."[9]

According to John Daugman and Andrew B. Watsen, the mathematicians who created the transforms to model the human visual system, the goal was efficient recognition by encoding natural scenes (*i.e.*, everyday macroscopic objects with the smallest number of possible neurons, which are tantamount to a wavelet coefficient) with just a few coefficients. As Field explains, "The reaction of a neuron is a 'wavelet coefficient'. If a neuron doesn't fire, the coefficient is zero. If it fires repeatedly and very fast, it is a big coefficient; if the response is sluggish, the coefficient is small. As in a wavelet transform, small receptive fields encode high frequencies [as represented by the S receptors/the high pass filter (fine resolution, little details, good localization in space)] while bigger receptive fields encode low frequencies [as represented by the L - M receptors/the low pass filter (coarser resolution, but good localization on frequency)]."[10] Consequently, our mammalian vision, which is mathematically constructed by employing wavelet transforms, is attuned to a small range of frequencies - a narrow bandwidth coincides with the fact that the confined waves of spherical harmonics can only vibrate (oscillate) at certain natural resonant frequencies. Field sums up by saying, "The visual neurons are also narrowly tuned to orientation. These are the bandwidths (typically about 1.5 octaves) of frequency and orientation needed to encode a natural scene with just a few neurons" and "structure in real scenes is only predictable for a small range of frequencies (one to two octaves) in a small range of orientations."[11]

Just as the human color visual system is trichromatic and, as a result, we visually construct reality into three dimensions, other animal classes' visual systems are dichromatic, tetrachromatic and pentachromatic. "Trichromacy is certainly not unique to humans; indeed, it would appear that virtually every animal class contains some species with trichromatic vision,"[12] says Varela. Dicromats, which include "squirrels, rabbits, tree shrews, some fishes, possibly cats and some New World monkeys",[13] perceive reality to be two-dimensional. Tetrachromats, which include "fishes that live close to the surface of the water like goldfish and diurnal birds like the pigeons and the duck",[14] perceive their reality in four dimensions. Pentachromats, which include some diurnal birds, perceive reality as being five-dimensional. So they see the same three-dimensional color space that human mammals call reality as being five-dimensional. So the same three-dimensional color space that human mammals call reality is also perceived as being simultaneously two-, four- and five-dimensional by other animal classes. "It should now be apparent, then, that the vastly different histories of structural coupling for birds, fishes, insects and primates have enacted or brought forth different perceived worlds of color. Therefore, our perceived world of color should not be considered to be the optimal 'solution' to some evolutionary posed 'problem.' Our perceived world of color is rather a result of one possible and viable phylogenic pathway among many others realized in the evolutionary history of living beings."[15]

2) <u>How other animals neurophysiologically create their world view of reality</u>: Out of the 1.6 billion species currently on earth (approximately sixteen billion species for the estimated four billion years of the Earth's age), man experiences a small, unique version of reality based on his neurophysiological processes. Also, other species simultaneously experience their own version of reality according to their physiological processes. For example, "horsefly's eyes are divided into 20,000 individual cells, each responding to a specific wavelength [or frequency], lengths of the electromagnetic spectrum or else a specific chemical molecule in the air which combines all of the receptors' input into an 'image' of the environment."[16] Along with other insects that have compound eyes, the horsefly constructs a multifaceted image of reality.

On the other hand, the lizard's dominant sense is their smell/taste/tongue, with which they build up a composite image of their environment. "Their tongue also serves as a navigating device, in order magnetically to sense direction."[17] Likewise, bacteria, birds and marine mammals use magnetic fields for their orientation. "Some fish use electrical discharges as an aid in navigation. However, water doesn't present a uniform color environment, and their color vision provides information that not only distinguishes one object from another, but also helps establish which was is up, which way to school with other fish and so forth."[18] Birds navigate by using the electromagnetic spectrum at .1 to 10 cps in order "to detect the very low frequency infrasounds given off by ocean waves and major topological features such as mountain ranges," according to Robin Baker in <u>Human Navigation and the Sixth Sense</u>.[19] Baker's thesis for this book is that "man has a magnetic sense of direction"[20] similar to that of birds, fish, bacteria and marine mammals.

Instead of utilizing the frequency range of what we call sound (18 to 20,000 cps or 10^1 to 10^4) only for hearing purposes as we do, bats and marine mammals (dolphins, whales, porpoises, seals and sea lions) utilize that portion of the electromagnetic spectrum, plus up to 100,000 cps, in order to maneuver in their environments. In caves and oceans, the bats and marine mammals respectively utilize echolocation. This ultrasonic, radar-like transmission/reception is normally outside the range of human hearing. For example, a bat's hearing is from 10,000 cps to 100,000 cps. Also known for their tremendous hearing ability are "barn owls, which are able to track the footsteps of a mouse from high overhead."[21] And even though the bee's visual system is trichromatic, just as man's is, their three different photoreceptor cells are not responsive to the frequency called red (429 to 492 trillion cycles per second), but to ultraviolet instead (over 750 trillion cycles per second). Consequently, bees cannot "see" red and we cannot "see" ultraviolet light. In fact, snakes can "see" the frequency range that we call infrared (which is less than the 429 trillion cycles per second) for what we call red. They construct their composite "images" from the heat (thermal energy) which is given off from the object.

3) In a 1953 paper to the French Academy of Sciences, Alfred Tomatis presented the following axiom: "The voice contains only the sound which the ear hears."[22] And, after further investigation, he demonstrated "the feedback loop between larynx and the ear: the larynx emits only the range that the ear controls. In other words, one can reproduce vocally only those sounds which one can hear."[23] In fact, Tomatis discovered that each of the world's 5,000 languages "has a specific frequency range within which most sounds in that particular language are spoken."[24] Tomatis developed his method "to reprogram the different stages of the human development through a symbolic experience,"[25] this experience being using the mother's voice to re-open the listening process. Based on an exhaustive review of scientific literature, Tomatis concludes that the mother's voice is not only an emotional nutrient to the child, but also prepares the child to acquire language after birth.[26] The author continues, "Hundreds of research studies on attachment show that this bond is primordial. <u>It is the base on which the sense of personal safety and the desire to communicate are built</u>."[27] The absence of this base, Tomatis suggests, may cause autism - a withdrawal from an incomprehensible world.

"For Tomatis, the listening process begins to develop early in prenatal life, at about 4 1/2 months before birth, the ear starts to function."[28] Of all of our senses, hearing is the first to develop <u>in utero</u>. While hearing is the first to develop at about four months before birth, vision, which is the dominant sensory system, is the last to develop <u>after</u> birth. And just hours after birth, the infant's olfactory sense is up and running. Taste is also present after birth, with infants preferring sweet to bitter, sour or salty. And skin receptors (for tactile sensations) are fully functioning at birth. Tomatis' findings and conclusions have been supported by other researchers as well. Tomatis proclaims that "among the many uterine sounds, the fetus is able to hear distinctly the voice of the mother."[29] "Tomatis has further stated that while in the womb, the higher frequencies of the mother's voice literally nourish the fetus. It is with this process that listening begins, and carries into childhood. The development of later communication skills, language acquisition, learning ability and social adjustment in particular, depends on the quality of this early listening."[30]

Affirmation of the early ear's functioning in accordance with language acquisition is echoed by Rivlin and Gravelle in <u>Deciphering the Senses</u>. "The child, according to linguist Noam Chomsky, is born with a set of innate language learning abilities centered in a small area on the brain's left temporal lobe."[31] Like sensory systems, however, they need to be stimulated at the proper age which, according to Piaget's work, is at a certain stage of sensormotor development, from one to eighteen months. It is also at four months that the researcher David Oates discovered that the backward reverse speech patterns were being verbally produced by the unconscious.

Tomatis further discovered in his research that "a high-frequency sound [similar to mother's voice] energizes the brain, whereas low-frequency sounds drain energy away".[32] "Tomatis notes that when our brain is 'well charged' [with higher frequencies] we can focus, concentrate, organize, memorize, learn and work for long periods of time, almost effortlessly."[33] As the author notes, "For Tomatis, the ear is primarily an apparatus intended to effect a cortical change, *i.e.*, to increase the electrical potential of the brain."[34]

"In fact, sound [as frequency between 18 to 20,000 cps] is transformed into nervous influx [waves] by the ciliform cells of the inner ear. The electrical energy obtained from the influx of nervous impulses reaches the cortex, which then distributes it throughout the body. This tones up the whole system and impacts greater dynamism."[35]

But most importantly, Tomatis discovered that the vestibular function (inner ear) determines balance, coordination, verticality (the last two determine spatial definition of the body in relation to its surrounding environment), muscle tone and the musculature of the eyes. The vestibular-cochlear system (which analyzes sounds and is important for language comprehension) is linked and acts as a relay station between the nervous system and the brain for all sensory information. The frequencies, turned into waves, then back into frequency, for touch, vision, smell, taste and hearing are all interpreted through our vestibular-cochlear system. "Only slightly less remarkable is Tomatis' description of the ear's involvement with the body. Because of its connections with the vital phuemogastric (vagus) nerve, the ear has a part in nearly everything we feel."[36]

Regarding music, which "has all the characteristics (pitch, timbre, intensity and rhythm) of spoken language, except semantic value,"[37] Tomatis determined that "children's songs and nursery rhymes harmonize body movements and motor functions by their effect on the vestibular system. They also increase the child's awareness of his body and help shape the body image."[38] "The critical range for musicality is 500 hertz to 4,000 hertz."[39]

4) (A) <u>The universality of the triadic and quadratic structure of RNA and DNA's encoded genetic information for all life forms.</u>

"The genetic code is nearly universal, shared by organisms as diverse as bacteria and humans."[40] A language shared across all of life must have been operating very early in the history of life - early enough to be present in the organisms that were common ancestors of all modern organisms from the simplest bacteria to human. A shared genetic vocabulary is a reminder of the kinship that bonds all on Earth. The complexity and diversity of the frequency patterns that constitute the human body are reflected at the various cellular, genetic, molecular and atomic levels. Even though the human body has approximately two hundred billion body cells, which are completely replaced every seven years, with each containing 50,000 to 100,000 genes, which are all composed of forty six chromosomes - twenty-three from each parent - which are comprised of a single anti-parallel, double-helix molecular strand of DNA, which is built of four (a quadratic structure) nucleotides [adenine (A), guanine (G), cytosine (C) and thymine (T)], which are further broken into triadic structures containing the three bases (codons) of phosphate, sugar and nitrogen. They form a vast network, rich in feed-back loops, in which genes (of which there are two hundred fifty-four different types) directly and indirectly regulate each other's activity. The term for this complete genetic set in an organism is a genome.

The cells' function is to carry out protein synthesis, which is carried out by DNA (deoxyribonucleic acid), along with RNA (ribonucleic acid), which has the same quadratic nucleotide as DNA (but contains uracil (U) instead of thymine (T)), serving as a messenger for transcription and translation between the two different chemical languages of nucleic acids (*i.e.*, RNA and DNA) and proteins. Also, just as DNA serves as a template or blueprint for building each unique human, it also serves as a blueprint for constructing the other 1.6 billion species on Earth. So all living organisms share the same DNA, with only the triadic (phosphate, sugar and nitrogen) bases (codons) differing from species to species.

As noted earlier in Cymantics, the pattern of form increases with complexity as the frequency increases so that at the body's cellular level it is quadratic, then triadic at the molecular level and pentagonal and hexagonal (five- and six-sided atomic structures) at the atomic level. The atomic structure of the base pairs AT and CG is pentagonal and hexagonal (five- and six-sided polygons whose atomic angles are L50°and L52° and L54°, respectively).

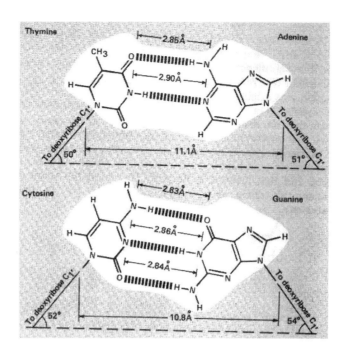

(B) When Candace Pert and Soloman Snyder of the National Institute of Mental Health in Maryland discovered opiate receptors in the brain in 1972, they revolutionized neurochemistry. They went on to discover that a chain of macromolecules, called peptides (of which there are sixty to seventy different types and which include endorphins, hormones, neurotransmitters, growth factors, etc.) act as messengers to interconnect the endocrine, immune and nervous systems. The peptide macromolecule is a short chain of amino acids which attaches itself to a specific cell receptor somewhere throughout the body, depending on the information that is to be delivered to a particular site. The sixty to seventy family members of peptides were <u>not only</u> found to be produced in the brain and then disbursed from there, but also found to be produced by the endocrine, immune and nervous systems. So, according to Candace Pert, "the three systems must be seen as forming a single psychosomatic network."[41]

Just as in mathematics, where networks and relationships imply nonlinearity (for example, a circular pattern), these peptides create a body network that is self-organizing, self-referring and self-actualizing. Historically, the limbic system in the brain was associated with our emotions. As it turned out, the researchers discovered a plethora of peptides in that area. "Peptides are the biochemical manifestation of emotions. They play a crucial role in coordinating activities of the immune system; they interlink and integrate mental, emotional and biological activities."[42] Just as the peptides color and change behavior and moods, "scientists now hypothesize that peptides may evoke a unique emotional 'tone.' The entire group of sixty to seventy peptides may constitute a universal biochemical language of emotions."[43]

The triadic molecular structure of the peptides which form the organizing aspect of "number as an archetype of order" (Jung), represents union. This is demonstrated by the fact "that each peptide mediates a particular emotional state. This would mean that all sensory perceptions, all thoughts and, in fact, all bodily functions are emotionally colored because they all involve peptides. Indeed, scientists observed that the nodal points of the central nervous system, which connect the sensory organs with the brain, are enriched with peptide receptors that filter and prioritize sensory perceptions [later, this filtered information is again re-filtered by the inner ear and yet again by the reticular activating system (r.a.s.), which is at the base of the brain, before our conscious mind (which is the beta state, 16 - 40 cps) becomes aware of it]."[44] "In other words, all of our perceptions and thoughts are colored by emotions. This of course, is also our common experience."[45]

In 1988, the triadic molecular structure of DNA's 4 bases (A, C, T and G) was empirically demonstrated to mimic the same ratios (*i.e.*, angles) as the intervals upon which music is based. The biologist David Dreamer of the University of California and the musician Susan Alejander produced a tape recording, "Sequencia", of the molecules for synthesizers, violin, cello and voice by utilizing the wavelength absorption spectra of adenine, cytosine, thymine and quanine. They determined that the "highest tones are associated with the lightest atoms in each molecule: hydrogen... they become sort of Es, Fs and F#s on our western scale. Oxygen, the next, are Fs and F#s on an octave below. Approximately 15 pitches out of 60 fall directly on the equal temperament scale and the entire spread is about 2 1/2 octaves. There are octave [*i.e.*, (2:1); the diameter of a circle represents an octave, $\pi/3$, 90°, 1.05 and $\sqrt{2}$] and Fifth [*i.e.*,(2:3), 60°, $\sqrt{3}$ and 1.5 interval, $\pi/2$] relationships within each base. These closely match with thirds, fourths and whole tones [*i.e.*, an octave, which a spiral represents]. The human DNA genetic code is in a helix structure which is a spiral, and a spiral is the involute of a sphere."[46] Demonstrate the logarithmic expansion principle: "In such a model, past time remains present as form and the formation grows through pulsating, rhythmic gnomonic expansion and thereby symbolize the evolution not of substance but of consciousness."[47] "The logarithmic spiral is so rich in geometric and algebraic harmonies that traditional geometers named it spira mirabilits, the miraculous spiral. While the radius of this spiral increases in a geometric progression, the radial angle increases in an arithmetic progression. These are the numerical progressions which yield all of the ratios from which the music scales are constructed."[48] In other words, these demonstrate the relationships to the nine partials (including the flat seventh partial)."

As the physicist David Bohm noted, "Recurrence is the basis of nature" and "the principle of repetitious recurrence also applies to the construction of individual coding sequences [of DNA]." Available evidence indicates that all of the coding base sequences were, at the inception eons ago, repeats of base oligomers. They therefore encode polypeptide chains of periodicities."[49]

In summary, our body, which is composed of 200 billion cells, represents an orchestra of sounds at the cellular, molecular, atomic and subatomic level. And at the molecular level, the peptides, which interlink all of our body's three systems, along with DNA, structurally represent musical intervals/ratios. Ratios represent an angle (the term "phase", which represents time can be substituted for "angle"), which is the interaction between parts or concepts.

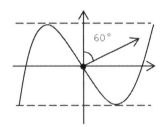

An <u>interaction</u> is the basis for the resonance phenomenon. The resonance/frequency is the same for the entire sphere, *i.e.*, Earth and its inhabitants, simultaneously. So since all living, earthly organisms share the same DNA, with different bases, the angles (or resonance, *i.e.*, phase) of our bases represent the same phase (*i.e.*, time) simultaneously. Remember L.W. Ditchburn's comment regarding the spherical waveform, which represents Earth and its inhabitants: "The phase is the same over the whole of any sphere centered on the origin."[50]

(C) <u>The ratios (angles) that determine the structures of DNA, RNA, music, singing and speech are the same intervals of time as our 0.8 – 1.2s lapse of consciousness and our .95 – 1s interval of consciousness.</u>

The same ratio of 1.5 or 2:3 (angle 60°) that determines the structure of DNA and RNA is the interval of time during which we lapse into unconsciousness: 0.8 – 1.2s, which is a 1.5 interval (1.2 ÷ .8). "It is well known that we are not able to observe continuously, even to think continuously. We do these things in certain intervals of time that may be called 'temporal quanta' (Stern 1897; Lehman 1905) or the 'conscious present,'"[51] states Dr. Bekesy. During nearly four decades of psychological experiments, Bekesy had "always been interested in the momentary lapses of consciousness in which momentary reductions in magnitude of sensation occur."[52] He further notes that "there is a certain periodic pattern of time in the activity of consciousness [*i.e.*, the beta state; one of the four brain wave clusters which oscillates from 16 – 40 cps]. One of these periodicities is 0.8 to 1.2 seconds long and it interjects a rhythm into the observations and recognitions of music, singing and speech. We tend to break both speech and music into temporal segments of this duration. This temporal pattern operates so as to enhance the reflected sounds that arise within one time unit to suppress the sounds that come after the unit has ended."[1] He continues, "Another way of observing this form of central inhibition is to record the number of syllables per word produced during continuous speech. Vierodt in 1868 noted that there is a definite preference for words of one or two syllables; about 45 percent of all words used are disyllabic. [...] The time required to pronounce a two-syllable word corresponds roughly to the temporal quanta defined above. Syllables pronounced during this period are likely to fuse into a single unit."[2]

Apparently, we are conscious one second, then unconscious for 0.8 to 1.2 seconds, then conscious again for one second, etc. But the temporal pattern which is the body is unaware of the unconscious lapse and consequently can start to react to an event 1 1/2 seconds before we are consciously aware of that same event. For example, if you are walking along and a ball comes flying at you, oftentimes your body will instantly react – without your conscious assessment of the situation and how to deal with it. Another example is recognizing a song on the radio or anticipating it before it starts to play. Your body was already aware of the probable event of the ball striking you and took evasive action starting during your 0.8 to 1.2 seconds of unconsciousness. Bekesy noted the body's continuous oscillatory nature by saying that "in the records of neural activity, for single nerve units, or larger groups, there does not seem to be any counterpart of this effect. We find for a continuous stimulus an uninterrupted series of nerve discharges. The momentary lapses seem to be of central origin and they can be regarded as momentary, periodic exhibitions of central activity."[3]

During his forty years of research, Bekesy demonstrated that the body, which has seventeen different senses and at least one hundred rhythmic cycles per day (*e.g.*, circadian [sleep/wake], ultradian [hormones], reproductive, etc.), localizes or externally projects sensations as in a hologram outside itself. "The funneling of sensations into a space outside the body is an important feature of neural funneling, for it controls practically all of our behavior."[4] Behavior, moods and thoughts are determined by the peptides, which are the biochemical manifestation of emotion. Consequently, there is an emotion (as frequency) which propels the frequency sensations (*i.e.*, the 60,000 thought patterns per day per human) outward from the body (localization). "For example, reflected light from any external object produces an image on the retina. The sensations exist only within our body, yet we localize the image outside the eye."[5]

Bekesy attributes this localization ability to the "fact that we are willing to make a fresh start after each lapse of consciousness. It might be said that we store the information obtained during the preceding quantum and concentrate on the next one." He continues, "When phenomena are complex, this activity produces a periodic shift of interest from one sensation to another. The shift of interest may be also a shift in conscious space, so that we begin to make a new localization of the sensation after each lapse."[6]

To summarize: the phase angles from 50° to 54°, representing the structure of DNA and RNA (for all earthly organisms), music and language, are the consequence of the natural resonant frequencies (which represent a confined sinewave form) of a sphere and due to the fact that frequencies oscillate (*i.e.*, blink on and off), the Earth and all inhabitants have the same unconscious lapse of 0.8 - 1.2s due to the nature of oscillation. And, as Ilya Prigogine mathematically demonstrates in From Being to Becoming: "[A]ll finite systems [*i.e.*, the spherical waveforms that represent all worldly phenomena] of quantum mechanics have a discrete energy spectrum and therefore, a purely periodic motion."[7] The analogy that our consciousness is the result of discrete packets of energy is echoed by Bekesy in reference to the 0.8 - 1.2s lapse of unconsciousness: "[I]n hearing and especially in speech and music, this separation of a continuous process into small, discrete [*i.e.*, the absorption/emission spectral lines of the electromagnetic spectrum] periods of time seems to be extremely important."[8]

This active role of the perception by the percipient is also echoed by David Bohm, physicist, in his book entitled The Special Theory of Relativity. He first demonstrates how tactile perception is evidently inherited the result of a set of active operations performed by the recipient."[9] He then details the experimental results of R.W. Ditchburn, which determines that the "eyeball is continually undergoing small and very rapid vibrations, which shift the image by a distance equal roughly to that between adjacent cells on the retina of the eye."[10]

(D) The human body as a self-organizing, self-regulating and self-actualizing (thought) pattern for organization: Discuss (a) social scientist Gregory Bateson's cybergenetic research; (b) the Santiago Theory of Consciousness (by the neurologists Humberto Maturana and Francisco Varela); and (c) neuroscientist Karl Pribam's postulated idea of the brain as a hologram.

"The pattern of organization of any system, living or non-living, is the configuration of relationships among the system's components that determines the system's essential characteristics. The structure of a system is the physical embodiment of pattern of organization."[11] Bohm goes on to demonstrate the pattern of organization, common to all living systems... is a network pattern."[12] "The first and most obvious property of any network is the nonlinearity - it goes in all directions. Thus, the relationships in a network pattern are nonlinear relationships. The concept of feedback [loops] is intimately connected with the network pattern."[13] And, just as feedback is the concept after which the famous mathematician John von Neumann modeled the digital computer, so the cybergeneticists in the 1950s and 1960s, a group of mathematicians and neuroscientists which included Norbert Wiener, John von Neumann, Gregory Bateson and Margaret Meade, attempted to understand the brain as a neural network. "The structure of the human brain is enormously complex. It contains about 10 billion nerve cells (neurons), which are interlinked in a vast network through 1,000 billion [1 trillion] junctions (synapses)."[14] Fritjof Capra states, "Mathematically, a feedback loop corresponds to a special kind of nonlinear process known as iteration (Latin for 'repetition'), in which a function operates repeatedly on itself. For example, if the function consists in multiplying the variable X by 3 (i.e., $f(x) = 3x$), the iteration consists in repeated multiplications. In mathematical shorthand this is written as follows:

$$X \rightarrow 3X$$
$$3X \rightarrow 9X$$
$$9X \rightarrow 27X$$

Each of these steps is called a 'mapping'. If we visualize the variable X as a line of numbers, the operation $x \rightarrow 3X$ maps each number to the other number on the line."[15]

The concept of feedback "as a general pattern of life, applicable to organisms and social systems"[16] got Gregory Bateson and Margaret Meade, both social scientists, interested in cybernetics. Bateson went on to develop a systems approach to mental illness and a cybernetic model of alcoholism, which led him to define "mental illness" as a systems phenomenon characteristic of living organisms." His systems approach led him to the realization "that mind is manifest not only in individual organisms, but also in social systems and ecosystems" and, consequently, that "relationships are the essence of the living world. Biological form consists of relationships, not parts, and he emphasized that is also how people think."[17]

(E) The mathematical, nonlinear network relationships central to feedback loops, biological forms social systems, ecosystems and thought systems are one of the three characteristics of self-organizing systems as identified by the neurophysiologists Humberto Maturana and Francisco Varela in the 1970s. The other two characteristics of the spontaneous emergence of new structures and new forms of behavior in open systems far from equilibrium set the stage for the development of their systems theory of cognition, called the Santiago Theory. In it, they correlate cognition, the process of knowing, with the process of life. They stress their concern with organization as a process, not structure, and they invent the term "autopoiesis" to describe their concept of circular organization. "<u>Auto</u>, of course, means 'self' and refers to the autonomy of self-organizing systems; and <u>poesis</u> – which shares the same Greek root as the word 'poetry' – means 'making.' So, <u>autopoiesis</u> means 'self-making.'"[18]

Originally, Maturana was interested in color perception (which Varela, his student, followed up on in his book the <u>Embodied Mind</u>), which "led me to a discovery that was extraordinarily important for me: The nervous system operates as a closed network of interactions, in which every change of the interactive relations between certain components always results in a change of the interactive relations of the same or of other components."[19] As Capra points out, "He hypothesized that the 'circular organization' of the nervous system is the basic organization of all living systems [which all have the same DNA and all have carbon]. 'Living systems…[are] organized in a closed casual circular process that allows for evolutionary change in the way the circularity is maintained, but not for the loss of the circularity itself'."[20]

Secondly, Maturana "postulated that the nervous system is not only self-organizing but also continually self-referring so that perception cannot be viewed as the representation of an external reality but must be understood as the continual creation of new relationships within the neural network: 'The activities of nerve cells <u>do not</u> reflect an environment independent of the living organism and hence, <u>do not</u> allow for the construction of an absolutely existing external world.'"[21] Capra concludes, "according to Maturana, perceptions and, more generally cognition, do not <u>represent</u> an external reality but rather <u>specify</u> one through the nervous systems's process of circular organization. From this premise, Maturana then took the radical step of postulating that the process of circular organization itself – with or without a nervous system – is identical to the process of cognition: 'Living systems are the cognitive systems, and living as a process is a process of cognition. This statement is valid for all organisms, with and without a nervous system.'"[22]

Francisco Varela describes the process of the brain as 'a highly cooperative system: the dense interactions among its components entail that eventually everything going on will be a function of what all the components are doing… as a result the entire system requires an internal coherence in intricate patterns, even if we cannot say exactly how this occurs.'"[23]

The Santiago theory of cognition reflects in Maturana's and Varela's conclusions regarding cognition "as the activity involved in the self-generation and self-perpetuation of autopoietic networks."[24] Capra interjects with, "In terms of our three key criteria of living systems - structure, pattern and process - we can say that the life process consists of all activity involved in the continual embodiment of the system's (autopoietic) pattern of organization in a physical (dissipative) structure."[25]

Maturana and Varela determined that "[t]he specific phenomenon underlying the process of cognition is structural coupling. As we have seen, an autopoietic system undergoes continual structural changes while preserving its weblike pattern of organization. It couples to its environment <u>structurally</u>, in other words, through recurrent [repetitious] interactions, each of which triggers structural changes in the system. The living system is autonomous, however, the environment only triggers the structural changes; it does not specify or direct them."[26]

So, the key to the Santiago Theory is that the "structural changes in the system constitute acts of cognition"[27] and "by specifying which perturbations form the environment and trigger its changes, the system 'brings forth a world,' as Maturana and Varela put it. Cognition, then, is not a representation of an independently existing, but rather a continual <u>bringing forth of a world</u> through the process of living."[28]

Maturana also connected self-awareness with language [which is based on the .95 - 1s second consciousness interval and is the result of the nature of the rhythm of periodic oscillations], which he approached through a "careful analysis of communication. Communication, according to Maturana, is not a transmission of information, but rather a <u>coordination of behavior</u> among living organisms through mutual structural coupling. Such mutual coordination of behavior is the key characteristic of communication for all living organisms, with or without nervous systems, and it becomes more and more subtle and elaborate with nervous systems of increasing complexity."[29]

Maturana calls learned communicative behavior "linguistic" and demonstrates that it requires a complex nervous system. He notes that "even very intricate forms of linguistic communication such as the so-called language of bees are not yet language."[30] According to Maturana, language arises where there is <u>communication about communication</u>. In other words, the process of 'languaging', as Maturana calls it, takes place where there is a coordination of behavior."[31]

Capra further emphasizes, "In human language a vast space is opened up in which words serve as tokens for the linguistic coordination of actions and are also used to create the notion of objects. For example, at a picnic we can use words as linguistic distinctions to coordinate our actions of putting a tablecloth and food on a tree stump. In addition, we can also refer to those linguistic distinctions (in other words, make a distinction of distinctions) by using the word 'table' and thus bringing forth an object."[32] Continuing, Capra concludes that "objects, then, in

Maturana's view, are linguistic distinctions, and once we have objects, we can create abstract concepts – the height of our table, for example – by making distinctions of distinctions of distinctions and so forth. Using Bateson's terminology, we could say that a hierarchy of logical types emerges with human language."[33] So in language we coordinate our behavior and together in language we bring forth one world. "The world everyone sees," write Maturana and Varela, "is not the world but a world, which we bring forth with others."[34] Our concepts, thoughts, ideas, emotions and movements, which are reflected in conversation, are caught on film and show that "every conversation involves a subtle and largely unconscious dance in which the detailed sequence of speech patterns is precisely synchronized not only with minute movements of the speaker's body but also with corresponding movements of the listeners. Both partners are locked into this precisely synchronized sequence of rhythmic movements and the linguistic coordination of their mutually triggered gestures lasts as long as they remain involved in their conversation."[35]

Another aspect of Maturana's concept of cognition was added by Varela's work in The Embodied Mind. Varela hypothesized "that there is a form of primary consciousness in all higher vertebrates that is not yet self-reflective but involves the experience of a 'unitary mental space,' or mental state."[36] These "mental states are transitory, continually arising and subsiding." Varela determined that an important feature of these transitory mental states was that the "experiential state is always 'embodied' that is embedded in a particular field of sensation. In fact, most mental states seem to have a dominant sensation that colors the entire experience."[37] Peptides, as the biochemical manifestation of emotion, color, all sensory perceptions, thoughts, behaviors and moods, would apparently seem to be the basis for our primary, transitory and mental states.

Varela's basis for the transitory experiential states is known in mathematics and physics as the resonance phenomenon. Resonance is the interaction between cells, molecules, atoms and sub-atomic particles and which, as Poincare proved, is the reason for dynamic, non-integratable, dissipative systems [and the existence of these interactions is based in the mathematical degrees of freedom] which creates "phase locking". In physics, resonance is the reinforced vibration of a body exposed to the vibration at about the same frequency of another body. In Varela's description then, phase locking (which is the phase/angle when the sinewave crosses the X axis and the pattern is locked into a recurrent (frequency/time) interval) occurs when various brain regions are interconnected in a network pattern so "that all their neurons fire in synchrony."[38] Varela cited many experiments in order to support his hypothesis "that cognitive experiential states [i.e., images, objects, events – in other words, reality] are created by the synchronizations of fast oscillations in the gamma and beta range that tend to arise and subside quickly. Each phase locking is associated with a characteristic relaxation time, which accounts for the minimum duration of the experience."[39]

This relaxation time coincides with Bekesey's 0.8 - 1.2s lapse of unconscious and is the result of the vibratory nature of a confined sinewave. Consequently, since all earthly organisms have the same DNA structure, with the same angles (1.5 interval, which represents the musical notes G:C, the numbers 2:3 and the angles of 84° - 90°) (phases), and as all worldly phenomenon are represented by spherical, harmonic waveforms within a small bandwidth of natural resonant frequency - approximately 1.5 octaves, 4 - 12 cps - then due to the periodic nature of oscillations and as Ditchburn notes in Light, "at any given time the phase is the same for the entire sphere,"[40] the Earth and all inhabitants - living and non-living - would oscillate or blink on and off simultaneously.

> In the movie 'Star Wars,' Luke Skywalker's adventure begins when a beam of light shoots out of the robot Artoo Detoo and projects a miniature three-dimensional image of Princess Leia. Luke watches spellbound as the ghostly sculpture of light begs for someone named Obi-wan Kenobi to come to her assistance. The image is a hologram, a three-dimensional picture made with the aid of a laser and the technological magic required to make such images is remarkable. But what is even more astounding is that some scientists are beginning to believe the universe itself is a kind of giant hologram, a splendidly detailed illusion no more or less real than the image of Princess Leia that starts Luke on his quest.[41]

Another example of a hologram is the gypsy's head in the crystal ball at the Haunted Mansion in Disneyland, and who can forget the delightful hologram of the "little blue lady" at the end of that ride? "Put another way, there is evidence to suggest that our world and everything in it - from snowflakes to maple trees to falling stars and spinning electrons - are also only ghostly images, projections from a level of reality so beyond out own it is literally beyond both space and time," says Michael Talbot, author of The Holographic Universe.[42] In fact, all earthly phenomenon (*i.e.*, objects) would appear "ghostly" or less dense if we consciously apprehended them at their natural resonant frequencies between 4 - 12 cps, with corresponding wavelengths of up to 6 miles long. But our conscious mind at 16 - 40 cps and apprehends the thoughtforms at faster frequencies (higher octaves), which gives the illusion of density and continuity (*i.e.*, matter), due to the fact that our neurophysiological functions cannot differentiate the processes outside of a certain range.

In his book, he goes on to identify "the main architects of this astonishing idea are two of the world's most eminent thinkers: University of London physicist David Bohm [now deceased], a protégé' of Einstein and one of the world's most respected quantum physicists, and Karl Pribam, a neurophysiologist at Stanford University and author of the classic neurophysiological textbook <u>Languages of the Brain</u>."[43]

Talbot goes on to explain that Bohm and Pribam arrived at their conclusion independent of each other but that it was a result of their frustration with standard theories to explain a wide range of phenomena such as the "ability of individuals with hearing in only one ear to determine the direction from which a sound originates; and our ability to recognize the face of someone we have not seen for many years even if that person has changed considerably in the interim."[44] The holographic model, whether of the universe, world, body, or brain, can explain "a wide range of phenomena so elusive they generally have been categorized outside the province of scientific understanding. These include telepathy, precognition, mystical feelings of oneness with the universe and even psychokinesis, or the ability of the mind to move physical objects without anyone touching them."[45]

"In 1980, University of Connecticut psychologist Dr. Kenneth Ring proposed that near-death experiences [NDEs] could be explained by the holographic model. In 1985, Dr. Stanislav Grof, Chief of Psychiatric Research Center and assistant professor of psychiatry at the Johns Hopkins University School of Medicine, published a book in which he concluded that existing neurophysiological models of the brain are inadequate and only a holographic model can explain such things as archetypal experiences, encounters with the collective unconscious, and other unusual phenomena experienced during altered states of consciousness. At the 1987 annual meeting of the Association for the Study of Dreams held in Washington, D.C., physicist Fred Alan Wolf delivered a talk in which he asserted that the holographic model explains lucid dreams (unusually vivid dreams in which the dreamer realizes he or she is awake). In his 1987 book entitled <u>Synchronicity: The Bridge Between Matter and Mind</u>, Dr. F. David Peat, a physicist at Queen's University in Canada, asserted that synchronicities [a term coined by Carl Jung] (coincidences that are so unusual and so psychologically meaningful they don't seem to be the result of chance alone) can be explained by the holographic mode. Peat believes that such coincidences are actually 'flaws in the fabric of reality.' They reveal that our thought processes are much more intimately connected to the physical world than has hitherto been suspected."[46]

In 1982, Dr. Alain Aspect, a physicist at the Institute of Theoretical and Applied Optics in Paris, led an experiment by a research team that proved the non-locality concept of quantum mechanics by demonstrating "that the web of subatomic particles that compose our physical universe – possesses what appears to be an undeniable 'holographic' property."[47]

The holographic properties of the microscopic world is translated into the macroscopic realm with the example in 1987 of physicist Robert G. John and clinical psychologist Brenda Dunn, both at Princeton University, conducting experiments wherein they "found that through mental concentration alone, human beings are able to affect the way certain kind of machines operate."[48]

Pribam apparently was started on his journey to understand reality within the framework of a holographic model, wondering where and how memories are stored in the brain. He was fortunate to be able to work with Karl Lashley at the Yerkes Laboratory of Primate Biology, then in Orange Park, Florida, in 1946. Lashley's research findings – experiments were done on rats where massive portions of their brains were cut out (even impairing their motor skills), but yet they somehow retained the memory of how to get from point A to point B in a maze – led him to the conclusion that the memories weren't localized in a specific brain area but instead were distributed through the entire brain. It wasn't until 1960 when he read about Dennis Gabor's construction of a hologram in "Scientific American" that he realized the solution to his puzzle.

The holographic property of the whole image being contained in even the smallest part is the result of the interaction (interference pattern) of waves whereby if the height (amplitude) of the two waves doesn't coincide, they will cancel each other, or if the height of the two waves does coincide, then the amplitude is squared (becoming intensity), and the waves will be in the phase so that the event will actualize in three-dimensional reality (or put another way, the sinewave as the basis of the spherical harmonic waveform is the basis for the hologram). Pribam realized if it "was possible for every portion of a piece of holographic film to contain all the information necessary to create a whole image, then it seemed equally possible for every part of the brain to contain all of the information necessary to recall a whole memory."[49]

During Pribam's own experiments, he discovered that the visual centers of the rat's brain (of which he removed 90 percent) and a cat's optic nerve (of which he removed ninety eight percent) were still able to complete their visual tasks even though seriously mutilated. Together with his research findings and the holographic concept, he came to the realization that the ten billion nerve cells in the brain with one trillion synapses (along with the "100,000 – 1,000,000 different chemical reactions occurring every minute within the brain") was causing the wavelike phenomenon of the inference patterns necessary for a hologram. "The hologram was there all the time in the wave – front nature of the brain-cell connectivity," observes Pribam.[50]

Talbot points out, "Holography also explains how our brains can store so many memories in so little space. The brilliant Hungarian-born physicist and mathematician John von Neumann once calculated that over the course of the average human lifetime, the brain stores something on the order of 2.8 X 10^{20} (280,000,000,000,000,000,000) bits of information. Interestingly, holograms also possess a fantastic capacity for information storage. By changing the angle [phase] at which the two lasers strike a piece of photographic film, it is possible to record many different images on the same surface. Any image thus recorded can be retrieved simply by illuminating the film with a laser beam possessing the same angle as the original two beams. By employing this method, researchers have calculated that one-inch square of film can store the same amount of information contained in fifty Bibles!"[51]

The realization came "that what the mystics had been saying for centuries was true, reality was 'maya', an illusion, and what was out there - the world of coffee cups, mountain vistas, elm trees and table lamps - might not even exist - was really a vast, resonating symphony of wave forms, a 'frequency domain', that was transformed in the world as we know it only <u>after</u> it entered our senses."[52] From <u>Sacred Geometry</u>, recall that "Our different perceptual faculties such as sight, hearing, touch and smell are a result then of various proportional reductions of one vast spectrum of vibratory frequencies. We can understand these proportional relationships as a sort of geometry of perception."[53] This prompted Pribam to seek out the work of David Bohm, who postulated that the entire universe possessed holographic properties.

Just as Pribam began his journey with a question, Bohm also had a similar question, but it concerned the state of interconnectedness that exists between unrelated subatomic events (for example: the double-slit photon experiment, whereby the two photons form a laser communicated instantaneously to each other as to the final destination; instantaneous communication of information is the definition for telepathy).

Although Bohm followed a traditional academic career as a protégé of Einstein and then as a contemporary, his research work as an assistant professor at Princeton University involved the behavior of electrons in metals at extremely high frequencies (plasmons) and demonstrated to him the incompleteness of the framework of quantum mechanics to entirely understand reality. His dissatisfaction with the prevailing framework led him to argue "that the way science viewed casuality was also much too limited. Most effects were thought of as having one or several causes".[54] However, Bohm felt that an effect could have an infinite number of causes. Bohm conceded that most of the time one could ignore the vast cascade of causes that had led to any given effect, but he still felt it was important for scientists to remember that no single cause-and-effect relationship was ever really separate from the universe as a whole.

Then, in 1980, Bohm published his book <u>Wholeness and the Implicit Order</u>, which detailed his thoughts regarding physics and philosophy. In it, he presents the principles behind the universe being "a kind of giant, flowing hologram"[55] or, in his words, a holomovement, which conveys a dynamic, active nature and not one that is static. [Remember from Poincare's work that static deterministic systems are (mathematically) integratable, but that dynamic nondeterministic systems are non-integratable and far from equilibrium. And, that the reason for their nonintegrability was the "existence of resonance between the degrees of freedom."]

Bohm describes what he means by the term "holomovement": "Our basic proposal was then that <u>what</u> is the holomovement and that everything is to be explained in terms of forms derived from this holomovement. Though the full set of laws governing its totality is unknown (and indeed, probably unknowable), nevertheless these laws are assumed to be such that from them may be abstracted relatively autonomous or independent subtotalities of movement (e.g. fields, particles, etc.), having a certain recurrence and stability of their basic patterns of order and measure)."[56]

He continues to explain that in the implicate and explicate orders, "the explicate order can be regarded as a particular or distinguished case of a more general set of implicate orders from which latter it can be derived. What distinguishes the explicate order is that what is thus derived is a set of recurrent and relatively stable elements that are <u>outside</u> of each other. This set of elements (e.g. fields and particles) then provides the explanation of that domain of experience in what mechanistic order yields and adequate treatment."[57]

Throughout the remainder of his book, Bohm presents analogies that demonstrate that "the relationships constituting the fundamental law are between the enfolded structures that interweave and inter-penetrate each other, throughout the whole of space, rather than between the abstracted and separated forms that are manifest to the senses (and to our instruments)."[58]

He continues, "What, then, is the meaning of the appearance of the apparently independent and self-existent 'manifest world' in the explicate order? The answer to this question is indicated by the root of the word 'manifest', which comes from the Latin *manus,"* meaning 'hand.' Essentially, what is manifest is what can be held with the hand - something solid, tangible and visibly stable."[59]

In relationship then to the implicate order, "which is, as we have seen, vast, rich, and in a state of unending flux of enfoldment and unfoldment, with laws most of which are only vaguely known,"[60], he describes what an electron is as "a 'particle' to be understood and a recurrent stable order of unfoldment in which a certain form undergoing regular changes manifests again and again, but so rapidly that it appears to be in continuous existence."[61] In other words, the electron, as energy is a process of interaction.

5) <u>How movement is determined by the eye.</u>

Bohm and Ditchburn pose the theory that fast and slow eyeball movements result in the construction of "objects as possessing a certain state of motion."[62]

Just as the movement of electrons is the basis of the electromagnetic spectrum and is itself the result of the confinement of a sinewave to a finite region (for example, the surface of a sphere), where the resultant spherical harmonic wave forms periodically vibrate only within the range of certain natural resonant frequencies (all worldly phenomenon at 4 - 12 cps), and wherein the confinement produces the electron waves that form patterns known as "standing waves", it is also the cause of a holographic projection (which mirrors Bekesy's concept of how our senses, such as tactile, olfactory and gustatory, externally project, localize or funnel "the sensations [that] exist only within our bod[ies]"[63] to a space outside of our bodies) and the resultant creation and alteration of space (which is the definition of magnetism), consequently demonstrating the properties of self-similarity, self-actualization, self-generation and a circular nature ("Reality is circular in nature"), or, as Bohm said in <u>The Holographic Paradigm</u>, "the holomovement is the ground of what is manifest." [64]

The concept of repetitive, circular patterns as periodic vibrations (natural resonant frequencies), as reflected as recurrence, is "one of the basic features of matter," and "the very structure of the holomovement is recurrence," comments Bohm.[65] But it is the movement of these circular patterns caused by confinement that represent relationships (the sinewave function being a non-linear relationship), or ratios of parts (or qualities since we are ultimately dealing with the psychological realm of All That Is), that result in the effects of angulation whereby "energies are controlled, specified and modified"[66], which is itself the result of interaction, and "[i]t is *interaction* [emphasis added] which is always important."[67] Similarly, as noted in <u>The Tao of Physics</u>, "The interaction between electrons and atomic nuclei is the basis of all solids, liquids and gases and also of all living organisms and of the biological processes associated with them."[68]

Then, at the microscopic level, interaction is the basis for the resonance phenomenon which, according to Linus Pauling, forms the molecular structure because it represents an energy exchange and was "introduced into quantum mechanics by Heisenberg [in 1926] in connection with the discussion of the quantum states of the helium atom."[69] Interaction is the basis of the four forces representing the unified field theory (electromagnetism, gravity and the strong and weak nuclear forces), which "become unified as one universal interaction at ultrahigh frequencies."[70]

Heinz Pagels goes on to say, "According to these unified theories, all the interactions we see in the present world are the asymmetrical remnant of a once perfectly symmetrical world."[71] Why, it may be asked, cannot Unity simply divide into two equal parts? Why not have a proportion of one term, a:a? The answer is simply that with equality there is no *difference* [emphasis added], and without difference there is no perceptual universe, for as the Upanishad says, "Whether we know it or not, all things take on their existence from that which perceives them."[72] In a static equational statement [According to Prigogine's chemical experiments and Poincare's mathematical deductions, our system is not only dynamical and non-integratable, but also far from equilibrium due to the existence of resonances] where one part nullifies the other, an asymmetrical division is needed in order to create the dynamics necessary for progression and extension from the Unity. Therefore, the Pi [the Golden Mean or ratio, the square root of five, "which philosophically represents the seat or basis of the created worlds"[73]] proportion is the perfect division of a unity: it is creative, yet the entire proportional universe that results from it relates back to it and is literally contained within it,"[74] which make it reflective of a hologram remnant of a once perfectly symmetrical world.

Movement, dynamism, creativity, duality, ordering (in a linear, temporal pattern according to number, as represented by frequency or vibration, which is the coded information of repetitive thought/concept packages) and energy are the psychophysical qualities that are represented by Jung's number two, the Father archetype, and are the result of the interaction between archetype two and archetype one, the Mother archetype, which manifests the psychophysical qualities of unity, transformation, rebirth, growth, fostering and matter. "In sum, that which we designate as matter or energy in the external world is an archetypal image just as the mind is."[75]

It follows then that at the macroscopic level, which is determined by the human perceptual range, the fact that our most dominant sense, the visual system, is the last to develop after birth takes on added significance because it develops as a process based on the intrinsic rotation of the eyeball around an axis which "coincides with the principal axis of crystal symmetry; the index ellipsoid is a sphere."[76] Crystallography is the study of the geometrical arrangement of atoms, which is called a system of points and generally structured as a lattice. Since all earthly organisms are carbon-based and thus have a quadratic atomic structure and a hexagonal crystalline molecular structure (which is derived from √3 and represents the structuring of forms), the angle of which at any given time coincides with all earthly DNA and consequently is also our

0.8 – 1.2s of unconsciousness (1.5 ratio), this is the result of the periodic, oscillatory nature of the spherical harmonic waveform, which is the result of a confined sinewave. "The angle between the principal (optical) directions and the crystallographic axes is the same for all wavelengths. Each principal index varies independently with wavelength so that the ratios of the principal indices vary with wavelength."[77] Hence, the angle between the optic axes varies with wavelength and, in the case of world phenomena, the resultant wavelength, which, along with telepathy, is one of the reasons why collectively we perceive relatively similar holographic images in a linear sequence of movement (which corresponds to the number 3 archetype). "The effect is to give the image [on the retina] in the region a corresponding linear movement,"[78] and also a fast movement along with a slow flick oscillatory movement ("In addition, it has a slower regular drift, followed by a 'flick' which brings the image more or less back to its original center"[79]), which, as Piaget, after many years of painstaking research on children from birth to ten years of age discovered, eventually allows the infant to mathematically construct space, time, permanent objects, causality and a separate sense of self as distinguished from the almost undifferentiated totality. Piaget convincingly demonstrates the aforementioned as the infant's experience in his book The Construction of Reality in a Child.

A slower drift or "flick" movement of the eyeball was determined not only in Ditchburn's experiments to counteract accommodation, "*i.e.*, the strength of [the nerve cells'] response tends to decrease, eventually falling below the threshold of what is perceptible,"[80] but also in Bekesy's experiments in order to explain adaption whereby an image lasts on the retina 1.5 seconds before it disappears. (Note: one hundred fifty images flashed in syncopation for one hundredth of one second (1/100) between the two retinas.) Movement is further enhanced, according to Bohm in The Implicate Order, where he proposes that an image flashes on one retina one hundredth of one second before the same image flashes on the other retina, producing the illusion of movement similar to the effect of a string of lights whereby "one of which comes on slightly later than the other."[81] In essence, then, instead of singular, static images, you perceive a flowing movement similar to that of a movie.

The length of time that an image remains on the retina before it disappears, 1.5 seconds, coincides with the amount of time that it takes for an image to be built upon the visual cortex. Even though a single image reaches the visual cortex every one hundredth (1/100) of one second, it must flash one hundred and fifty times, or for 1.5 seconds, before it is consciously acknowledged by the brain. These processes occur during our 0.8 – 1.2s lapses of consciousness, and they are indiscernible to us because "it is found that there is an interval of time, of the order of one tenth of a second, which is 'speciously' experienced as a single moment, in the sense that people do not seem to be able clearly to discriminate changes that take place in times less than this."[82] So since the information from the retina is flashed onto the visual cortex every one hundredth of one second, it happens too quickly for our senses to apprehend, but this mathematical construct of an image/event second by second is periodically broken up, due to the oscillatory nature of spherical harmonics, by our lapse of consciousness (which is the basis for all DNA, music and language), and consequently, our conscious minds at 16 - 40cps (beta-gamma waves) bridge the gap between the second of consciousness to 0.8 - 1.2s of unconsciousness to another second of consciousness so smoothly that we are not aware of any discontinuity. But discontinuity is due to the discrete, discontinuous (quantized) nature of the energy of the electromagnetic spectrum.

Though the rhythm of this interval is the basis for the structure of DNA, music and language, it also allows for the recurrence or repetitious build-up of one hundred and fifty images per second on the visual cortex. These composite images of the mathematical transforms (metaphorically utilizing the *Fourier Transform*) energy as frequency into incoming waves back into frequency (on the retinal cells), and then into waves again, so mosaic patterns or features from the retinal image are abstracted and "the response of the nerves connected to a given retinal cell will therefore depend less on the light intensity at the point in question than on the way in which the light intensity *changes* [emphasis added] with the position [of the eyeball]. This means that the excitation of the optic nerve does not correspond to the pattern of light on the retina, but rather to a modified pattern in which contrasts are heightened and in which a strong impression is produced at the boundaries of objects, where the light intensity varies sharply with position."[83] The coded information continues to travel as a wave through the optic nerves of each eye, which carries one half the retinal image to the opposite brain hemisphere and the image on the right retina is eventually built up, again as a frequency, analogous to the pixels on a computer monitor or television, on the left hemisphere of the visual cortex as well, but one hundredth of a second later, which gives the illusion of movement to the series of images.

On its way to the visual cortex, the wavelike image is processed through the inner ear, which determines balance, spatial order and verticality, the reticular activating system (r.a.s.), which acts as a filter to screen out frequency as information that is not compatible to three-dimensional reality, and then on to the "part of the thalamus known as the lateral geniculate nucleus (LGN). For every one fiber entering the LGN from the retina, more than eighty enter the same point from the other areas of the brain, including connections returning from the cortex."[84] This process takes about one hundredth of one second but occurs one hundred and fifty times, as a build-up on our visual cortex, within our lapse of consciousness of 0.8 - 1.2s, in order to create the illusion of matter's density for the then "funneled" image outward as a holographic projection.

An instance where the phenomenon was experienced was in the spring of 2000, while the author was walking down an outdoor breezeway on the way to her office. At the time, she was unaware of having been experiencing that unconscious 0.8 - 1.2s interval during which an image was building upon her visual cortex, not then being familiar with the concept of the build-up of an image from the retina onto the visual cortex.

The event lasted no longer than the time it takes to lift a foot and take a step, but in that short interval the breezeway's familiar solid red brick walls and the concrete sidewalk did not exist, and in their place was instead a volume of vacant space (for lack of a better term) and incomplete, indistinct geometric shapes (some rectangular, some circular). Not only disconcerting, the experience was somewhat frightening in that the conscious thought running through her mind was to hurry and finish forming the sidewalk lest her foot (likewise unformed), would step into nothingness. Then it was over as quickly as it occurred, except for some residual dizziness. At the time, she did not realize she may be experiencing the mathematical construction of an image on the visual cortex. Realizing now the concept and necessity of the periodic lapse of consciousness for this process, and in explaining it to another person, the author comprehends this process because had she been required to consciously experience the image build-up second by second, she never would have completed her walk.

In summary, Bohm states that "the perceived picture [the image on the visual cortex] is therefore not just an image or reflection of our momentary sense impressions, but rather is the outcome of a complex process leading to an ever-changing (three-dimensional) *construction* [emphasis added] which is present to our awareness of an 'inner show.' This construction is based on the abstraction of what is invariant in the relationship between a set of movements produced actively by the percipient himself and the resulting changes in the totality of his sensual 'inputs.'"[85] Each second-by-second constructed image of reality comes together as a movie on a screen (which is our visual cortex) where the "movie plot and the metaphors of Reverse Speech are characters and stage settings for this internal movie"[86] as they reflect the archetypal thoughtforms the collective unconscious of sinewave forms.

Part D

Musical Concepts

> "Music is the medium through which we express our feelings of joy and sorrow, love and patriotism, penitence and praise. It is the charm of the soul, the instrument that lifts minds to higher regions, the gateway into the realms of imagination. It makes the eye to sparkle, the pulse to beat more quickly. It causes emotions to pass over our being like waves over the far reaching sea."
>
> – Carl E. Seashore.[1]

Music is the result of the interaction of the effects of angulation as it represents the ratio of one frequency to another frequency. When a non-periodic sinewave is confined to a sphere, the result is a periodical natural resonant frequency pattern, or "standing wave, which consist[s] of waves propagating back and forth between the boundaries, [which] lead[s] to resonances in vibrating systems."[2] This movement then represents music.

According to Tomatis, "The critical range for musicality is 500 hz to 4,000 hz (hertz),"[3] and music is composed of melody and rhythm. "Music has all the characteristics (pitch, timbre, intensity, rhythm) of spoken language, except semantic value,"[4] Tomatis points out. And children's songs and nursery rhymes harmonize body movements and motor functions by their effect on the cochlear vestibular system of the ear. They also increase the child's awareness of his body and help shape his body information, according to Tomatis.[5]

"The psychological attributes of sound, namely pitch, loudness [intensity], time [rhythm], and timbre, depends upon the physical characteristics of the sound wave: frequency [the number of waves per second], amplitude [the intensity/height of the wave], duration [wavelength], and form,"[6] states Carl E. Seashore. He goes on to mention that the form of the sound wave "determines its harmonic constitution, which gives us the experience of timbre."[7]

After forty years of research and a career in the science of music, Seashore summed up his findings by saying: "On the basis of our experiments in measuring these sensory capacities, the sense of pitch, the sense of time, the sense of loudness [intensity/amplitude], and the sense of timbre are elemental, by which we mean that they are largely inborn and function from early childhood."[8]

Over the next few pages, he gives the definitions for these basic capacities: "The terms 'frequency,' double vibrations (d.v.),' 'the number of vibrations per second,' 'cycles,' and 'waves' are synonymous and may be used interchangeably to designate frequency and pitch."[9]

Then he states further that "for psychological purposes, the intensity of tone is expressed in terms of decibels (db). Like pitch and loudness, the decibel is a psychological unit representing the degree of loudness. Its physical counterpart, intensity, is expressed in terms of units of electrical energy."[10] He defines the "wave form: timbre [tone]…in terms of the form of the sound wave,"[11] and says that "timbre is determined primarily by the number, the order, and the relative intensity of the fundamental ["the mode of vibration or component of sound with the lowest frequency"[12]] and its overtones as expressed in the waveform."[13]

Timbre is further described by Seashore as the "distinguishing or characteristic quality of a sound."[14] He adds that "the investigations of Helmholtz proved that the timbre of a sound is determined by the proportions in which the various natural harmonics are heard in it."[15] Harmonics refers to the vibrational modes of a system that are the whole number ratios of intervals.

Seashore goes on to describe duration (time, rhythm): "pitch and intensity are always recorded against time, expressing the duration of notes, pauses, or any specific feature of these."[16] Then he adds, "Rhythm adjusts the strain of attention. In poetry and music for instance, the rhythm enables us to anticipate the magnitude of units which are to be grasped."[17]

He continues, "Genetically, the ordinary measure in poetry and music is determined by what is known as the attention wave. Our attention is periodic. All our mental life works rhythmically, that is, by periodic pulsation of effort or achievement with unnoticed intermittence of blanks."[18] As demonstrated by Bekesy, our lapse of consciousness, or periodic attention, corresponds to the interval of 0.8 - 1.2s, which is the ratio 1.5, or the musical note G, the ratio of numbers 2:3 and also the angles from 84° to 90°.

This harmonic interval, which Bekesy pointed out is the basis of music, language and speech and, by extrapolation, is also the basis of our DNA (not only human DNA, but all earthly DNA), corresponds to the twelve frequency ratios within an octave. Our present even-tempered (diatonic) scale has seven notes (C, D, E, F, G, A and B), but the twelve steps (semitones), which represent the flats and sharps as the average of the frequency of the note above and below it. Therefore, the entire octave is divided into C, C#, D, D#, E, F, F#, G, G#, A, A# and B.

The reason for the twelve steps or semitones is explained in <u>Psychology of Music</u>: "It is found that on the whole, our present half-tone step is as small a step as the average of an unselected population can hear with reasonable accuracy, enjoy and reproduce in the flow of melody and harmony in actual music."[19]

These twelve steps or ratios of successive notes to the tonic in the major mode are as follows:

Notes	Ratios
C:D	9:8
C:E	5:4
C:F	4:3
C:G	3:2
C:A	5:3
C:B	15:8
C^1:C	2:1 (an octave)

In the A minor mode, the ratios are: 9:8 (A:B), 6:5 (A:C), 4:3 (A:D), 3:2 (A:E), 8:5 (A:F), 9:5 (A:G), and 2:1 (A:A) (an octave).

As demonstrated by Sir James Jeans, the frequency ratios between the twelve notes represent "a frequency ratio of 1.05946, since this is the twelfth root of 2."[20] The square root of 2 is used because "the exact interval of 2 is spread equally over the twelve semitone intervals which make the octave." 2:1 is C^1:C, which represents an octave.[21]

"Frequency ratios within the octave are as follows (C=1):

$$\begin{aligned}
C\# &= 1.05946 \\
D &= (1.05946)^2 = 1.1225 \\
D\# &= (1.05946)^3 = 1.1892 \\
E &= (1.05946)^4 = 1.2599 \\
F &= (1.05946)^5 = 1.3348 \\
F\# &= (1.05946)^6 = 1.4142 \\
G &= (1.05946)^7 = 1.4983 \\
G\# &= (1.05946)^2 = 1.5874 \\
A &= (1.05946)^8 = 1.6818 \\
A\# &= (1.05946)^{10} = 1.7818 \\
B &= (1.05946)^{11} = 1.8877 \\
C^1 &= (1.05946)^{12} = 2.0000"^{22}
\end{aligned}$$

The octave corresponds to a 2 to 1 ratio frequency, just as hydrogen does to oxygen in the water molecule, H_2O, having the molecular shape of a right △, whose ∠ = 90° and whose height/amplitude or hypotenuse = √2, so that the frequency doubles when you increase the octave, and it is a general law that the frequency is proportional to the square root of the tension [of a string] and that the period is exactly proportional to the length of the string, so that the frequency of vibration varies inversely as the length of the string. The frequency interval of 1.05, π/3, which corresponds to our interval of consciousness, is what both the melody and harmony are built upon, and it is also the ratio that determines the lunar and solar year in the eclipse cycle.[23]

As pointed out in <u>Psychology of Music</u>, "While all music is objectively due to physical sound waves, we must bear in mind that we can never be directly aware of the rate of vibrations as such, for we hear it as musical pitch. This is one of the wondrous transformations from matter to mind."[24]

Then pitch (frequency) represents the 120 discrete tones which, as the rest of the electromagnetic spectrum, are quantized by musical instruments which "are inherently resonant systems and therefore respond to only certain frequencies."[25]

The quantized aspect of frequency is demonstrated by the following table[26] of middle C, or 261 cps:

$$C = 261.6 \text{ cps}$$
$$C\# = 277.2 \text{ cps}$$
$$D = 293.6 \text{ cps}$$
$$D\# = 311.1 \text{ cps}$$
$$E = 329.6 \text{ cps}$$
$$F = 349.2 \text{ cps}$$
$$F\# = 370.0 \text{ cps}$$
$$G = 392.0 \text{ cps}$$
$$G\# = 415.3 \text{ cps}$$
$$A = 440.0 \text{ cps}$$
$$A\# = 466.2 \text{ cps}$$
$$B = 493.9 \text{ cps}$$
$$C^1 = 523.2 \text{ cps}$$

The twelve intervals between notes (semitones) (which interestingly, is a number that parallels the twelve months of the year, the twelve astrological signs of the zodiac, the twelve hours of the clock face, the twelve disciples of Christ, the twelve tribes of Israel, the twelve Titans and the twelve planets [numerologically, these can be reduced to the number three, for example one plus two equals three, which represents Jung's archetype number 3, which constitutes Union]) represent a logarithmic relationship which "is one on which equal distances represent the same factor anywhere along the scale (in contrast to a linear scale, on which equal distances represent equal increments)."[27]

Logarithms, which are the basis of our senses, especially hearing: "hearing tends to follow logarithmic relationships"[28] are defined as follows: "The logarithm to base 10 of a number X equals the power to which 10 must be raised in order to equal X. That is, if $X = 10^Y$, $Y = \log X$. For example, $100 = 10^2$, so $2 = \log 100$ (here $X = 100$, $Y = 2$); or $1000 = 10^3$ so $3 = \log 1000$ ($x = 1000$, $Y = 3$)."[29] A direct correspondence with geometry demonstrates that "logarithmically developed forms always carry this element of the retention of past time and thereby symbolize the evolution not of substance, but of consciousness."[30]

The significance of the logarithm of the twelfth root of the square root of 2, *i.e.*, 1.05946, "represents the power of multiplicity which can extend itself both towards unlimited expansion and towards utterly minute infiniteness."[31] The author Robert Lawlor continues: "This figure perfectly represents the growth patterns of cellular fission in living organisms."[32] "In a vital sense, the geometric root is an archetypal expression of the assimilative, generating, transformative function which is root."[33]

Thus, the principle of transformation and growth (or, as it is referred to in <u>Sacred Geometry</u>, the Principle of Alternation [The Taoist, Yin & Yang or duality], which is represented by the √2, or, in case of the musical intervals, as the twelfth root of √2, 1.05, π/3, 90°) is at the basis of music, language, speech and the structure of all earthly DNA and is represented by the same or the notes G# and A♭ as the minor sixth interval of frequency as our lapse of consciousness, which is 0.8 - 1.2s, or a ratio of 1.5 (1.2 ÷ .8). An example of a logarithmic or gnomic relationship is demonstrated in the Pythagorean formula $a^2 + b^2 = c^2$. Also, Hero of Alexandria defined it as follows: "A gnomen is any figure which, when added to an original figure, leaves the resultant figure similar to the original."[34]

These resultant forms can be found in nature, as demonstrated by Jill Purce in <u>Mystic Spiral</u>, as the "trunks of eucalyptus trees, the horns of rams and reindeer, our skeletal bones, mollusk shells, snakes' coils, the cochlea of the ear, an elephant's trunk, an umbilical cord, the sunflower."[35] The geometric and arithmetic progressions of logarithmic ratios yield spiral-like forms such as the double helix shapes of DNA and RNA. These spiral forms result from the gnomonic growth of triangles, which represent the groupings of the four DNA bases of A, C, T and G, and hexagons, which represent the shape of the carbon-based atomic, crystalline structure of all earthly organisms, for example oxygen, hydrogen, nitrogen and carbon.

Nature's forms then represent a cacophony of sound from the subatomic to the cellular level. This is empirically demonstrated by David Dreamer's and Susan Alejander's recording of the interaction of the DNA's molecular structure, "Sequentia". They found that the lighter atoms, for example hydrogen, represented the interval ratio that became Es, Fs and F#s and that oxygen matched the frequency of Fs and F#s, but at an octave below that of hydrogen. In fact, all of the ninety-two naturally occurring elements in our periodic chart can be paralleled with a frequency reflecting various octaves of the electromagnetic spectrum. For example, hydrogen, at the magnetic electric level of 1.008 cps - 2.02 cps, parallels our delta brain waves from 0 - 4 cps (also, the Note "C" and the color red), and potassium at 1.222 to 2.44 cps reflects the same brain level. Then at 4.03 cps, hydrogen still reflects the Note "C", but parallels our theta brain waves, and potassium, at 4.89 cps, represents the Note D# and the color orange/yellow and parallels our theta waves. Then hydrogen at 8.06 cps, still the Note "C", parallels our alpha waves, as does potassium at 9.77 cps. Finally, hydrogen at 16.13 - 32.26 cps parallels out beta waves (conscious mind state), as does potassium at 19.55 - 39.10 cps.

The concept of the interconnectedness is a result of the narrow frequency range of 4 - 14 cps and the periodic nature of spherical harmonic waveforms, of which all earthly forms are composed, which find forms of expression in music, whose structure represents our lapse of consciousness, the ratio of 1.5, 2:5 or π/2, language and DNA, and was the life's work of Johannes Kepler. Even though he was the author of three of the planetary laws, a scientist and mathematician, these accomplishments were a result of a lifelong obsession with "seeking evidence for a harmony of the world such as was handed down as a legend from antiquity"[36] from the Egyptians to the Pythagoreans. He found his world harmony in the form of musical laws, for example, the ratio or interval of one frequency to another, and demonstrated it in his <u>Harmonics Mundi Libri V (Five Books on World Harmony)</u> in 1619.

Kepler discovered that the angles of the planets of our solar system, as measured from the Sun at their closest (aphelion) and furthest (perihelion) points within twenty-four hours, paralleled the musical intervals and in most cases represented chords (three notes or more). As Rudolf Haase in <u>Cosmic Music</u> pointed out, "Kepler's planetary harmonics, therefore, hold true to this day; they are a reality that belongs as much to the eternal state of the cosmos as do his famous planetary laws."[37]

Posthumously, Kepler's view of the interconnectedness of reality was borne out in 1953 by Heinrich Husmann in his Husmann Theory of Consonance, which was the result "of very careful experiments and their mathematical interpretation. At the core of these is the discovery that, as a result of the nonlinearity of human hearing [as a result of logarithmic relationships of our senses], there are sounds that arise in the ear besides those that reach the eardrum."[38]

Haase continues, "These inner sounds are of two different kinds. First, there are <u>subjective overtones</u>: every incoming tone acquires an additional overtone row in the ear with the same construction as that occurring objectively in nature, so that these subjective (or auricular) overtones considerably amplify those already entering [in other words, as the wave's amplitude is squared, it actualizes or manifests as an object/image/event in a three-dimensional reality]. Secondly, there arise in the ear whenever two or more notes are sounded [hence with every interval which is $12\sqrt{2}$, or 1.05, if it is a note and encompasses the symbolic representation of $\sqrt{2}$ as the Principle of Alternation, *i.e.*, duality or Yin & Yang] so-called combination tones [for example, the triadic and quadratic structure of DNA and RNA would represent chords, as would their hexagonal/crystalline structures]."[39] These either add or subtract the frequencies of the given tones, hence we also speak of "summation" or "difference tones". This concept of a differential response also correlates to the process of our three-dimensional color channel visual system.

The combination tones in the ear are formed from the incoming frequencies (which would be in the 20 - 20,000 cps range) and result in seventy-two overtones per interval. Haase further states, "First of all, it appears that the coincidence of overtones and combination tones will only be possible if the interval in question is made from a ratio of whole numbers."[40] [harmonics or octaves is based on this concept]

Then, in summation, he adds, "In other words, the interval proportions on which our musical system has been founded since antiquity have arisen neither by accident nor from speculation, but correspond exactly to a physiologically explicable disposition of our ear."[41] Finally, he says, "This means, however, that traditional Western music is finalistically oriented, directed toward a goal, and that this goal has always been man himself."[42] [because it is based on our 0.8 - 1.2s lapse of consciousness, which is the result of the periodic nature of a confined sinewave, or spherical harmonic waveform].

The cosmologies of the world's great religions (as they try to express the intangible) of the Sumerians, Egyptians, Hindus, Hebrews, Greeks and Christians are shown to be based on the primacy of number (Jung's archetype of order) via tone-mandalas and tuning systems in Dr. Ernest McClain's book, The Myth of Invariance: The Origin of the Gods, Mathematics and Music from the Rg Veda to Plato. In the book, he demonstrates that music is one avenue capable of developing and projecting a philosophical framework. By citing extensive passages from the Egyptian Book of the Dead, the Rg Veda, the Bible, and Plato's Republic, he demonstrates the recurrence of similar number ratios and mathematical logic as it is expressed in the sacred hymns, as they appear in the ancient cultures of Babylon (Sumeria), Egypt, Greece and Israel.

Glossary

Archetype: As understood by Jung, an unobservable general structure of psychic behavior patterns common to the entire human species, which consists of emotionally charged concept clusters that form associations around a center and magnetize ever more associative material to itself. Archetypes underlie mankind's religious, mythical and scientific conceptions.

Autopoiesis: A theory of living systems by Maturana and Varela, whereby the organization common to all living systems is a nonlinear network of production and transformation processes in which each part participates so that the whole becomes self-referring and self-actualizing.

Bell's Theorem: A mathematical proof that demonstrates that reality is non-local, *i.e.*, an event at a distance can influence an event locally. This interconnectedness of reality, *i.e.*, Jung's *Unus Mundus*, is the basis for the superluminal transfer of information, *i.e.*, telepathy.

Brain wave clusters: Rhythmic electrical impulses arranged in frequency patterns; for example, fast beta waves, at 16 - 40cps, constitute the conscious state and slower alpha waves, at 8 - 15cps, constitute a relaxed state; whereas theta waves, at 5 - 8cps, constitute a meditative or near sleep state (this frequency also represents the base resonant frequency of all worldly phenomenon) and delta waves, at 0 - 4cps, represent the sleeping state.

Chakra: Sanskrit for "wheel"; these are seven energy centers located along the spine (our axis of symmetry), which are rotating energy vortices roughly corresponding to the colors red through purple (10^{14} on the electromagnetic spectrum as visible light to the human eye) and our organs from the base of the spine to the head.

Circle, parts of:

<u>Cartesian Coordinate System</u>:

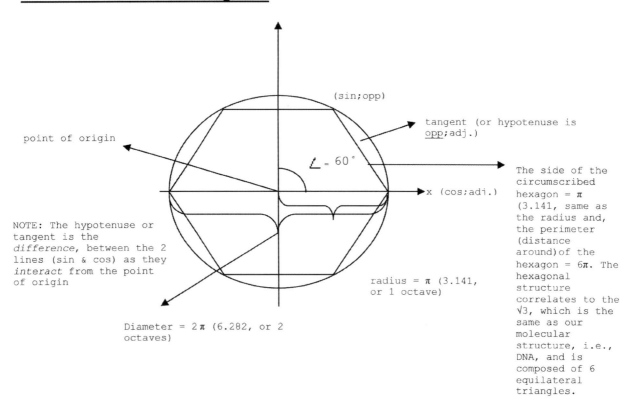

<u>Cartesian Coordinate System</u>

(y) = sin = height   sin = opp.
                                   hyp.

(x) = cos = width   cos = adj.
                                   hyp.

(z) = tangent = depth   tan = opp.
                                   adj.

Note: a circle represents a two-octave scale, so that the radius, or π (3.141), represents one octave and the diameter, or 2π (6.282), represents two octaves.

Note: A hexagon consists of 6 equilateral triangles.

Collective unconscious: The psychic realm where all creative concepts are constellated from a creative, living matrix (root for matter and mother), resulting in all unconscious and conscious functionings, according to Jung.

Crystallography: The branch of math that deals with a system of discontinuous or discrete regular points which form an atomic or molecular structure.

Cybernetics: A comparative study of the functions of the human brain with those of a computer.

Dissipative structures: The chemist Ilya Prigogine discovered ordered molecular patterns in allegedly chaotic chemical systems which were far from equilibrium. He noted that self-organizing principles are inherent in dynamical systems, so that dynamism equals order. (Note: Jung equated "number" as an archetype of order and the Father archetype as representing dynamism.)

Electromagnetic spectrum: Composed of electromagnetic waves, which are able to propagate without a medium, ranging from 10^1 (power and telephone waves) to 10^{24} (gamma rays). This spectrum includes what is perceived as visible light to humans, $10^{14} - 10^{15}$, which is in cycles per second (cps) or as is commonly known as frequency.

Electrons: The only stable elementary particles, which don't have an internal structure (*i.e.*, can't be broken down any further, taus, muons and neutrinos, all of which are composed of, decay to or are the interaction of an electron) belonging to a family of particles called leptons, which includes photons.

Emotion: Noun, from the Latin emovere; verb, e-out; movere - to move, stir up, agitate, psychical excitation, to move out of the psyche.

The Fourier Transform, Analysis, Series: The transform shows that any wave can be written as an unique sum of sinewaves. The analysis shows that any wave, when confined by boundaries, is a rotating (circular) informational pattern composed of infinite coordinate points and can be decomposed into the frequencies (events/images) that compose it. The series shows that any periodic function (one that represents itself), such as a wave, can be expressed as a sum of sines and cosines.

Fractal geometry: An extension of classical geometry, whose author, French mathematician Benoit Mandelbrot, uses it to describe nature's irregular shapes; for example, coastlines, lighting, leaves, etc.

Frequency/Vibration/Oscillation: The number of repeated circular patterns (a rotating circle generates sinewaves, which are the basis of a hologram) within a certain time period - measured in cycles per second.

Function: As it applies to a sinewave function, a formal, numerical relationship (*i.e.*, interaction) between the "X" and "Y" coordinates, which are represented by numbers (archetypes of order) on the Cartesian graph.

Geometry: The measurement of the earth and its forms, in order to establish spatial order.

Harmonics (in music): The vibration modes of a system that represents the ratios of whole number intervals; for example, 2:3 = 1.5 (this ratio also correlates to the unconscious interval of 0.85 - 1.25s) (3 ÷ 2). The term "first harmonic" refers to the fundamental frequency (sound) of an octave; for example, the note "C".

Harmonic motion (in math and physics): A motion (frequency as number) that repeats itself at regular intervals, hence it is called "periodic" (a term which always implies a period of 2 π, the diameter of a circle).

Holographic: A method that uses laser light (photons) to produce three-dimensional images by splitting the laser beam into two beams and recording on a photographic plate the patterns of wave interference. (Note: this method/process is symbolic of the one becoming two and producing three, etc.).

Isomorphic: Two or more forms having the same or similar appearance due to similar atomic ratios or proportions.

Logarithm: A number multiplied by itself (squared) and then continually multiplied by the original number; for example, 10^2 = 10 x 10 = 100 and 100 x 10 (original number) = 1,000. So the log of 100 = 2 (*i.e.*, 10^2), and the log of 1,000 = 3 (*i.e.*, 10^3) for base 10. (Note: The entire electromagnetic spectrum from 10^1 to 10^{24} is an logarithm for the base 10 as is our human neurophysiological system.)

Matrix: Latin for source, original, womb. "Mater" is derived from matrix. Matter and "mother" are both derived from "mater". Also, in math it is a rectangular array of numbers.

Matter: According to Quantum Theory is both wavelike and particle-like depending upon the observed experiment. As a wave, matter is a broad distribution of energy and information that moves from point A to point B and, as a particle (when the sinewave is collapsed and a probability becomes an actuality), it is represented as a tiny concentration of energy ($E-MC^2$). Matter is considered an <u>aspect</u> of energy.

Metaphor: A figure of speech comparing one thing to another.

Natural resonant frequency: A system or object that is the result of a confined sinewave to a surface; whereby, it can only vibrate at certain frequencies as well as absorbing only similar frequencies.

Number: Jung calls number "an archetype of order" (note: the term "order" refers to placing concepts in a linear order of time sequences, *i.e.*, daily events) and a primary means to ordering a seemingly chaotic multiplicity of images (*i.e.*, frequency) into linear succession.

Octave: A scale of eight natural tone divisions from C to C^1 is called an octave.

Peptides: A chain of macromolecules (amino acids), which include endorphins, hormones, neurotransmitters, growth factors, etc., that act as messengers to interconnect the endocrine, immune and nervous systems in a non-linear manner. They interlink and integrate mental, emotional and biological activities and are synonymous with emotion.

Phase: The phase of a wave and the angle of a triangle are the same (meaning that the coordinates of a point, which would be the result of that angulation [or comparison/interaction of two opposites] would have a definite "time" of actualization), so that the hypotenuse of a triangle and the height or amplitude of a wave are also the same. Then, according to Quantum Theory, in order for a probability to become actualized (manifested), the amplitude (height) has to be squared (multiplied by itself). So for two waves to be "in phase", their <u>angles</u> have to be similar.

Phase entanglement: In Quantum Mechanics, this term refers to a state (of a system; for example, an object) of parallel-polarization between two particles, so that what one particle is doing is determined by the other particles' phase (angle; for example a ratio, such as 2:3).

Polarization: The same as saying that two different particles have the same angle.

Proportion: An equivalency relationship between two ratios (differences). It demonstrates simultaneous difference <u>and</u> sameness, which is a holographic property.

Psyche: As understood by Jung, everything conscious, that which is associated with the ego complex; everything unconscious, that which is known to the psyche, but unknown to the ego complex until it crosses the threshold of consciousness and assimilates itself as a conscious content; and everything that constitutes the psychoid system, that which never crosses the conscious threshold, such as the psychic element mixing with inorganic matter. Psyche in Greek means soul.

Quantum Mechanics: Quantum is a German word for a study of a quantity of something. Mechanics is study of motion. Quantum mechanics is a branch of physics that deals with the probabilities of events happening (being actualized).

Ratio: A measure of differences (note: the concept of a "word" or language [remember: language, music and all earthly DNA is based on the $12\sqrt{2}$ or the 1.05 interval, or the 18:19 ratio] comes from the Greek term "logos", which means "to reason", whose root is "ratio") determined by the relationship between two whole numbers; for example, the ration of 2:3 (the perfect fifth) equals the interval of 1.5∠, which is also the same as the = 60°, and the height or amplitude equals $\sqrt{3}$, so the ratio of 2:3 defines the hexagonal form for the molecular structure of all earthly DNA.

Reticular Activating System (R.A.S.): Located at the base of the brain's hypothalamus (medulla oblongata) and acts as a filtering system on the incoming frequency data, *i.e.*, second-by-second events, the conscious mind.

Reverse Speech: A term and concept developed by David John Oates that is an expression of the right brain and the collective unconscious in the form of backward speech, which is mostly metaphoric in content, as compared to forward speech, which is an expression of the left brain and the conscious mind.

Rheomode: A language concept developed by the physicist David Bohm, whereby experimentation with flowing language forms develops insight into the unbroken wholeness of existence (non-local causality).

Scaling function: "Φ" or "phi" is a mathematical method created by the Fourier Transform of a low-pass filter, as represented by the L-M visional color channel receptors that gives an image of a signal (frequency) at a given resolution. It represents the $\sqrt{5}$ (whose angle is 45° and whose interval is 2.24), which defines the pentagonal cellular structure of DNA.

Synchronicity: Jung described it as an excited state (constellation) of archetypal contents that simultaneously occur in both inner and outer reality. Jung believed that synchronistic events seemed to demonstrate the unity of existence, which he called the unus mundus (one world) and physicists call non-local casualty.

Topology: "Topos" means position or situation in Greek. It is a branch of geometry that deals with the invariant relationships or patterns of numbers ("archetypes of order").

Uncertainty Principle: In physics, an elementary particle, such as an electron, doesn't simultaneously have a precise position and a precise momentum.

Unified Field Theory: Its purpose is to explain mathematically in a single set of equations the interrelationships between the four universal forces: electromagnetism, gravity and the strong and weak nuclear forces.

Vision, three-color channel: A theory proposed in 1957 to explain the human visual system as a differential response to the electromagnetic spectrum frequencies in order to determine three dimensions. In other words, the frequency of color (10^{14}) as visible light determines our human perception of objective reality as having three dimensions; whereas cats have a two-color channel visional system and perceive reality as being two-dimensional and birds have four and five color visional systems and perceive the same reality as us but in four or five dimensions.

Wave (sine):

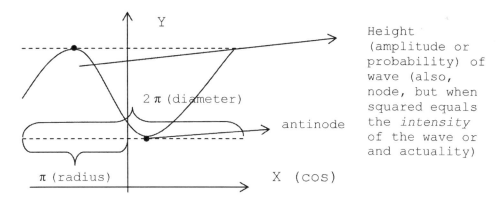

Note: a rotating circle generates a sinewave and also electricity and magnetism.

Wavelet: A little (compressed) wave, as an extension of Fourier analysis, transforms the information of a signal (wave) into frequency (represented by numbers), which gives an image of an object.

Bibliography

About the Tomatis Method, Tim Gilmor, Paul Madaule, and Billie Thompson, Listening Centre, Toronto, Ont., Canada (1989)

Archetypes: A Natural History of the Self, Dr. Anthony Stevens, Quill, New York (1983) (International Standard Book Number[1] 0-688-00785-6 and ISBN 0-688-01976-5 (pbk.))

Archetypes and the Collective Unconscious: The Collected Works of C. G. Jung, Volume 9, Part 1, C. G. Jung, Bollingen Series XX (Translated by R.F.C. Hull), Princeton University Press, Princeton, New Jersey (1959, new material copyright 1969) (Library of Congress Card Catalog Number 75-156, ISBN 0-691-09761-5 and 0-691-01833-2 (pbk.)

Archetypes of the Zodiac, Kathleen Burt, Llewellyn Publications, St. Paul, Minnesota (1993) (ISBN 0-87542-088-5)

Astrology, Psychology and the Four Elements, Stephen Arroyo, CRCS Publications, Sebastopol, California ((1975) (ISBN 0-916-360-02-4)

Aura Awareness, C. E. Lindgren, D, Litt, Jennifer Baltz, Blue Dolphin Publishing Inc., Nevada City (1997) (ISBN 0-9652490-5-0)

The Chakras, C. W. Leadbeater, The Theosophical Publishing House, Wheaton, Illinois (1927) (Fifth Quest Book printing, 1987) (Library of Congress Card Catalog Number 73-147976, ISBN 0-8356-0422-5)

Cheiro's Book of Numbers: The Complete Science of Numerology, Cheiro, Prentiss Hall, New York, Arco Publishing, Inc. (1964) (ISBN 0-688-01170-X)

The Construction of Reality in the Child, Jean Piaget, Ballentine Books, New York (1954) (Library of Congress Card Catalog Number 54-8278, ISBN 345-24300-5-195)

The Cosmic Code: Quantum Physics as the Language of Nature, Heinz R. Pagels, Bantam Books, New York (1982) (ISBN 0-553-24625-9)

Cosmic Music: Musical Keys to Interpretation of Reality, (Essays by Marius Schneider, Rudolf Haase, Hans Erhaard Lauer), edited with an introduction by Joscelyn Godwin (translated by Marton Radkai and Joscelyn Godwin), Inner Traditions, Rochester, Vermont (1989) (ISBN 0-89281-070-X)

Cymantics, Wave Phenomena, Vibrational Effects, Harmonic Oscillations with their Structure, Kinetics and Dynamics, Hans Jenny, Basilius Presse AG, Basel (English Version: D. Q. Stephenson, Basle) (1974) (ISBN 3-85-560-033-3)

The Dancing Wu Li Masters: An Overview of the New Physics, Gary Zukov, Bantam New Age Books, New York (1986) (ISBN 0-533-26382-X)

Deciphering the Senses: The Expanding World of Human Perception, Robert Rivlin and Karen Gravelle, Simon and Schuster, New York (1984)

A Dictionary of Symbols, J. E. Cirlot (translated from the Spanish *Diccionario de Simbolos Tradicionales* by Jack Sage), Philosophical Library, New York (1962)

DNA and Replication, Arthur Kornberg, W. H. Freeman and Company, San Francisco (1980) (ISBN 0-7167-1102-8)

Egyptian Mysteries: New Light on Ancient Spiritual Knowledge, Lucie Lamy (Translation from French by Deborah Lawlor), The Crossroad Publishing Company, New York (1981) (Library of Congress Card Catalog Number 81-66806)

The Elementary Theory of Nuclear Shell Structure, Structure of Matter Series, Maria Goeppert Mayer and J. Hans D. Jensen, John Wiley & Sins, Inc. (New York) and Chapman & Hall (London) (1955) (Library of Congress Card Catalog Number 55-7037)

The Elements of Creation Myth, R.J. Stewart, Element Books Limited, England (1989) (ISBN 1-85230-106-6)

The Embodied Mind, Francisco J. Varela, Evan Thompson and Eleanor Rosch, The MIT Press, Cambrige, MA (1991) (ISBN 0-262-22042-3)

The Essential Plato, Introduction by Alain de Botton from the 1871 translation of Plato by Benjamin Jowett, Quality Paperback Book Club, Inc. (1999)

Experiments in Topology, Stephen Barr, Thomas Y. Crowell Company, New York (1964) (Library of Congress Card Catalog Number 64-10866)

First Concepts of Topology, The Geometry of Mapping of Segments, Curves, Circles and Disks, Volume 18, W. G. Chinn and W. G. Steenrod, The Mathematical Association of America (1966) (Library of Congress Card Catalog Number 66-20367, ISBN 0-88385-600-X for complete set and ISBN 0-88385-618-2 for Volume 18)

The Fourier Series, Georgi P. Tolstov (translated from the Russian by Richard A. Silverman, Dover Publications, Inc., New York (1962) (Library of Congress Card Catalog Number 75-41883, ISBN 0-486-63317-9)

Fractals Everywhere, Second Edition, Michael F. Barnsley, Academic Press Professional (a division of Harcourt Brace & Company), Boston, Massachusetts (1993) (ISBN 0-12-079061-0)

The Fractal Geometry of Nature, Benoit B. Mandelbrot, W. H. Freeman and Company, New York (1977, 1982, 1983), (ISBN 0-7167-1186-9)

From Being to Becoming, Ilya Prigogine, W.H. Freeman & Company, San Francisco, (1980) (ISBN 0-7167-1107-9

Fundamentals of Musical Acoustics, Second, Revised edition, Arthur H. Benade, Dover Publications, Inc., New York (1976) (ISBN 0-486-26484-X)

Fundamentals of Physics, David Halliday and Robert Resnick (with assistance from John Merrill), John Wiley & Sons, Inc. (1988, Third Edition) (ISBN 0-471-81989-1)

Fundamentals of Trigonometry, Second Edition, Earl Swokowski, Prindle, Weber & Schmidt, Inc., Boston, Massachusetts (1971) (Library of Congress Card Catalog Number 68-18419)

Geometry and the Imagination, Second Edition, D. Hilbert and S. Cohn-Vossen (translation by P. Nemenyi), AMS Chelsea Publishing (American Mathematical Society), Providence, Rhode Island (1999) (ISBN 0-8218-1998-4)

The Gnostic Gospels, Elaine Pagels, Vintage Books (a division of Random House), New York (1979) (ISBN 0-679-72453-2 (pbk.))

A Guide to the World's Languages, Volume I: Classification, Merritt Ruhlen, Stanford University Press, Stanford, California (1987) (ISBN 0-8047-1984-6)

The Holographic Paradigm and Other Paradoxes, Exploring the Leading Edge of Science, Edited by Ken Wilber, Shambala Publications, Inc., Boulder, Colorado and London, England (1982) (ISBN 0-87773-235-3 and ISBN

0-394-52823-9 (Random House), ISBN 0-87773-238-8 (pbk.), and ISBN 0-394-71237-4 (Random House: pbk.))

The Holographic Universe, Michael Talbot, Harper Perinnial, a Division of Harper Collins Publishers (1991) (Library of Congress Card Catalog Number 90-55555, ISBN 0-06-092258-3)

The Human Aura, Walter J. Kliner, The Citadel Press, Secaucus, New Jersey (1965) (ISBN 0-8065-0545-1)

Human Navigation and the Sixth Sense, Robin Baker, Simon and Schuster, New York (1981)

I Ching, In Ten Minutes, R. T. Kaser Avon Books, New York (1994) (Library of Congress Card Catalog Number 93-11886, ISBN 0-380-77153-5)

The Individual and the Nature of Mass Events (A Seth Book), Jane Roberts, Prentiss-Hall Press, New York (1981) (ISBN 0-13-457242-4)

The Interpretation of Fairytales, Marie-Louise von Franz, Shambala, Boston and London (1996) (ISBN 0-87773-526-3)

The Interpretation of Nature and the Psyche, C. G. Jung (Synchronicity: An Acausal Connecting Principle) and W. Pauli (The Influence of Archetypal Ideas on the Scientific Theories of Kepler), Bollingen Series LI, Pantheon Books (1955) (Library of Congress Card Catalog Number 54-11743)

Jung and Tarot: *An Archetypal Journey*, Sallie Nichols, Samuel Weiser, Inc., York Beach, Maine (1980) (Library of Congress Card Catalog Number 80-53118, ISBN 0-87728-515-2)

Language and Mind, Enlarged Edition, Noam Chomsky, Harcourt Brace Jovanovich, Inc., (1972) (Library of Congress Card Catalog Number 70-187121, ISBN 0-15-549257-8 (paperbound) and 0-15-147810-4 (hardbound))

Light, R. W. Ditchburn, Ph.D., Unabridged Republication of 1961 Interscience Publishers Edition, Dover Publications, Inc., New York (1991) (ISBN 0-486-66667-0 (pbk.))

Man and His Symbols, (Illustrated), C. G. Jung and M. L. von Franz, Joseph L. Henderson, Jolande Jacobi, Aniela Jaffe, Dell Publishing, a division of Bantam Doubleday Dell Publishing Group, Inc. New York ((1964) (ISBN 0-440-35183-9)

Man's Religions, (Seventh Edition), John B. Noss and David S. Noss, MacMillan Publishing Company, New York (1984) (ISBN 0-02-388470-3)

Mathematical Foundations of Quantum Mechanics, John von Neumann (translated from German by Robert T. Beyer), Princeton University Press, Princeton, New Jersey (1955; renewed 1983) (Library of Congress Card Catalog Number 53-10143, ISBN 0-691-08003-8)

The Mathematical Traveler, Exploring the Grand History of Numbers, Calvin C. Clawson, Plenum Press, New York and London (1994) (ISBN: 0-306-44645-6)

Music, Physics and Engineering (formerly *Musical Engineering*), Second Edition, Harry F. Olson, Dover Publications, Inc., New York (1952) (Library of Congress Card Catalog Number 66-28730)

The Mystery of the Aleph, Amir D. Aczel, Pocket Books, a division of Simon & Schuster, Inc., New York, NY (2000) (ISBN:0-7434-2299-6)

The Mystical Spiral, Journey of the Soul, Jill Purce, Thames and Hudson, Ltd., London (1974, reprinted 1980) (Library of Congress Card Catalog Number 79-67664)

The Myth of Invariance: The Origin of the Gods, Mathematics and Music From the Rg Veda to Plato, Ernest G. McClain, Nicolas-Hays, Inc., York Beach, Main (1976) (ISBN 0-89254-012-5)

The Mythic Image, Joseph Campbell, Bollingen Series C, Princeton University Press, Princeton, New Jersey (1974) (Library of Congress Card Catalog Number 79-166363, ISBN 0-691-01839-1)

The Nature of the Chemical Bond, Third Edition, Linus Pauling, Cornell University Press, Ithaca, New York (1960) (ISBN 0-8014-03330-2)

Number, The Language of Science: A Critical Survey Written for the Cultured Non-Mathematician, Fourth Edition, Revised and Augmented Ninth Printing, Tobias Dantzig, Ph.D., The MacMillan Company, New York (1967)

Number and Time, Studies in Jungian Thought, Reflections Leading Toward Unification of Depth Psychology and Physics, Marie Louise von Franz (translated by Andrea Dykes, James Hillman, General Editor), Northwestern University Press, Evanston (1974) (Library of Congress Card Catalog Number 73-84647, ISBN 0-8101-0532-2)

Numerology and the Divine Triangle, Faith Javane and Dusty Bunker, Whitford Press, Atglen, Pennsylvania (1979) (ISBN 0-914918-10-9)

On the Nature of the Psyche: Volume 8 from the Collected Works of C. G. Jung, C. G. Jung (Translation R. F. C. Hull) Princeton University Press, Princeton, New Jersey (1960) (Library of Congress Card Catalog Number 75-106803, ISBN 0-691-01751-4)

The Origin of Satan, Elaine Pagels, Random House, New York, (1995) by Elaine Pagels (ISBN 0-679-40140-7)

Oversoul Seven and Museum of Time, Jane Roberts, Prentiss Hall Press, New York (1984) (ISBN 0-13-647446-2)

Philosophical Foundations of Physics: An Introduction to the Philosophy of Science, Rudolf Carnap (Edited by Martin Gardner), Basic Books, Inc. (1966) (Library of Congress Card Catalog Number 66-16499)

Philosophy of Mathematics and Natural Science, Hermann Weyl (Revised and Augmented English Edition Based on a Translation by Olaf Helmer), Princeton University Press, Princeton, New Jersey (1949)

The Power of Myth, Joseph Campbell, Doubleday, New York (1988) (ISBN 0-385-24773-7)

Presence of the Past (Morphic Resonance and the Habits of Nature), Rupert Sheldrake, Vintage Books, New York (1988) (ISBN 0-394-75990-7)

Psyche and Matter, Marie-Louise von Franz, Shamala Publications, Inc., Boston, Massachusetts, and London (Random Century House) (1988), translation of *Psyche und Materie*, "*C. G. Jung Foundation Book*" (ISBN 0-87773-902 (alk. paper))

Psychic Politics: An Aspect Psychology Book, Jane Roberts, Prentiss-Hall, Inc., Englewood Cliffs, New Jersey (1976) (ISBN 0-13-731715-X)

Psychological Reflections, C. G. Jung, Princeton University Press, New Jersey (1953) (ISBN 0-691-01786-7)

Psychology and Alchemy, Illustrated, Second Edition, C. G. Jung (translated by R. F. Hull, Bollingen Series XX, Princeton University Press (1968) (Library of Congress Card Catalog Number 75-156, ISBN 0-691-09771-2 and ISBN 0-691-01831-6 (pbk.))

Psychology of Music, Carl E. Seashore, Dover Publications, Inc., New York (1967) (Library of Congress Card Catalog Number 67-27877)

The Psychology of Ritual, Murray Hope, Element Books Limited, Longmead, England (1988) (ISBN 1-85230-043-4)

The Physical World of Late Antiquity, S. Sambursky, Princeton University Press, Princeton, New Jersey ((1962) (ISBN 0-691-08476-9)

Quantum Healing, Exploring the Frontiers of Mind/Body Medicine, Deepak Chopra, M. D., Bantam Books, New York (1989) (ISBN 0-553-34869-8)

Quantum Reality, Beyond the New Physics: An Excursion into Metaphysics ... And the Meaning of Reality, Nick Herbert, Anchor Press, Doubleday, New York ((1985) (ISBN 0-385-23569-0 (pbk.))

Quantum Theory, David Bohm, Dover Publications, Inc., New York (1951, 1979), (ISBN:0-486-65969-0)

Reverse Speech: Voices From the Unconscious, David John Oates, Promotion Publishing, San Diego, California (1996) (ISBN 1-57901-000-8)

Reverse Speech: The Hobbyist Course (Study Guide), An Overview of Basic Theory, Analysis Procedures and Self-Use Instructions, David John Oates (1995)

Reverse Speech: Metaphor Dictionary (Study Guide), An Aid in the Analysis of Metaphors that Occur Universally in the Unconscious Mind, David John Oates (1996)

The Revolution in Physics: A Non-Mathematical Survey of Quanta, Loius de Broglie, (translated with additions form the French *La Physique Nouvelle et Les Quanta* by Ralph Niemeyer), Routledge & Kegan Paul, Ltd., Broadway House, London, printed in Great Britain by Lund, Humphries & Co., Ltd. and London & Bradford (1936)

Sacred Geometry: Philosophy and Practice, Robert Lawlor, Thames and Hudson, Ltd., London, 1982 (Reprinted 1997) (Library of Congress Card Catalog Number 88-51328, ISBN 0-500-81030-3)

Science and Music, Sir James Jeans, Dover Publications, Inc., New York, (Library of Congress Card Catalog Number 68-24632, ISBN 0-486-61964-8)

The Science of Musical Sound, John R. Pierce, Scientific American Books (W. H. Freeman and Company), New York and San Francisco (1983) (ISBN 0-7167-1508-2 and ISBN 0-7167-1509-0 (pbk.))

The Science of Sound, Thomas D. Rossing, Addison-Wesley Publishing Company, Reading Massachusetts (ISBN 0-201-06505-3)

Science, Order and Creativity: a Dramatic New Look at the Creative Roots of Science and Life, David Bohm and F. David Peat, Bantam Books, New York (1987) (ISBN 0-553-34449-8)

Sensory Inhibition, Georg von Bekesy, Princeton University Press, Princeton, NJ (1967) (Library of Congress Card Catalog Number 66-17713)

The Seth Material, Jane Roberts, Prentiss Hall Press, New York, (1979) (ISBN 0-553-27948-3)

Seth: Dreams and Projections of Consciousness, Jane Roberts, Stillpoint Publishing, Walpole, New Hampshire (1986) (Library of Congress Card Catalog Number 86-60443, ISBN 0-913299-25-1)

The Signature of God: Astonishing Biblical Discoveries, Grant R. Jeffrey, Frontier Research Publications, Inc., Toronto, Ontario (1996) (ISBN 0-921714-28-9)

Sound Health Resources*,* Sharry Edwards (1997)

The Special Theory of Relativity, David Bohm, W.A. Benjamin, New York (1965)

The Structure of Magic: A Book About Language and Therapy, Richard Bandler and John Grinder, Science and Behavior Books, Inc., Palo Alto, California, (1975) (Library of Congress Card Catalog Number 75-12452, ISBN 08314-0044-7)

The Symbolic Species: The Co-Evolution of Language and the Brain, Terrence W. Deacon, W. W. Norton & Company, Inc., New York, (1997) (ISBN 0-393-03838-6)

Synchronicity: The Bridge Between Matter and Mind, F. David Peat, Bantam Books, New York ((1987) (ISBN 0-553-34321-1)

The Tao of Physics: An Exploration of the Parallels Between Modern Physics and Eastern Mysticism, Second Edition, Fritjof Capra, Bantam New Age Books, New York (1983) (ISBN 0-553-26379-X)

Thoughts and Language, Lev Vygotsky, Massachusetts Institute of Technology Press, Cambridge, Massachusetts and London, England (1986) (ISBN 0-262-22029-6)

Transformations of the Myth Through Time, Joseph Campbell, Harper & Row, Publishers, New York (1990) (ISBN 0-06-055189-5)

Unconditional Life: Discovering the Power to Fulfill Your Dreams, Deepak Chopra, M. D., Bantam Books, New York (1991) (ISBN 0-553-37050-2)

The Unknown Reality: A Seth Book, Volume Two, Jane Roberts, Prentiss-Hall, Inc., Englewood Cliffs, New Jersey (1979) (ISBN 0-13-938696-3 (v. 2))

The Web of Life, Fritjof Capra, Anchor Books, New York (1996) (ISBN 0-385-47675-2)

Webster's New Universal Unabridged Dictionary, Second Edition, Dorsett and Baber, Simon & Shuster Division of Gulf & Western Corporation, New York (1979), (Library of Congress Card Catalog Number 83-42537, ISBN 0-671-41819-X)

Wholeness and the Implicit Order, David Bohm, ARK Paperbacks, London and New York (1983) (ISBN 0-7448-0000-5)

The World According to Wavelets: The Story of a Mathematical Technique in the Making, Second Edition, Barbara Burke Hubbard, A. K. Peters, Ltd., Wellesley, Massachusetts (1998) (ISBN 1-56881-072-5)

Postscript

The information in this book has a practical application, which is reversing a negative cognitive set (*i.e.*, worldview) to a positive cognitive set, and thus eliminating the need for a person to try to destroy themselves through addictive behaviors, since all addiction is aimed at destroying the self due to erroneous judgments concerning themselves in relationship to the universe. This can be accomplished consciously by utilizing a theta-wave interaction when concisely explaining the book's contents.

A chart demonstrating the correlations between planets, angles, astrological signs, colors, musical intervals and note frequencies, senses, molecular structures, elements, the bonding strengths of the electron shells' sublevels and the binding nuclear strengths of the neutrons and protons and chakras as harmonic intervals (numerical ratios) of the electromagnetic spectrum:

	Notes	**Interval**	**Frequency ratio from origin**	**DNA Letter**
	C:C	Unison	1:1	T
	C#:C	Semitone or minor 2nd	1.059463:1	
	D:C	Whole tone or major 2nd	1.122462:1	
	D#:C	Minor 3rd	1.189207:1	
	E:C	Major 3rd	1.259921:1	C
	F:C	Perfect 4th	1.334840:1	
(or) Diminished 5th (or) "Lapse of consciousness ratio: 1.2s%0.85 = 1.5 or 2:3	F#, G♭:C	Augmented 4th	1.414214:1	G
	G:C	Tritone Perfect 5th	1.498307:1	
	G#, A♭–C	Minor 6th	1.587401:1	A
	A:C	Major 6th	1.681793:1	
	A#, B♭:C	Minor 7th	1.781797:1	
		Major 7th	1.887749:1	
		Octave	C′:C	

Notes:
1) Oscillation or vibration/frequency (c.p.s.) as cycles per second is based on the Principle of Alternation, which is "expressed geometrically in the ancient Taoist symbol of Yin and Yang" (<u>Sacred Geometry</u>, pg. 42) and is expressed by √2. "Everything alternates towards its opposite. The truth of every progression or evolution is rhythmic alternation and oscillation" (pg. 42).

<u>**Cents from origin**</u>	<u>**Natural Element**</u>	<u>**Number ratio**</u>	*<u>Archetype</u>*	<u>Angle</u>
0	Oxygen	√1	*#2, Father*	58°
100		^{12}√2; 15:16		60°
200		8:9		65°
300		5:6		68°
400	Nitrogen	4:5	*#3, Union*	62°–73°
500		3:4 (or) 6:8		75°–76°
600	Carbon's valence #	√2 (or) 32:45	*#4, Self*	78°–83°
700	Hydrogen	2:3	*#1, Mother*	84°–90°
800	Hydrogen	5:8	*#1, Mother*	above 90°
900		3:5		above 90°
1000	Carbon	√3 or 5:9	*#4, Self*	above 90°
1100		8:15		above 90°
1200		1:2, or 2		

(continued) So, for example, you divide 1.25 by 0.8s, which equals 1.5, which is the ratio 2:3 or the musical note G and the angles 84°– 90°. Since ^{12}√2 for G = 1.498307 and ^{12}√2 for F#G♭ = 1.414214←(√2), von Békésy rounded off and used 1.414 or the √2 for his assertion.

Notes: The bonding strength information was obtained from Linus Pauling's <u>The Nature of the Chemical Bond</u> and refers to the electron's bonding strength per the sublevel orbitals of s, p, d and f as it was proven by Hultgren in 1932 to be equal to the square root of the number of orbitals. For example, the s sublevel orbitals equals 1, hence the bonding strength equals √1. And p = √3 w/3 orbitals; d = √5 + f = √1.

Frequency from Mid C	**Brain wave**	**Color as (10^{14}) visible light**
261.6 cps	Beta; (4 octaves lower/ Mid C) 16-40 cps	Red
277.2 cps		Red/Orange
293.6 cps		Orange
311.1 cps		Orange/Yellow
329.6 cps	Alpha; (5 octaves lower) 8-15 cps	Yellow
349.2 cps		Yellow/Green
370.0 cps	Theta; (6 octaves lower) 5-8 cps	Green
392.0 cps	Delta; (7-8 octaves lower) 0-4 cps	Green/Blue
415.3 cps		Blue
440.0 cps		Blue/Violet
466.2 cps		Violet
493.9 cps		Violet/Red
523.2 cps		

So s = √1, at 1; p = √3 = 1.732; d = √5 = 2.236 + f = √7 = 2.645. When there is a hybridization of sublevel orbitals, *i.e.* sp, then the bonding strength reflects √2 or 1.414, which is the musical notes $F^{\#}$ + G^{b} and the ratio 32:45. Hybridization occurs at the octave level of C':C, so that sp^3 = √4, or 2:1 and the ratio 1:2. *Note: in order to determine the ratio of 5:6, divide 6/5 = 1.2, which is the note $D^{\#}$.

*Note: the bonding strength is also dependent on the angulation of the orbitals. Hence the p level is strongest @ 90°=√2.

Notes:

1) Per the chemist Hans Jenny, as the frequency increases so does the form's complexity.
2) As you go up an octave, the frequency doubles, and as you go down an octave, you divide the frequency.
3) In order to determine a ratio, you divide. For example, middle C @ 261.6 cps is divided into C$^\#$ @ 277.2 cps and the ratio (as well as the ratios between all of the 12 notes) is 1.059463, which is the twelfth root of the square root of 2 ($\sqrt{2}$).

Frequency of visible light	Astrological Sign Element	Atomic Form	Planets
429-492 trillion cps	Aries/Fire	Square	Mars
429-508 trillion cps	Taurus/Earth		Venus
492-508 trillion cps	Gemini/Air		Mercury
492-526 trillion cps	Cancer/Water		Moon
508-526 trillion cps	Leo/Fire	Triangle	Sun
508-600 trillion cps	Virgo/Earth		Mercury
526-600 trillion cps	Libra/Air		Venus
526-650 trillion cps	Scorpio/Water	Circle	Mars
600-650 trillion cps	Sagittarius/Fire	Circle	Jupiter
650-700 trillion cps	Capricorn/Earth	Hexagon	Saturn
700-750 trillion cps	Aquarius/Air		Uranus
750+ trillion cps	Pisces/Water		Neptune

Note: the binding strength refers to the subatomic energy of the protons and neutrons in the nucleus as demonstrated by Maria Goeppert-Mayer and J. H. D. Jensen in the <u>Elementary Theory of Nuclear Shell Structure</u>. The nuclear forces prefer an equal number of protons and neutrons in the nucleus for stability, but at what Geoppert refers to as the "magic numbers" of 2, 8, 20, 28, 50, 82 and 126 protons with equal neutrons, there appears to be the same closure effect that exists between the electron orbital closures of 2.8.

Note:
1) The number of complete vibrations which occur in a second is called the frequency of the vibration, for example how many times the circular thought pattern (archetype) repeats itself. The designation for this occurrence is "cps" or "cycles per second".
2) A <u>ratio</u> measures <u>differences</u>, while a proportion demonstrates equivalency between two ratios, *i.e.* "a" is to "b" as "c" is to "d", or $\overset{\text{ratio}}{(a:b)} \overset{}{(::)} c:d. \overset{\text{proportion}}{}$

Principle of Alternation: (√2) Yin & Yang (Duality)	Chakras	Physiological System
Masculine	root (base of spine); 1st	reproductive
Feminine		
Masculine	spleen; 2nd	elimination & assimilation
Feminine		
Masculine	solar plexus; 3rd	digestive (stomach, liver)
Feminine		
Masculine	heart; 4th	immune and circulatory
Feminine		
Masculine	throat; 5th	respiratory
Feminine	brow; 6th	autonomic nervous system
Masculine	crown; 7th	central nervous system
Feminine		

Notes:
1) From <u>Sacred Geometry</u>, pg. 12, "√2 is the functional number of a square. Pi (π, 3.14…) is the functional number of a circle and √3 is the functional number of a hexagon [*i.e.*, the atomic structure of carbon]."

Notes:
1) The sinewave function represents a formal numerical relationship and, consequently, an <u>interaction</u> of numbers as principles or coded information (signals) for concepts and thoughtforms, *i.e.* archetypes.
2) The closure numbers of the electrons' shell capacity @ 2,8,18 and 32 reflect the ratios of 2:8 = 4; 8:18 = 2.25; 18:32 = 1.77, or √16, √5 and the √3, respectively.
3) The planets associated with the astrological signs reflect the mundane rulers, rather than the esoteric or exalted planets that could also be used.

Glands	**Taste**	**Touch**
ovaries/testes	pungent, spicy	pungent, spicy
spleen and pancreas	sour, acidic	hot, warm
adrenal	astringent, salty	warm, sun
thymus	all taste	cool, misty
thyroid and parathyroid		soft, smooth
pituitary	sweet	
pineal	balanced	crystal, ice
	bitter, salty	mystical

Notes:

*1) The intervals between the "magic" nuclear numbers is 2:8 = 4~√16, 8:20 = 2.5~√6; 20:28 = 1.4 or √2; 28.50 = 1.7 or √3; 50:82 = 1.6 or 3.5, + 82:/26 = 1.5 or 2:3, which is the ratio for our lapse of consciousness.

Smell	Sound	Euler's Topological Connectivity Number	Bonding strength of electron subshell levels
rose, ginger and basil	e (as in red)	#2	s = √1
almond bergamot	o (as in home)		
lemon, rosemary	a-o-m (ahh-ooo-mmm)	#3	
pine, spring rain	a (as in ah)	#4	Hybrid: sp = √2
		#1	
gardenia, magnolia	u (as in blue)		
cedarwood	om (as in home)		p = √3 (or) 1.732
lavendar, mist	ee (as in bee)		
			Hybrid: sp^3 = √4 = 2

197

Nuclear bonding strength	Interval	Notes	Frequency ratio from origin
		C#′:C	2.11892:1
		D′:C	2.2449:1
		D#′:C	2.37839:1
		E′:C	2.5198:1
		F′:C	2.6696:1
		F#:C	2.828:1
Ratio of 20/28 neutrons & protons equals √2		G′:C	2.996:1
Ratio of 82/126 neutrons & protons equals 1.5; 2:3		G#′:C	3.1747:1
Ratio of 50/82 neutrons & protons = 1/64		A#′:C	3.363:1
		A#′:C	3.563:1
Ratio of 28/50 neutrons & protons equals 1.785		B:C	3.7753:1
		C″:C	3.999(4.0):1
		C#″:C	4.2376:1

DNA Letter	Cents from origin	Natural element	Number ratio	Archetype	Bonding strength of electron sublevels
	1300				
	1400		√5, 2.23		d = √5 = 2.24
	1500				
	1600		√6; 2.44		Hybrids: spd = √6 = 2.44
	1700		√7; 2.64		Sublevel f = √7 = 2.64
	1800		√8; 2.82		Hybrids: sp^3d^4f = √8 = 2.82
	1900		√9; 3		sp^3d^5 = √9 = 3
	2000		√10; 3.16		sp^3d^5f = √10 = 3.16
	2100		√11; 3.31		$sp^3d^5f^2$ = √11 = 3.31
	2200		√12; 3.46		$sp^3d^5f^3$ = √12 = 3.46
	2300		√14; 3.74		$sp^3d^5f^4$ = √14 = 3.74
	2400		√16; 4		$sp^3d^5f^7$ = √16 = 4
	2500		√18; 4.24		$sp^3d^5f^9$ = √18 = 4.24

Frequency from Middle C at 261.6	Nuclear bonding strength
554.40 cps	
587.40 cps	
622.20 cps	
659.20 cps	Ratio of neutrons + protons; 8:20 protons
698.40 cps	
740.0 cps	
784.0 cps	
830.6 cps	
880.0 cps	
932.4 cps	
1,046.4 cps	
1,108.8 cps	Ratio of 2:8 protons + neutrons
1,174.8 cps	

Planets/Signs

Mars/Aries

Venus/Taurus

Mercury/Gemini

Moon/Cancer

Sun/Leo

Mercury/Virgo

Venus/Libra

Mars/Scorpio

Jupiter/Sagittarius

Saturn/Capricorn

Uranus/Aquarius

Neptune/Pisces

Mars/Aries

Correlations for Unison Interval	
Notes	C:C
Frequency Ratio from Origin	1:1
DNA Letter	T
Cents from Origin	0
Natural Element	Oxygen
Number Ratio	√1
Archetype	#2, Father
Angle	58°
Frequency from Mid C	261.6 cps
Brainwave	Beta; (4 octaves lower/ Mid C) 16-40 cps
Color as (10^{14}) Visible Light	Red
Frequency of Visible Light	429-492 trillion cps
Astrological Sign/Element	Aries/Fire
Atomic From	Square
Planets	Mars
Principle of Alteration: (√2) Yin and Yang Duality	Masculine
Chakras	Root (base of spine); 1st
Physiological System	Reproductive
Glands	Ovaries/Testes
Taste	Pungent, Spicy
Touch	Pungent, Spicy
Smell	Rose, Ginger, and Basil
Sound	E (as in Red)
Euler's Topological Connectivity Number	#2
Bonding Strength of Electron subshell levels	S = √1
Nuclear Bonding Strength	–
Notes	C#:C
Frequency Ratio from Origin	2.11892:1
Cents from Origin	1300
Number Ratio	–
Bonding Strength of Electron Sublevels	–
Frequency from Middle C at 261.6	554.40 cps
Nuclear Bonding Strength	–
Planets/Signs	Mars/Aries

Correlations for Semitone or Minor 2nd Interval	
Notes	C#:C
Frequency Ratio from Origin	1.059463:1
DNA Letter	-
Cents from Origin	100
Natural Element	-
Number Ratio	$^{12}\sqrt{2}$; 15:16
Archetype	-
Angle	60°
Frequency from Mid C	277.2 cps
Brainwave	-
Color as (10^{14}) Visible Light	Red/Orange
Frequency of Visible Light	429-508 trillion cps
Astrological Sign/Element	Taurus/Earth
Atomic From	-
Planets	Venus
Principle of Alteration: ($\sqrt{2}$) Yin and Yang Duality	Feminine
Chakras	-
Physiological System	-
Glands	-
Taste	-
Touch	-
Smell	-
Sound	-
Euler's Topological Connectivity Number	-
Bonding Strenth of Electron subshell levels	-
Nuclear Bonding Strength	-
Notes	D':C
Frequency Ratio from Origin	2.2449:1
Cents from Origin	1400
Number Ratio	$\sqrt{5}$; 2.23
Bonding Strength of Electron Sublevels	$d = \sqrt{5} = 2.24$
Frequency from Middle C at 261.6	587.40 cps
Nuclear Bonding Strength	-
Planets/Signs	Venus/Taurus

Correlations for Whole Tone or Major 2nd Interval	
Notes	D:C
Frequency Ratio from Origin	1.1224262:1
DNA Letter	-
Cents from Origin	200
Natural Element	-
Number Ratio	8:9
Archetype	-
Angle	65°
Frequency from Mid C	293.6 cps
Brainwave	-
Color as (10^{14}) Visible Light	Orange
Frequency of Visible Light	492-508 trillion cps
Astrological Sign/Element	Gemini/Air
Atomic From	-
Planets	Mercury
Principle of Alteration: ($\sqrt{2}$) Yin and Yang Duality	Masculine
Chakras	Spleen; 2nd
Physiological System	Elimination & Assimilation
Glands	Spleen and Pancreas
Taste	Sour, Acidic
Touch	Hot, Warm
Smell	Almond, Bergamot
Sound	O (as in Home)
Euler's Topological Connectivity Number	-
Bonding Strength of Electron subshell levels	-
Nuclear Bonding Strength	-
Notes	D#:C
Frequency Ratio from Origin	2.37839:1
Cents from Origin	1500
Number Ratio	-
Bonding Strength of Electron Sublevels	-
Frequency from Middle C at 261.6	622.20 cps
Nuclear Bonding Strength	-
Planets/Signs	Mercury/Gemini

Correlations for Minor 3rd Interval	
Notes	D#:C
Frequency Ratio from Origin	1.189207:1
DNA Letter	-
Cents from Origin	300
Natural Element	-
Number Ratio	5:6
Archetype	-
Angle	68°
Frequency from Mid C	311.1 cps
Brainwave	-
Color as (10^{14}) Visible Light	Orange/Yellow
Frequency of Visible Light	429-526 trillion cps
Astrological Sign/Element	Cancer/Water
Atomic From	-
Planets	Moon
Principle of Alteration: ($\sqrt{2}$) Yin and Yang Duality	Feminine
Chakras	-
Physiological System	-
Glands	-
Taste	-
Touch	-
Smell	-
Sound	-
Euler's Topological Connectivity Number	-
Bonding Strenth of Electron subshell levels	-
Nuclear Bonding Strength	-
Notes	E':C
Frequency Ratio from Origin	2.5198:1
Cents from Origin	1600
Number Ratio	$\sqrt{6}$; 2.44
Bonding Strength of Electron Sublevels	Hybrids: spd = $\sqrt{6}$ = 2.44
Frequency from Middle C at 261.6	659.20 cps
Nuclear Bonding Strength	Ratio of neutrons + protons; 8:20 protons
Planets/Signs	Moon/Cancer

Correlations for Major 3rd Interval	
Notes	E:C
Frequency Ratio from Origin	1.259921:1
DNA Letter	C
Cents from Origin	400
Natural Element	Nitrogen
Number Ratio	4:5
Archetype	#3, Unison
Angle	62-73°
Frequency from Mid C	329.6 cps
Brainwave	Alpha; (5 octaves lower) 8-15 cps
Color as (10^{14}) Visible Light	Yellow
Frequency of Visible Light	508-526 trillion cps
Astrological Sign/Element	Leo/Fire
Atomic From	Triangle
Planets	Sun
Principle of Alteration: ($\sqrt{2}$) Yin and Yang Duality	Masculine
Chakras	Solar Plexus; 3rd
Physiological System	Digestive (Stomach, Liver)
Glands	Adrenal
Taste	Astringent, Salty
Touch	Warm, Sun
Smell	Lemon, Rosemary
Sound	A-O-M (ahh-ooo-mmm)
Euler's Topological Connectivity Number	#3
Bonding Strength of Electron subshell levels	—
Nuclear Bonding Strength	—
Notes	F':C
Frequency Ratio from Origin	2.6696:1
Cents from Origin	1700
Number Ratio	$\sqrt{7}$; 2.64
Bonding Strength of Electron Sublevels	Sublevel f = $\sqrt{7}$ = 2.64
Frequency from Middle C at 261.6	698.40 cps
Nuclear Bonding Strength	—
Planets/Signs	Sun/Leo

Correlations for Perfect 4th Interval	
Notes	F:C
Frequency Ratio from Origin	1.334840:1
DNA Letter	-
Cents from Origin	500
Natural Element	-
Number Ratio	3:4 (or) 6:8
Archetype	-
Angle	75-76°
Frequency from Mid C	349.2 cps
Brainwave	-
Color as (10^{14}) Visible Light	Yellow/Green
Frequency of Visible Light	508-600 trillion cps
Astrological Sign/Element	Virgo/Earth
Atomic From	-
Planets	Mercury
Principle of Alteration: ($\sqrt{2}$) Yin and Yang Duality	Feminine
Chakras	-
Physiological System	-
Glands	-
Taste	-
Touch	-
Smell	-
Sound	-
Euler's Topological Connectivity Number	-
Bonding Strenth of Electron subshell levels	-
Nuclear Bonding Strength	-
Notes	F#:C
Frequency Ratio from Origin	2.828:1
Cents from Origin	1800
Number Ratio	$\sqrt{8}$; 2.82
Bonding Strength of Electron Sublevels	Hybrids: $sp^3d^4f = \sqrt{8} = 2.82$
Frequency from Middle C at 261.6	740.0 cps
Nuclear Bonding Strength	-
Planets/Signs	Mercury/Virgo

Correlations for Augmented 4th Interval	
Notes	F#, Gb:C
Frequency Ratio from Origin	1.414214:1
DNA Letter	G
Cents from Origin	600
Natural Element	Carbon's valence #
Number Ratio	√2 (or) 32:45
Archetype	#4, Self
Angle	78-83°
Frequency from Mid C	370.0 cps
Brainwave	Theta; (6 octaves lower) 5-8 cps
Color as (10^{14}) Visible Light	Green
Frequency of Visible Light	526-600 trillion cps
Astrological Sign/Element	Libra/Air
Atomic From	-
Planets	Venus
Principle of Alteration: (√2) Yin and Yang Duality	Masculine
Chakras	Heart; 4th
Physiological System	Immune and Circulatory
Glands	Thymus
Taste	All Taste
Touch	Cool, Misty
Smell	Pine, Spring Rain
Sound	A (as in ah)
Euler's Topological Connectivity Number	#4
Bonding Strength of Electron subshell levels	Hybrid: sp = √2
Nuclear Bonding Strength	Ratio of 20/28 neutrons & protons = √2
Notes	G':C
Frequency Ratio from Origin	2.996:1
Cents from Origin	1900
Number Ratio	√9; 3
Bonding Strength of Electron Sublevels	sp^3d^5 = √9 = 3
Frequency from Middle C at 261.6	784.0 cps
Nuclear Bonding Strength	-
Planets/Signs	Venus/Libra

Correlations for Tritone Perfect 5th Interval	
Notes	G:C
Frequency Ratio from Origin	1.498307:1
DNA Letter	-
Cents from Origin	700
Natural Element	Hydrogen
Number Ratio	2:3
Archetype	#1, Mother
Angle	84-90°
Frequency from Mid C	392.0 cps
Brainwave	Delta; (7-8 octaves lower) 0-4 cps
Color as (10^{14}) Visible Light	Green/Blue
Frequency of Visible Light	526-650 trillion cps
Astrological Sign/Element	Scorpio/Water
Atomic From	Circle
Planets	Mars
Principle of Alteration: ($\sqrt{2}$) Yin and Yang Duality	Feminine
Chakras	-
Physiological System	-
Glands	-
Taste	-
Touch	-
Smell	-
Sound	-
Euler's Topological Connectivity Number	#1
Bonding Strenth of Electron subshell levels	-
Nuclear Bonding Strength	Ratio of 82/126 neutrons & protons equals 1.5; 2:3
Notes	G#':C
Frequency Ratio from Origin	3.1747:1
Cents from Origin	2000
Number Ratio	$\sqrt{10}$; 3.16
Bonding Strength of Electron Sublevels	$sp^3d^5f = \sqrt{10} = 3.16$
Frequency from Middle C at 261.6	830.6 cps
Nuclear Bonding Strength	-
Planets/Signs	Mars/Scorpio

Correlations for Minor 6th Interval	
Notes	G#, Ab:C
Frequency Ratio from Origin	1587401:1
DNA Letter	A
Cents from Origin	800
Natural Element	Hydrogen
Number Ratio	5:8
Archetype	#1, Mother
Angle	above 90°
Frequency from Mid C	415.3 cps
Brainwave	–
Color as (10^{14}) Visible Light	Blue
Frequency of Visible Light	600-650 trillion cps
Astrological Sign/Element	Sagittarius/Fire
Atomic From	Circle
Planets	Jupiter
Principle of Alteration: ($\sqrt{2}$) Yin and Yang Duality	Masculine
Chakras	Throat; 5th
Physiological System	Respiratory
Glands	Thyroid and Parathyroid
Taste	–
Touch	Soft, Smooth
Smell	Gardenia, Magnolia
Sound	U (as in Blue)
Euler's Topological Connectivity Number	–
Bonding Strength of Electron subshell levels	–
Nuclear Bonding Strength	Ratio of 50/82 neutrons & protons = 1/64
Notes	A#′:C
Frequency Ratio from Origin	3.363:1
Cents from Origin	2100
Number Ratio	$\sqrt{11}$; 3.31
Bonding Strength of Electron Sublevels	$sp^3d^5f^2 = \sqrt{11} = 3.31$
Frequency from Middle C at 261.6	880.0 cps
Nuclear Bonding Strength	–
Planets/Signs	Jupiter/Sagittarius

Correlations for Major 6th Interval	
Notes	A:C
Frequency Ratio from Origin	1.681793:1
DNA Letter	-
Cents from Origin	900
Natural Element	-
Number Ratio	3:5
Archetype	-
Angle	Above 90°
Frequency from Mid C	440.0 cps
Brainwave	-
Color as (10^{14}) Visible Light	Blue/Violet
Frequency of Visible Light	650-700 trillion cps
Astrological Sign/Element	Capricorn/Earth
Atomic From	Hexagon
Planets	Saturn
Principle of Alteration: ($\sqrt{2}$) Yin and Yang Duality	Feminine
Chakras	Brow; 6th
Physiological System	Autonomic Nervous System
Glands	Pituitary
Taste	Sweet
Touch	-
Smell	-
Sound	-
Euler's Topological Connectivity Number	-
Bonding Strenth of Electron subshell levels	-
Nuclear Bonding Strength	-
Notes	$A^{\#\prime}$:C
Frequency Ratio from Origin	3.563:1
Cents from Origin	2200
Number Ratio	$\sqrt{12}$; 3.46
Bonding Strength of Electron Sublevels	$sp^3d^5f^3 = \sqrt{12} = 3.46$
Frequency from Middle C at 261.6	942.4 cps
Nuclear Bonding Strength	-
Planets/Signs	Saturn/Capricorn

Correlations for Minor 7th Interval	
Notes	A#, Bb:C
Frequency Ratio from Origin	1.781797:1
DNA Letter	-
Cents from Origin	1000
Natural Element	Carbon
Number Ratio	√3 or 5:9
Archetype	#4, Self
Angle	above 90°
Frequency from Mid C	466.2 cps
Brainwave	-
Color as (10^{14}) Visible Light	Violet
Frequency of Visible Light	700-750 trillion cps
Astrological Sign/Element	Aquarius/Air
Atomic From	-
Planets	Uranus
Principle of Alteration: (√2) Yin and Yang Duality	Masculine
Chakras	Crown; 7th
Physiological System	Central Nervous System
Glands	Pineal
Taste	Balanced
Touch	Crystal, Ice
Smell	Cedarwood
Sound	om (as in Home)
Euler's Topological Connectivity Number	-
Bonding Strength of Electron subshell levels	p = √3 (or) 1.732
Nuclear Bonding Strength	Ratio of 28/50 neutrons & protons equals 1.785
Notes	B:C
Frequency Ratio from Origin	3.7753:1
Cents from Origin	2300
Number Ratio	√14; 3.74
Bonding Strength of Electron Sublevels	$sp^3d^5f^4$ = √14 = 3.74
Frequency from Middle C at 261.6	1,046.4 cps
Nuclear Bonding Strength	-
Planets/Signs	Uranus/Aquarius

Correlations for Major 7th Interval	
Notes	-
Frequency Ratio from Origin	1.887749:1
DNA Letter	-
Cents from Origin	1100
Natural Element	-
Number Ratio	8:15
Archetype	-
Angle	Above 90°
Frequency from Mid C	493.9 cps
Brainwave	-
Color as (10^{14}) Visible Light	Violet/Red
Frequency of Visible Light	750+ trillion cps
Astrological Sign/Element	Pisces/Water
Atomic From	-
Planets	Neptune
Principle of Alteration: ($\sqrt{2}$) Yin and Yang Duality	Feminine
Chakras	-
Physiological System	-
Glands	-
Taste	Bitter, Salty
Touch	Mystical
Smell	Lavender, Mist
Sound	ee (as in Bee)
Euler's Topological Connectivity Number	-
Bonding Strenth of Electron subshell levels	-
Nuclear Bonding Strength	-
Notes	C″:C
Frequency Ratio from Origin	3.999(4.0):1
Cents from Origin	2400
Number Ratio	$\sqrt{16}$; 4
Bonding Strength of Electron Sublevels	$Sp^3d^5f^7 = \sqrt{16} = 4$
Frequency from Middle C at 261.6	1,108.8 cps
Nuclear Bonding Strength	Ratio of 2:8 protons + neutrons
Planets/Signs	Neptune/Pisces

Correlations for Octave Interval	
Notes	C′:C
Frequency Ratio from Origin	–
DNA Letter	–
Cents from Origin	1200
Natural Element	–
Number Ratio	1:2 or 2
Archetype	–
Angle	–
Frequency from Mid C	523.2 cps
Brainwave	–
Color as (10^{14}) Visible Light	–
Frequency of Visible Light	–
Astrological Sign/Element	–
Atomic From	–
Planets	–
Principle of Alteration: ($\sqrt{2}$) Yin and Yang Duality	–
Chakras	–
Physiological System	–
Glands	–
Taste	–
Touch	–
Smell	–
Sound	–
Euler's Topological Connectivity Number	–
Bonding Strenth of Electron subshell levels	Hybrid: $sp^3 = \sqrt{4} = 2$
Nuclear Bonding Strength	–
Notes	C#‴:C
Frequency Ratio from Origin	4.2376:1
Cents from Origin	2500
Number Ratio	$\sqrt{18}$; 4.24
Bonding Strength of Electron Sublevels	$sp^3d^5f^9 = \sqrt{18} = 4.24$
Frequency from Middle C at 261.6	1,174.8 cps
Nuclear Bonding Strength	–
Planets/Signs	Mars/Aries

Notes:

*1) The intervals between the "magic" nuclear numbers is 2:8 = 4~√16, 8:20 = 2.5~√6; 20:28 = 1.4 or √2; 28.50 = 1.7 or √3; 50:82 = 1.6 or 3.5, + 82:/26 = 1.5 or 2:3, which is the lapse of consciousness.

Notes:

1) The definition of number, according to Carl Jung, is "the archetype of order", so that it represents principles, concepts, thought patterns, for example. It is coded, numerical information.
2) Angulation, or in physics terms, the phase/time of a wave, represents the principle of leverage, or how energies are controlled, specified and modified and ultimately is the

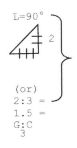

result of interaction of differences (*i.e.*, ratios/proportions; 2:3 = 1.5 = G:C and is our lapse of consciousness interval).

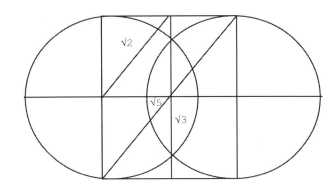

per *Sacred Geometry*, "Unity creates by division," pg. 23

*The interval of an octave corresponds to a 1:2 ratio, *i.e.* middle C = 261.6cps and C′ = 523.2cps, so that mathematically and philosophically a musical octave simultaneously demonstrates division and then multiplication and consequently growth or transformation by the asymmetrical division of 1:√2 = 1.414, which is the frequency of F$^\#$, G$^\flat$ and the angles 78° - 83°.

3) According to <u>Sacred Geometry</u>, the square root symbolically represents transformation and growth from the aspect of three-dimensional reality. The square roots of √2, √3 and √5 permeate ancient Egyptian monuments' tombs, rituals and pyramids, per <u>Egyptian Mysteries</u>

by Lucie Lamy, and also ancient India, as demonstrated by Ernst McClain in <u>The Myth of Invariance</u>.

4) The √2 represents the Principle of Alternation, which reflects generative growth and the dance of the opposites, (principles), *i.e.* the Taoist Yin and Yang as it reflects duality; male and female concepts/principles. √2 represents a proportion, which is the comparison of equivalent ratios, which measures differences, so paradoxically it represents sameness and yet difference, for example an octave. Remember: the octave as well as a hologram is a reflection of the whole within the parts and both the hologram and an octave are based on the sinewave and when a sinewave is confined to a surface, *i.e.* a sphere (the earth), movement results, which is the basis of the electromagnetic spectrum. It produces vibrations called natural resonant frequencies, which by nature can only be expressed within a certain narrow bandwidth or frequency range, *i.e.* 4 - 12cps.

5) √3 represents the formative process. For example, it reflects the structure of form, as in the hexagonal atomic structure of carbon (all earthly organisms are carbon-based, so that the angles represented by √3 = 1.7 or 5:9 would simultaneously be the same at any given moment, which would mean, according to Ditchburn's assertion, "that the phase [angle/time] is the same at any given time over the entire sphere." Also, according to Petr Beckmann in <u>A History of π</u>, pg. 27, "The Babylonians [Sumerians] knew of course that the perimeter of a hexagon is exactly equal to 6 times the radius of the circumscribed circle," *i.e.* 6r/c or π = C/2r (or 6 equilateral triangles).

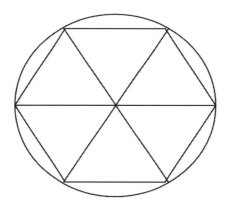

6) √5 represents a dynamical, asymmetrical division of unity, which is necessary for progression and extension or actualization/manifestation of a "ghostly" thoughtform (archetypal) image from the natural resonant frequency level of 5 - 8cps to a thicker, denser image, reflecting the harmonics of our senses from $10^1 - 10^{14}$→

visible lite. In other words, the beta brain wave level, of 16 -40cps is transforming the 5 - 8cps and alpha, 8 - 15cps thought images (thoughtforms) into what appear to be solid, concrete objects.

Electron Shell Orbitals

The shell used to be designated by a letter, *i.e.* the first shell = K. Now they are referred to by a quantum number, hence K = 1, L = 2, M = 3, N = 4, etc. These are 4 sublevels of s, p, d and f, whose number of orbitals are 1, 3, 5, and 7, respectively, and whose bonding strength reflects the square root of their numbers, *i.e.* s = $\sqrt{1}$ = 1; p = $\sqrt{3}$ = 1.7; d = $\sqrt{5}$ = 2.24; and f = $\sqrt{7}$ = 2.64. Each orbital can only have 2 electrons, whose spins are opposite to each other, *i.e.* S = (↑↓); p = (↑↓) (↑↓) (↑↓), etc.

	Letter and Quantum No.:			
Shell	K = 1	L = 2	M = 3	N = 4
Sublevel	S(↑↓)	S(↑↓) Pooo	S(↑↓) Pooo dooooo	S(↑↓) Pooo dooo foooo
Sublevel capacity	2	2, 6	2, 6, 10	2, 6, 10, 18
Shell capacity	2	8	18	32

Ratios:

Sublevel capacity of L = 2:6 or 3~$\sqrt{9}$
Sublevel capacity of M = 2:6 or 3 + 6:10 = 1.66 ~ 3:5
Sublevel capacity of N = 2:6 or 3 + 6:10 = 1.66 ~ 3:5, + 10:14 = $\sqrt{2}$ or 1.4
Shell capacity of K:L = 2:8 = 4~$\sqrt{16}$
Shell capacity of L:M = 8:18 = 2.23 or $\sqrt{5}$
Shell capacity of M:N = 18:32 = 1.7 or $\sqrt{3}$

Notes:

1) According to Sacred Geometry, pg. 24, "By definition, a square is four equal straight lines joined at right angles [90°]. But a more important definition is that the square is the fact that any number [as an archetype of order, *i.e.*, concept or thought pattern] when multiplied by itself is a square [as in a logarithm, which is the

basis of our senses]. The ear especially reflects this principle (cosmic music, pg. 122) according to the 1953 Husmann Theory of Consonance, whereby the non-linearity of the ear's structure produces subjective overtones, *i.e.*, inner sounds that arise in the ear to match or amplify the incoming sounds. These overtones and undertones [See: Lambdoma chart, next pg.] are octaves of two fundamentals, *i.e.* C:C'. Remember: when the peak/height/amplitude/phase (different terms for the same thing) is matched, then per physics the intensity (sound) is squared and the probability wave actualized or manifested, *i.e.* a thought form becomes concretized". So when a number, as in a logarithm, is squared, or multiplied by itself, *e.g.* cell reproduction and how a root system generates, the result is harmonic octaves, which reflect the whole within the parts, *i.e.* hologram. "The cross symbolizes multiplication."

Lambdoma

Notes:

1) According to Sacred Geometry, pg. 26, "The side of a square is called its root ($\sqrt{}$). The side of the primary square (square 1) is $\sqrt{1}$ [representing the bonding strength of the "s" sublevel of the electron's shell], and that of square 2 is $\sqrt{2}$ [representing the bonding strength of the hybrid "sp" sublevel of the electron's shell and also 1.414, etc.]. The diagonal of square 2 is equal to 2, exactly twice the side of the primary square." For example,

$$\frac{root}{diag.} : \frac{root}{diag.} :: \frac{1}{\sqrt{2}} : \frac{\sqrt{2}}{2} : \frac{2\sqrt{2}}{4} : \frac{4}{4\sqrt{2}} : \frac{4}{8}$$

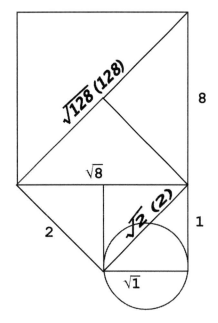

Pythagoream theroem:
$a^2 + b^2 = c^2$

Simultaneously the diameter of a circle

"The ratios are diagonal to side; 1:√2 and circumference to diameter; π, [3.14]," pg. 12.

Square #1 = $1^2 + 1^2$ = 2 or $\sqrt{2}$ = 1.414
Square #2 = $2^2 + 2^2$ = 8 or $\sqrt{8}$ = 2.828
Square #3 = $8^2 + 8^2$ = 128 or $\sqrt{128}$ = 11.313

Lambdoma

According to <u>Cosmic Music</u>, pgs. 91-109 by Rudolf Haase, the Lambdoma diagram.

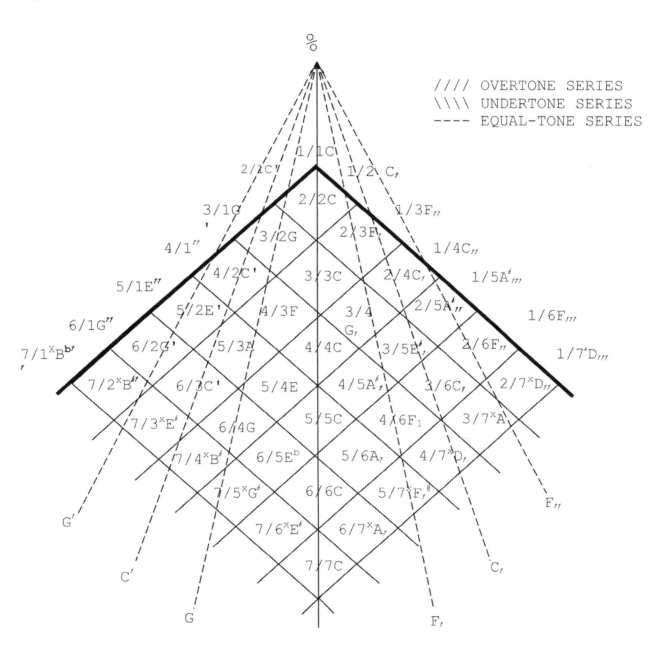

Endnotes

Part One: Chapter One (references described fully in bibliography)
1. Individual and Nature, Roberts, p. 83
2. Ibid., pg. 107 & 108
3. Ibid., pg. 109
4. Ibid.
5. Ibid.
6. Ibid., p. 114
7. Ibid.
8. Archetypes and the Collective Unconscious, Jung, p. 3
9. Ibid., p. 5
10. Ibid.
11. Psyche and Matter, von Franz, p. 1
12. On the Nature of the Psyche, Jung, p. 95
13. Psyche and Matter, von Franz, p. 4
14. Ibid., p. 6
15. Ibid.
16. Essential Plato, Botton, p. 43
17. Psyche and Matter, von Franz, p. 52
18. Essential Plato, Botton, p. 423
19. Ibid, p. 442 & 443
20. Ibid, p. 420
21. Mystic Spiral, Purce, Thames and Hudson, p. 15
22. Sacred Geometry, Lawlor, Thames, and Hudson, p. 22
23. Wholeness and the Implicit Order, Bohm
24. Cosmic Code, Pagels
25. Holographic Paradigm, Wilber, p. 23
26. Seth Material, Roberts
27. Dancing Wu Li Masters, Zukav, p. 193
28. Cymantics, Jenny, p. 9
29. Unconditional Life, Chopra, p. 68
30. Ibid., p. 85
31. Synchronicity, Peat, p. 18
32. Ibid., p. 81
33. Psyche and Matter, von Franz, p. 211
34. Ibid., p. 213
35. Seth: Dreams and Projections, Roberts, p. 9
36. Ibid., p. 46

37 Ibid., p. 218
38 Interpretation of Nature, Jung, Foreword
39 Psyche and Matter, von Franz, p. 66
40 Individual and Nature, Roberts, p. 98
41 Astrology, Arroyo, p. 7
42 Ibid., p. 28
43 Ibid., p. 31
44 Ibid., p. 33
45 Ibid., p. 42
46 Ibid., p. 73
47 Archetypes of the Zodiac, Burt, p. 56
48 Ibid., p. 28
49 Reverse Speech, Oates, p. 27
50 Ibid., p. 28
51 Ibid., p. 32
52 Ibid., p. 36
53 Ibid., p. 48
54 Ibid., p. 61
55 Human Aura, Kilner, p. 3
56 Chakras, Leadbeater, p. 5
57 Aura Awareness, Lindgren, p. xiv
58 Ibid.
59 Ibid.

Part One: Chapter Two (references described fully in bibliography)
1 Interpretation of Fairytales, von Franz, p. 1
2 Transformations of the Myth, Campbell, p. 31
3 Ibid., p. 74
4 Psyche and Matter, von Franz, p. 52
5 Ibid., p. 11
6 Ibid., p. 11 & 12
7 Physical World, Sambursky, p. ix
8 Psyche and Matter, von Franz, p.12
9 Physical World, Sambursky, Introduction
10 Ibid,
11 Ibid,
12 Psyche and Matter, von Franz, p. 12
13 Ibid., p. 281
14 Oversoul Seven, Roberts, p. 129
15 Ibid., p. 130
16 Psyche and Matter, von Franz, p. 177
17 Ibid., p. 151
18 Psychology and Alchemy, Jung, p. 252
19 Power of Myth, Campbell, p. 23
20 Ibid., p. 23-24
21 Individual and Nature, Roberts, p. 101
22 Man's Religions, Noss, p. 29

23. for example, the hero of a religion, Osiris, Zarathrusta, Jesus, Attis, etc. exemplify the good, and the villains such as Seth or Satan, whose progression of mere irritant in the Old Testament to "Evil incarnate" in the New Testament is chronicled by Elaine Pagels, in <u>The Origin of Satan</u>
24. Man and His Symbols, Jung & von Franz, p. 68
25. Ibid.
26. Egyptian Mysteries, Lamy, p. 17
27. Ibid.
28. Ibid., p. 14
29. Ibid., p. 15
30. Mystical Spiral, Purce, Thames, and Hudson, p. 12
31. Elements of Creation Myth, Stewart, p. 31
32. Ibid., p. 32
33. Ibid., p. 33

Part One: Chapter Three (references described fully in bibliography)
1. Man and His Symbols, Jung, p. 68
2. Ibid., p. 88
3. Psychological Reflections, Jung, p. 9
4. Gnostic Gospels, Pagels p. 147
5. Man's Religions, Noss, p. 29
6. Ibid., p. 10
7. Ibid.
8. Archetypes and the Collective Unconscious, Jung, p. 118
9. Ibid., p. 117
10. Ibid.
11. Psychology of Ritual, Hope, p. 74 & 75
12. Ibid., p. 77
13. The reason for this is that music, language and DNA are based on our .95s - 1s consciousness interval, which is 1.05 (*i.e.*, π/3) the $^{12}\sqrt{2}$.] (see: Conclusion, Neurophysiological and Musical Concepts)
14. Psychology of Ritual, Hope, p. 79 & 80
15. Ibid.
16. Unconditional Life, Chopra, p. 37
17. Ibid., p. 38
18. Ibid., p. 40
19. Fractal Geometry, Mandelbrot, p. 3
20. Fractals Everywhere, Barnsley, p. 1
21. Ibid.
22. Wholeness and the Implicit Order, Bohm, p. 50
23. Ibid.

Part One: Chapter Four (references described fully in bibliography)
1. Mystery of the Aleph, Aczel, Introduction
2. Ibid.
3. Ibid., p. 160
4. Ibid., p. 171
5. Ibid., p. 172

6. Quantum Theory, Bohm, p. 32
7. Ibid, p. 33
8. Unknown Reality, Roberts, p. 531
9. Ibid., p. 532
10. Individual and the Nature, Roberts, p. 83

Part Two: Chapter One (references described fully in bibliography)
1. Individual and Nature, Roberts, p. 81
2. Ibid., p. 82
3. Seth: Dreams and Projections, Roberts, p. 177
4. Ibid., p. 182
5. Interpretation of Nature, Jung, p. 87
6. Ibid., p. 88
7. Chakras, Leadbeater, p. 5 & 7
8. Ibid, p. 7

Part Two: Chapter Two (references described fully in bibliography)
1. Transformation of Myth Through Time, Campbell, p. 47
2. Ibid, p. 132
3. Ibid, p. 140
4. Power of Myth, Campbell, p. 71
5. Elements of Creation Myth, Stewart, p. 18
6. Ibid., p. 94 & 95
7. Dictionary of Symbols, Cirlot, p. xxxv
8. Ibid., p. xxvi
9. Nature of the Psyche, Jung, p. 15
10. Man and His Symbols, Jung, p. 88
11. Ibid., p. 84 & 85
12. Ibid., p. 85
13. Egyptian Mysteries, Lamy, p. 26
14. Ibid.
15. Mystical spiral, Purce, p. 25
16. Ibid., p. 14
17. Symbolic Species, Deacon, p. 22
18. Mythic Image, Campbell, p. 36
19. Seth Material, Roberts, p. 330
20. Ibid., p. 266
21. Ibid.
22. Ibid., p. 266 & 267
23. Number and Time, von Franz, p. 143
24. Philosophy of Mathematics, Weyl, p. 61
25. Ibid., p. 64
26. Ibid., p. 66
27. Number and Time, von Franz, p. 72
28. Ibid., p. 73 & 74
29. Number, The Language of Science, Dantzig, p. 7
30. Ibid.
31. Cosmic Music, Godwin, p. 143

32. Ibid.
33. Ibid.
34. Number and Time, von Franz, p. 87
35. Fundamentals of Musical Acoustics, Benade, p. 25
36. Interpretation of Fairytales, von Franz, p. 1
37. Ibid., p. 10
38. Archetypes and the Collective Unconscious, Jung, p. 5
39. Ibid., p. 252
40. Ibid., p. 253
41. Cosmic Code, Pagels, p. 238
42. Ibid., p. 239
43. Science, Order, and Creativity, Bohm and Peat, p. 16
44. Ibid., p. 147
45. Ibid.
46. Ibid., p. 7
47. Man's Religions, Noss, p. 29
48. Man and His Symbols, Jung and von Franz, p. 68
49. Ibid.
50. Mythic Image, Campbell, p. 47
51. Ibid. p. 48

Part Two: Chapter Three (references described fully in bibliography)
1. Web of Life, Capra p. 282 & 283
2. Ibid., p. 283
3. Ibid., p. 284
4. Quantum Healing, Chopra, p. 74 & 75
5. Unconditional Life, Chopra, p. 62
6. Ibid., p. 63
7. Ibid., p. 82
8. Ibid., p. 83
9. Unknown Reality, Roberts, p. 435
10. Ibid., p. 551
11. Ibid., p. 553
12. Ibid. p. 560
13. Sensory Inhibition, von Bekesy, p. 202
14. Ibid., 218
15. Ibid., 219
16. Quantum Healing, Chopra, p. 149
17. Ibid.

Part Two: Chapter Four (references described fully in bibliography)
1. Web of Life, Capra, p. 126
2. Experiments in Topology, Barr, p. 5
3. First Concepts of Topology, Chinn & Steenrod, p. 54
4. Quantum Healing, Chopra, p. 188
5. Ibid., p. 189
6. Myth of Invariance, McClain, p. 3
7. Ibid., p.2

8   Presence of the Past, Sheldrake, p. 108
9   Ibid.
10 Ibid., p. 109
11 Ibid.

Part Three: Chapter One (references described fully in bibliography)
1   Webster's New Universal, Dorset and Baber, p. 388

Part Three: Chapter Two (references described fully in bibliography)
1   Psyche and Matter, von Franz, p. 280
2   Ibid.
3   Embodied Mind, Varela, Thompson, and Rosch, p. 167
4   Sacred Geometry, Lawlor, p. 20
5   Egyptian Mysteries, Lamy, p. 9
6   Ibid., p. 8
7   Ibid.
8   Mystical Spiral, Purce, p. 10
9   Ibid., p. 7
10 Ibid., p. 15
11 Seth Material, Roberts, p. 267
12 Number and Time, van Franz, p. 144
13 Ibid., p. 143
14 Ibid., p. 145
15 Construction of Reality, Piaget, p. 424
16 Ibid., p. 429

Part Three: Chapter Three (references described fully in bibliography)
1   Web of Life, Capra, p. 173
2   Unknown Reality, Roberts, p. 160
3   Ibid., p. 161
4   Ibid., p. 162
5   Ibid.
6   Structure of Magic, Bandler & Grinder, p. 24
7   Ibid., p. 37
8   Ibid., p. 162
9   Ibid., p. 159
10 Ibid.
11 Ibid.

Part Three: Chapter Four (references described fully in bibliography)
1   Wholeness and the Implicate Order, Bohm, p. 178
2   Ibid., p. 179
3   Ibid.
4   Ibid., p. 200
5   Special Theory of Relativity, Bohm, p. 198
6   Ibid., p. 164
7   Ibid., p. 206
8   Ibid., p. 200

9. Ibid., p. 198
10. Ibid., p. 197
11. Ibid., p. 208
12. Holographic Universe, Talbot, p. 20
13. Ibid., p. 29
14. Ibid., p. 39

Part Four: Chapter One (references described fully in bibliography)
1. Number and Time, von Franz, p. 33
2. Ibid., p. 28
3. I Ching, Kaser, p. ix
4. Philosophical Foundations of Physics, Carnap, p. 62
5. Signature of God, Jeffrey, p. 10
6. Ibid.
7. Sacred Geometry, Lawlor, p. 10
8. Number and Time, von Franz, p. 52
9. Ibid., p. 44
10. Double Helix, Watson & Crick, p. 32
11. Number and Time, von Franz, p. 76
12. World According to Wavelets, Hubbard, p. 10
13. Ibid., p. 117
14. Number, The Language of Science, Dantzig, p. 12
15. Cymantics, Jenny, p. 133 & 134
16. Ibid., p. 106
17. Number and Time, von Franz, p. 74
18. Psyche and Matter, von Franz, p. 15
19. Ibid.
20. Ibid., p. 16
21. Ibid.
22. Numbers and Time, von Franz, p. 105
23. Note: numbers designated with an asterisk (*) are from the Real Time Chart, which is copyrighted.
24. Numbers and Time, von Franz, p. 124
25. Ibid., p. 174
26. Ibid., p. 144

Part Four: Chapter Two (references described fully in bibliography)
1. Embodied Mind, Varela, Thompson, and Rosch, p. 171
2. World According to Wavelets, Hubbard, p. 197
3. Special Theory of Relativity, Bohm, p. 56
4. Ibid., p. 57

Part Four: Chapter Three (references described fully in bibliography)
1. Cymantics, Jenny, p. 97
2. Ibid., p. 104
3. Wholeness and the Implicit Order, Bohm, p. 27
4. Ibid., p. 29
5. Ibid., p. 30

6. Ibid., p. 32
7. Embodied Mind, Varela, Thompson, and Rosch, p. 178
8. Ibid., 179
9. Ibid., p. 181
10. Unknown Reality, Roberts, p. 462
11. Cosmic Code, Pagels, p. 305
12. Language and Mind, Chomsky, p. 42
13. Sacred Geometry, Lawlor, p. 44
14. Reverse Speech, Oates, p. 22
15. Ibid., p. 59
16. Ibid., p. 218
17. Ibid., p. 25
18. Structure of Magic, Bandler, p. 15
19. Ibid., p. 179
20. Unknown Reality, Roberts, p. 150

Part Four: Chapter Four (references described fully in bibliography)
1. Web of Life, Capra, p. 284
2. Ibid.
3. Unknown Reality, Roberts, p. 151
4. Reverse Speech, Oates, p. 34
5. Ibid., p. 79
6. Psyche and Matter, von Franz, p. 3

Conclusion (references described fully in bibliography)
1. Unknown Reality, Roberts, p. 301
2. Sacred Geometry, Lawlor, p. 8
3. Ibid., p. 82
4. Note: The $12\sqrt{2}=1.05$, which is what the intervals or notes of music and our 17 different senses are based upon. Also birdsong and human language are based on the 122
5. Note: Ptolemy correlated the 12 zodiacal signs [personality patterns] with the tones of the musical system, which then was correlated several centuries later by Kepler with the planets' orbits.

Appendices: Part A (references described fully in bibliography)
1. Tao of Physics, Capra, p. 58
2. Unknown Reality, Roberts, p. 667
3. Quantum Reality, Herbert, p. 104
4. Note: The momentum (or rotation) of the sinewave happens when it confronts a boundary system, such as our consciousness interval of .95s to 1s. The rotation of the 2 dimensional wave results in a sphere.
5. Mathematical Foundations, von Neumann
6. Sacred Geometry, Lawlor, p. 6
7. Cymantics, Jenny, p. 165

Appendices: Part B (references described fully in bibliography)

1. Sacred Geometry, Lawlor p. 6
2. Philosophy of Mathematics and Natural Science, p. 144
3. Sacred Geometry, Lawlor, p. 8
4. Ibid.
5. Ibid.
6. Ibid., p. 30
7. Note: [DIAGRAM] Each side of the first square equals 1 so that the square root of 1 squared plus the square root of 1 squared equals the square root of 2.
8. Note: A ratio is determined by 2 numbers, and numbers represent concepts as mentioned previously by Jung and von Franz. Consequently a square root represents the difference or comparison between two concepts.
9. End of Certainty, Prigogine, p. 38
10. Ibid., p. 112
11. Nature of the Chemical Bond, Pauling, p. 32
12. From Being to Becoming, Prigogine, p. 112
13. Sacred Geometry, Lawlor, p. 56
14. Ibid., p. 58
15. Ibid.
16. Geometry and the Imagination, Hilbert, p. 289
17. Web of Life, Capra, p. 150
18. Holographic Paradigm, Wilber, p. 181
19. Ibid., p. 90
20. End of Certainty, Prigogine, p. 38
21. Web of Life, Capra, p. 191
22. Ibid., p. 192
23. Ibid., p. 135
24. Unknown Reality, Roberts, p. 446
25. Ibid., p. 390
26. Light, Ditchburn, p. 33
27. Seth: Dreams and Projections, Roberts, p. 99
28. Cosmic Code, Pagels, p. 233
29. Ibid.
30. Tao of Physics, Capra, p. 58
31. Quantum Reality, Herbert, p. 103
32. Light, Ditchburn, p. 55
33. Ibid.

Appendices: Part C (references described fully in bibliography)

1. Embodied Mind, Varela, Thompson, and Rosch, p. 159
2. Ibid.
3. Sacred Geometry, Lawlor, p. 46
4. Embodied Mind, Varela, Thompson, and Rosch, p. 164
5. Ibid.
6. Ibid., p. 181
7. World According to Wavelets, Hubbard, p. 237
8. Ibid., p. 236

9. Ibid., p. 235
10. Ibid., p. 236
11. Ibid.
12. Embodied Mind, Varela, Thompson, and Rosch, p. 164
13. Ibid.
14. Ibid.
15. Ibid., p. 181
16. Ibid.
17. Ibid.
18. Ibid., p. 183
19. Human Navigation, Baker, p. 46
20. Ibid., p. 78
21. Ibid., p. 45
22. About the Tomatis Method, Gilmor, p. 8
23. Ibid., p. 196
24. Ibid.
25. Ibid., p. 9
26. Ibid., p. 16
27. Ibid., p. 13
28. Ibid., p. 14
29. Ibid., p. 7
30. Ibid.
31. Deciphering Senses, Rivlin & Gravelle, p. 90
32. About the Tomatis Method, Gilmor, p. 36
33. Ibid., p. 52
34. Ibid., p. 83
35. Ibid., p. 113
36. Ibid., p. 77
37. Ibid., p. 70 & 71
38. Ibid., p. 72
39. Ibid., p. 78
40. DNA, Kornberg, p. 321
41. Web of Life, Capra p. 204 & 205
42. Ibid., p. 135
43. Ibid., p. 282
44. Ibid., p. 283
45. Ibid., p 284
46. Sound Health Resources, Edwards, p. 4
47. Ibid.
48. Ibid., p. 3
49. Sound Health Resources, Edwards, p. 3
50. Light, Ditchburn, p. 35
51. Sensory Inhibition, von Bekesy, p. 215
52. Ibid., p. 216
53. Ibid.
54. Ibid., p. 202
55. Ibid., p. 216
56. Ibid., p. 218

57. Ibid., p. 220
58. Ibid.
59. From Being to Becoming, Prigogine p. 250
60. Sensory Inhibition, von Bekesy, p. 218
61. Ibid., p. 198
62. Ibid., 164
63. Web of Life, Capra p. 158
64. Ibid., p. 82
65. Ibid.
66. Ibid.
67. Ibid., p. 124
68. Ibid., p. 62
69. Ibid., p. 73
70. Ibid., p. 97
71. Ibid., p. 96
72. Ibid.
73. Ibid., p. 97
74. Ibid., p. 267
75. Ibid.
76. Ibid.
77. Ibid.
78. Ibid.
79. Ibid.
80. Ibid., p. 288
81. Ibid., p. 290
82. Ibid.
83. Ibid.
84. Ibid.
85. Ibid., p. 291
86. Ibid.
87. Ibid., p. 292
88. Ibid.
89. Ibid.
90. Ibid.
91. Ibid., p. 293
92. Light, Ditchburn, p. 97
93. Holographic Universe, Talbot, p. 1
94. Ibid.
95. Ibid., p. 3
96. Ibid., p. 2
97. Ibid, p. 5
98. Ibid.
99. Ibid., p. 17
100. Ibid., p. 20
101. Ibid., p. 29
102. Ibid., p. 39
103. Ibid., p. 21
104. Ibid., p. 31

105 Sacred Geometry, Lawlor, p. 5
106 Holographic Paradigm, Wilber, p. 51
107 Ibid., p. 90
108 Science, Order, and Creativity, Bohm, p. 178
109 Ibid.
110 Ibid., p. 185
111 Ibid.
112 Ibid.
113 Ibid., p. 186
114 Holographic Paradigm, Wilber, p. 51
115 Sensory Inhibition, von Bekesy, p. 220
116 Holographic Paradigm, Wilber, p. 51
117 Ibid., p. 90
118 Sacred Geometry, Lawlor, p. 8
119 Unknown Reality, Roberts, p. 520
120 Tao of Physics, Capra, p. 60
121 Nature of the Chemical Bond, Pauling, p. 12
122 Cosmic Code, Pagels, p. 233
123 Ibid.
124 Sacred Geometry, Lawlor, p. 55
125 Ibid., p. 46
126 Ibid., p. 47
127 Psyche & Matter, von Franz, p. 16
128 Light, Ditchburn, p. 532
129 Ibid., p. 522
130 Special Theory of Relativity, Bohm, p. 200
131 Ibid., p. 198
132 Ibid., p. 197
133 Ibid., p. 200
134 Sensory Inhibition, von Bekesy, p. 18
135 Special Theory of Relativity, Bohm, p. 198
136 Science of Sound, Rossing, p. 56
137 Science, Order, and Creativity, Bohm and David, p. 200
138 Reverse Speech, Oates, p. 218

Appendices: Part D (references described fully in bibliography)
1 Psychology of Music, Seashore, p. 64
2 Quantum Reality, Herbert, p. 116
3 Method, Tomatis, p. 78
4 Ibid., p. 71
5 Ibid., p. 72
6 Psychology of Music, Seashore, p. 2
7 Ibid.
8 Ibid., p. 3
9 Ibid., p. 17
10 Ibid., p. 19
11 Ibid., p. 20
12 Ibid., p. 95

13. Ibid., p. 96
14. Ibid., p. 63
15. Ibid.
16. Ibid.
17. Ibid., p. 64
18. Ibid., p. 19
19. Ibid., p. 140
20. Science and Music, Jeans, p. 25
21. Ibid., p. 63
22. Ibid., p. 29
23. Sacred Geometry, Lawlor, p. 51
24. Psychology of Music, Seashore, p. 128
25. Music, Physics, and Engineering, Olson, p. 59
26. Science and Music, Jeans, p. 29
27. Science of Sound, Rossing, p. 72
28. Ibid., p. 73
29. Ibid., p. 71
30. Ibid.
31. Sacred Geometry, Lawlor, p. 28
32. Ibid.
33. Ibid., p. 29
34. Ibid., p. 65
35. Mystical Spiral, Purce, p. 66
36. Cosmic Music, Schneider, Haase,& Lauer, p. 111
37. Ibid., p. 121
38. Ibid.
39. Ibid.
40. Ibid., p. 122
41. Ibid.
42. Ibid., p. 123

Made in the USA
San Bernardino, CA
20 April 2018